Foreign Exchange

Founded in 1807, John Wiley & Sons is the oldest independent publishing company in the United States. With offices in North America, Europe, Australia, and Asia, Wiley is globally committed to developing and marketing print and electronic products and services for our customers' professional and personal knowledge and understanding.

The Wiley Finance series contains books written specifically for finance and investment professionals as well as sophisticated individual investors and their financial advisors. Book topics range from portfolio management to e-commerce, risk management, financial engineering, valuation and financial instrument analysis, as well as much more.

For a list of available titles, please visit our web site at www.Wiley Finance.com.

Foreign Exchange

A Practical Guide to the FX Markets

TIM WEITHERS

John Wiley & Sons, Inc.

Published by John Wiley & Sons, Inc., Hoboken, New Jersey.
Published simultaneously in Canada.

Library of Congress Cataloging-in-Publication Data:

Weithers, Timothy M. (Timothy Martin), 1956–
    Foreign exchange : a practical guide to the FX markets / Tim Weithers.
        p.   cm.—(Wiley finance series)
    Includes bibliographical references and index.
    ISBN-13: 978-0-471-73203-7 (cloth)
    ISBN-10: 0-471-73203-6 (cloth)
    1. Foreign exchange market.   2. International finance.   I. Title.   II.
Series.
    HG3851.W44   2006
    332.4'5—dc22
                                                    2005038005

Printed in the United States of America.

10   9   8   7   6   5   4   3   2   1

Dedication:

To my boys: Michael, Stephen, and Peter

Contents

Preface

I have been teaching about foreign exchange for more than a dozen years now and thinking about money and trade for even longer. At the University of Chicago, on my way to a Ph.D. in economics, I enrolled in the 1980s in an international trade course ("with money"—as opposed to "real" trade) with Jacob Frenkel [who, from 1991 through 2000, was governor of the Bank of Israel (i.e., Israel's counterpart to Alan Greenspan/Ben Bernanke) and who subsequently served as president of the international division of an investment bank and then chairman and CEO of the Group of Thirty (G-30)]. The University of Chicago is proud of its role in instituting the "quarter system" (the summer being one of the "quarters"—that is, in establishing what most people would call the trimester system in which three 10-week sessions constitute the academic year). Mr. Frenkel distributed what seemed to me like a particularly thick syllabus for a 10-week term. Chicago graduate students in the Department of Economics were required to take courses in a relatively large number of different fields. International trade was not one of my areas of specialization, so I stopped by Mr. Frenkel's office to ask if he could tell me which were the more important papers. His succinct response: "Zey are oll important!" While I was reading the material, some of the journal articles seemed to refer to the exchange rate as, say, Dollars per Pound, while others appeared to take the exchange rate to indicate Pounds per Dollar; it was truly confusing! This was my first exposure to the ambiguity and frustration associated with foreign exchange.

Engaging in that fascinating phenomenon that I believe psychologists refer to as the "continuing cycle of child abuse," I went on to teach economics at Fordham University for several years. After my wife and I had our third son, I joined an amazing little partnership called O'Connor and Associates, a proprietary option trading firm based in Chicago that had its own in-house Education Department (of which I was the third full-time instructor). Many businesses refer to internal development programs as "training"; one of my colleagues was always quick to point out, "You train animals; you educate people." While the name of this business has changed repeatedly over the years (O'Connor and Associates, LLP; SBC/OC; Swiss Bank Corporation (SBC), SBC Warburg; SBC

Warburg Dillon Read; Warburg Dillon Read; UBS Warburg; and UBS) and while my title has changed (though slightly less often), I am still teaching (and still enjoy teaching) for "the Bank." Up until a few years ago, with rare exception, the only people whom our group, now called Financial Markets Education, taught were internal employees; more recently, we have opened many of our more popular classes to UBS's top clients. We have both invited them into our regularly scheduled courses and, on occasion, taught dedicated seminars for them. Foreign Exchange has been, and continues to be, one of our best attended and most demanded courses.

In addition, starting back in the Fall of 1997, the University of Chicago began offering a financial engineering graduate degree, organized by the Department of Mathematics, through its Masters of Science in Financial Mathematics. At that time, Niels Nygaard, the director of the program, sought teaching assistance from what he referred to as the "practitioner" community. I have taught Foreign Exchange, among other things, every year since the start of that program (with friends and former colleagues, Al Kanzler and Jeff Krause).

This book is a synthesis of what I teach at UBS, what I teach at the University of Chicago, and also what I find interesting about foreign exchange (FX) that may not have made its way into either of the two aforementioned forums. I have assumed no prior exposure to foreign exchange (which, obviously, depending on the reader, may be grossly inaccurate); because I start from the basics, though, it's my belief that this book is self-contained. More importantly, I would like to think that this book is practical, insightful, and useful for anyone who is, or who will be, working in the area of foreign exchange.

The organization of the book is as follows:

Chapter 1 describes what I believe foreign exchange is all about in very general terms, identifies the most important currencies, and provides (in an Appendix) a relatively exhaustive listing of the names for, and standardized abbreviations of, money from around the globe.

Chapter 2, for those who have not worked in the financial community, is a brief exposition on prices and markets that might differ slightly from what you may have heard in a college economics or finance course, but an understanding of these concepts is essential, and will set the stage for what follows.

Chapter 3 serves as an introduction to interest rates. The phenomenon of interest, through which money tends to multiply, distinguishes foreign exchange from many of the traditional asset classes. Compounding conventions, day count, discounting, and examples of actual market rates are all discussed here.

Chapter 4 gives some historical perspective and color on the evolution and development of the foreign exchange markets. Moreover, it contains some information about the current state of the FX markets (as of late 2005).

In Chapter 5 we introduce the FX spot market. Everything in foreign exchange revolves around spot. If you understand the following statement: "I buy 10 bucks, Dollar-Swiss, at the offer of one-twenty-five—the figure," you may skip to Chapter 6.

Chapter 6 presents FX forwards—in as intuitive a fashion as I have been able to devise over the years. FX forward valuation and forward points, while they could be viewed as being somewhat mechanical, are the source of a great deal of confusion, and this chapter is an attempt to eliminate any obfuscation and to empower the reader with some solid intuition regarding the pricing of these useful and frequently traded instruments.

FX futures, although not terribly significant as a fraction of FX trading volume, can be a source of market information (in a world dominated by nontransparent, over-the-counter transactions) and are covered in Chapter 7.

The subject of Chapter 8, Cross-Currency Interest Rate Swaps, is really a "funding" or interest rate topic; these instruments are most easily explained after our discussion of FX forwards (really being nothing more than "bundlings" of FX forwards into single contracts). They are very important for the world of international debt issuance.

Options follow in Chapter 9 [in which we start by comparing and contrasting the way most people understand and talk about options (that is, from the equity point of view) versus their foreign exchange counterparts]. There is always the question of where to start and where to end with options; terminology, graphical representations, option spreads, theoretical valuation, option risk measures (or "the Greeks"), and strategies all deserve treatment. We save the more formal, quantitative modeling issues for an Appendix.

In FX, exotic (or non-standard) options are really not all that "exotic"—trading more, and more liquidly, in this product area than in any other. In this sense, they constitute an important component of the FX markets. Even if one does not trade FX exotic options, everyone dealing with foreign exchange should still have an understanding of, and appreciation for, what these instruments are all about because, as Chapter 10 attempts to point out, they can have a significant impact on the movement and behavior of the FX spot market.

Once we have laid out the spectrum of products found within the world of foreign exchange, we circle back and talk about exchange rates within their larger economic context in Chapter 11. This includes a discussion of the pros and cons of fixed versus flexible exchange rate systems or regimes, beggar-thy-neighbor policies, and the implications of monetary policy for the foreign exchange markets.

While a firm believer in the efficiency and benefits of free markets, anyone writing about FX is compelled to address the numerous currency crises that have occurred throughout history; selected documentation of these incidents are the focus of Chapter 12.

Most academic economists and the majority of finance professors, who are quick to articulate their belief in market efficiency, would, therefore, rule out the potential usefulness or effectiveness of technical analysis as a tool for understanding and predicting foreign exchange movements; while in no way an instruction manual or course on the finer points of charting, Chapter 13 attempts to survey some of the methods used by those who practice this "art."

The book winds down with a view to the future of the FX markets and circles back to gold and other precious metals, not themselves foreign exchange, in an Appendix to the final chapter.

Because I consider them an integral part of the learning process, I have included a number of examples and exercises within the text and at the end of several of the chapters; there is no doubt that one learns by doing problems and, by working through these practice exercises, one will advance one's understanding of, facility with, and confidence in engaging in foreign exchange transactions. Answers to these homeworks can be found at the end of the book.

Finally, while intended for those who work in the real world, I would like to think that this book will also be relevant and helpful for those in the academic world: students of finance, economics, international trade, and/or international business.

Acknowledgments

I would like to thank Joe Troccolo, my manager at UBS, my teacher, and my mentor for over 12 years; it was in his classroom that I was first introduced to real finance (and by that, I generally mean the opposite of academic finance). Thanks also to my associates in Financial Markets Education: Walter Braegger, Joe Bonin, Onn Chan, Lindsey Matthews, Radha Radhakrishna, Kai Hing Lum, and Spencer Morris; you are a collegial, stimulating, and wonderfully critical and supportive group. Finally, much of what I know about FX, I have learned from my friends and colleagues in foreign exchange at UBS and its legacy institutions; thanks to Ed Hulina (who taught me to navigate the Merc Floor), Ellen Schubert, Mark Schlater, Fabian Shey, Carol Gary-Tatti (who created the FX screen shots found in this book and helped in many other ways), Ed Pla, Urs Bernegger, Daniel Katzive, Raj Kadakia, Ramon Puyane, John Meyer, Dan Denardis, Heinz Henggeler, Paul Richards, Maryellen Frank, Brian Guidera, Brian Jennings, Andy Robertson, Denise Giordano, Christine Gilfillan, Matt Slater, Jason Perl, Dave Toth, and many, many others. Thanks also to my former and exceptional summer interns: Eric Dai, David Alpert, and Kaitlin Briscoe.

I would also like to acknowledge the invaluable support and cheerful assistance of Martha Ciaschini and Rob Greco who run the Information Center in our UBS office in Stamford, Connecticut. It would be difficult for me to do my job without your help.

Knowing about a particular topic, especially a specialized or technical topic, and even teaching about such a topic, is one thing; bringing a book to life on that material is quite another. From the original conception of this book (in which he can claim no small part), Bill Falloon has been incredibly supportive. He is a man who loves the financial markets (their history, their excitement, their lore and legend); in this we are kindred souls. Moreover, the encouragement and assistance of Laura Walsh, Bill's colleague at John Wiley & Sons, Inc., has also been vital in the completion of this work. Thanks are also due to Emilie Horman and Todd Tedesco of John Wiley & Sons and the staff at Cape Cod Compositors.

Finally, I'd like to offer a blanket recognition and expression of gratitude to all of my students at both UBS and the University of Chicago, for helping me develop many of the ideas in this book. Of course, any remaining errors are entirely mine.

CHAPTER 1

Trading Money

INTRODUCTION

When many of us think of foreign exchange, what comes to mind are those little booths in the airport at which we can exchange, say, our United States Dollars for British Pounds Sterling when on our way to or from a vacation or business trip. Indeed, in some ways, there is nothing more complicated about the market for foreign exchange than that; it is all about buying and selling money.

But there are two things to note up front about **foreign exchange** that make it appear a bit daunting.

First, the realm of foreign exchange is rife with incomprehensible slang, confusing jargon, a proliferation of different names for the same thing, and the existence of convoluted conventions that make working in this field (unless you have already gained a facility with the rules) a real challenge. Banks and other financial institutions can't even agree as to what this business area or "desk" should be called: **FX, Currencies, Treasury Products, ForEx or Forex, Bank Notes, Exchange Rates, . . .**

Second, and more fundamentally, what constitutes "foreign" depends upon where you consider "home" (e.g., whether you are from the U.S. or the U.K.). Having taught about this product for years, working for a large global bank, I know that what is "foreign" for me may very well be "domestic" for you. For that reason, I will make every attempt to avoid the use of the expressions "foreign" and "domestic" in our explanations—not so much out of my hope that this book may achieve some degree of international success, but out of my inclination to want to avoid any ambiguity (and also based on the fact that I, as an "ugly American," would almost always revert to thinking in terms of U.S. Dollars). This will keep me honest. We see later, though, in the context of options that perspective really can and does matter!

Over the years, I have developed a mantra (which I always share with my classes):

> **"Foreign Exchange:**
> **It's not difficult;**
> **It's just confusing."**

I genuinely believe this. As we explore the market conventions used by the FX community, the reasons for this statement will become clear.

Furthermore, of all the complicated financial instruments about which I lecture on a daily basis, the product area, far and away, that generates the most questions (and anxiety) is foreign exchange. The interesting thing is that many of the questions asked in my classroom come from people who work in foreign exchange; in the course of doing their jobs, they often internalize mental shortcuts and rules of thumb and stop thinking about what is going on under the surface; at least one reason for this is that speed is frequently rewarded in the marketplace.

It is our intention to do four things in this book:

1. We'd like to make you familiar with the market conventions associated with foreign exchange as well as conveying an understanding of the practical mechanics required to participate in the FX markets.
2. We hope to provide you with a solid grounding in the theory and the relationships that are relevant for foreign exchange products, valuation (what some people call "pricing"), arbitrage, and trading.
3. We intend to empower you with the intuition to efficiently and expediently analyze what is transpiring in the currency markets and infer what might be the ramifications of various sorts of news.
4. And finally, we would like everyone to take away an understanding of the underlying economic phenomena that drive this fascinating maelstrom of financial activity.

TRADING MONEY

Understanding that the FX market involves exchanging one country's currency for the currency of another country (or region), it is clearly all about trading money. Why is trading money so important? A long time ago,

David Hume, a friend of Adam Smith (the founder of modern economics and champion of free markets), wrote:

> *Money is not, properly speaking, one of the subjects of commerce; but only the instrument which men have agreed upon to facilitate the exchange of one commodity for another. It is none of the wheels of trade: It is the oil which renders the motion of the wheels more smooth and easy. (David Hume,* Of Money *(1752))*

Now, if that is true (that money should not be the object of trade), then why is the foreign exchange market so large? Its magnitude (i.e., trading volume) is, surprisingly and significantly, greater than the flows required by the entire amount of global international trade. Indeed, foreign exchange constitutes the largest financial market in the world.

To answer the question of why the FX market is so big, it is worth thinking a bit about money, maybe a bit more (or at least a bit differently) than we usually do.

THE ROLES MONEY PLAYS

Economists ascribe three functions (or roles) to money. **Money serves as**

1. **A medium of exchange.**
2. **A unit of account.**
3. **A store of value.**

A Medium of Exchange

The first function is served because money, as Hume noted, is meant to facilitate trade. Prior to the emergence of money (I always thought it was interesting that "to discover" and "to invent" are the same word in Latin), people had to barter, that is, they had to trade goods for goods. This, no doubt, made transactions potentially problematic, even though barter may have been enjoyed by some wheeler-dealers at the time. Unless I had some of what you wanted, you had some of what I wanted, and we could arrive at some mutually agreeable rate of exchange, the lack of a universally acceptable product limited the extent of trade.

Over the ages, a variety of things have served in this role as money. It has been documented that, at one time, large numbers of bronze knife blades traded hands as part of lumpier transactions and, while still seemingly an instrument of barter, these are recognized as one of the first commonly accepted **commodity currencies**. Other non-precious metal money include sheep, shells, whale teeth, tobacco, nails, oxen, fish-hooks, jewels, elephant tails, and wampum. What distinguishes these from instruments of barter is the fact that they were generally accepted in a transaction with no thought to their consumption usage, but simply as a means of payment that would later be spent again.

Some strange things have served as mediums of exchange. Perhaps one of the most unusual is the money of Yap. For centuries, inhabitants of this Micronesian island group have employed extremely large stones, known as "rai," as currency in various transactions. Interestingly, while they occasionally change hands (in terms of ownership), they generally do not change location.

There is also a fascinating account of money that was written by a British economist (turned Royal Air Force officer) named R. A. Radford who, during World War II, was shot down, captured, and spent time in a German prisoner of war camp.[1] Within that environment, the generally accepted medium of exchange was the cigarette. Prices were quoted and transactions carried out using cigarettes as payment. As with all other forms of money, value fluctuated with demand and supply. For example, with an influx of Red Cross packages containing cigarettes, prices tended to jump, but, over time, as the supply of cigarettes was exhausted, prices (of other goods in terms of cigarettes) tended to fall—a phenomenon known as "deflation" (the opposite of the more familiar sustained aggregate price increases commonly referred to as "inflation").

One might think that large stones and coffin nails would not be particularly relevant to the study of foreign exchange, but, as mediums of exchange, our examples all serve to highlight the central role of money in facilitating trade.

Economists have identified money, defined as a commonly accepted means of payment, as a critical factor in fostering trade, in encouraging specialization, in allowing for the division of labor, and in promoting economic development in the large—leading, quite literally, to the "wealth of nations" (a phrase which, although constituting part of the title of his revolutionary book published in 1776, was not coined by Adam Smith).[2]

Indeed, some people have even tried to identify or equate wealth and money, although anyone who has lived through a hyperinflation knows that the value of money can be fleeting (as experienced by generations of inhabitants of South America as well as individuals in Germany in 1923 during which it literally required a wheelbarrow of Marks to buy a loaf of bread).

In general, though, by serving as a generally acceptable (and accepted) vehicle of payment, money circumvents what economists refer to as "the double coincidence of wants," a circumstance that makes barter a particularly inefficient mechanism of exchange.

Why is money "commonly accepted?" Good question. Why did Native Americans willingly take strung shell beads (wampum) in exchange for real products like corn and meat? One might think of the "greater fool theory" (that is, I'll buy something for a high price today in the expectation that there is somebody out there—an even bigger fool—who will buy it from me at an even higher price in the future), but that explanation is rather naïve. In general, one accepts money as a means of payment (for one's labor or one's goods) in the belief that that same money can subsequently be employed in the acquisition of other goods and services. George J. W. Goodman (who published under the pen name Adam Smith) properly wrote, "All money is a matter of belief."

"Common acceptance" is an essential characteristic of money. Of course, over the years, the U.S. government has insisted upon the acceptance of their money "for all debts public and private" (a stock epithet that continues to appear on the face of U.S. paper currency to this day—see Figure 1.1)—though there is no formal federal law or statute that man-

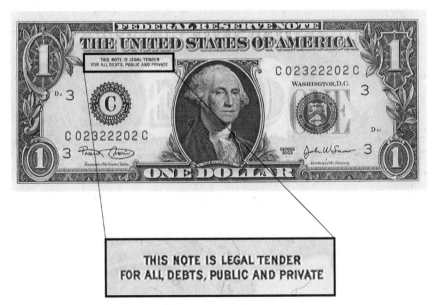

FIGURE 1.1   "This Note Is Legal Tender for All Debts, Public and Private"

dates that private businesses in the United States must accept cash as a form of payment.[3] Interestingly, back in the 1800s, the U.S. government did not allow the payment of U.S. paper money for one's tax liabilities, insisting, instead, on the delivery of real money (e.g., precious metal or "specie").

Money can achieve common acceptance either due to formal governmental proclamation ("fiat") or due to the explicit or implicit acknowledgment of the market participants. Why has the U.S. Dollar enjoyed its status as a universal currency since World War II? Because, in short, individuals and institutions around the world have been willing to hold this money (i.e., to accept it as payment and often to maintain a stock of it "in reserve"). Prior to the global acceptance of the U.S. Dollar, this status was long enjoyed by the British Pound (on whose empire, as was said at one time, "the sun never sets").

U.S. paper currency, which is occasionally referred to as "fiat currency," once was backed by real money (i.e., gold and/or silver). In the United States, you may have seen silver certificates—Dollar bills with blue seals on them—or heard of gold certificates (see Figure 1.2). This paper money, at one time, could literally be exchanged for gold (up until April 5, 1933) or silver (up until June 24, 1968) through the U.S. Treasury via the Federal Reserve Bank—the central bank of the United States. Almost all of the world's major currencies were once backed by gold and/or silver; today, U.S. Dollars (and the others) are no longer convertible into precious metal. Gold and silver are now recognized as commodities (even though they have been employed in the manufacture of money for millennia and are still minted/coined for investors and collectors). We return to discuss the market for gold, silver, platinum, and other precious metals at the end of this book (in the Appendix following the final chapter).

Regardless of its form, money generally continues to serve its role as a medium of exchange, though currency substitutes (credit cards, checks, debit cards, wire transfers, money orders, charge cards, etc.) increasingly impinge on the role of cash money. And, with the increasingly sophisticated ability to reproduce and print counterfeit currency, which requires constantly vigilant and continuously sophisticated measures on the part of the United States Treasury and the other central banks of the world to counteract such activity, the trend toward electronic money will no doubt continue.

We will return to a more formal definition of money, from a banking perspective, later on.

The second role of money is as **a unit of account**, that is, we measure things in currency units. We consider the size of our bank accounts, the profitability of our businesses, and the magnitude of our pension funds (and

FIGURE 1.2   Five Dollar Silver Certificate and Ten Dollar Gold Note

therefore the financial security of our retirement) all in terms of money. On a larger (or more macro) scale, gross domestic product (GDP, the sum of the market value of all goods and services produced within a given country in a given year) is reported in monetary terms. The GDP of the United States in 2004 was approximately 12,000,000,000,000 (12 trillion). Japan's gross domestic product in 2004 was about 505,000,000,000,000 (505 trillion). Did Japan really produce approximately 42 times more than the United States in 2004?

No. Japan shows a larger GDP than does the United States because the Japanese GDP figure is reported in Japanese Yen and the U.S. GDP number is reported in U.S. Dollars, and Yen are small in value when compared to a Dollar. Of course, if you were to convert these GDPs into either one of the two currencies, then you would be comparing apples and apples. Practically, though, there are several issues to consider when doing these sorts of conversions; typically, aggregate numbers or indices such as GDP figures are used to track the growth in various economic variables or series. There is a potential disconnect when converting to one currency because the value of currencies themselves change over time (and this may obscure what is happening in real terms—or "behind the veil of money" as economists are fond of saying). For example, if Japan produced exactly the same output in 2005 as it did in 2004 (and, measured in Yen, this number was precisely the same), but the exchange rate between Yen and Dollars were to double (i.e., it took twice as many Yen in 2005, relative to 2004, to buy a fixed amount of Dollars), then, looking at Japanese GDP in U.S. Dollar terms, it would seem to indicate that the Japanese economy "halved" in magnitude over that time period, while, by definition, it would have really (that is, in real terms) remained exactly the same.[4] Yes, foreign exchange can be confusing.

While we calculate and report things in currency units (which, on the surface, seems to make sense, allowing us to aggregate the value of all the various and varied products and services produced in a given country in a given year), obviously employing money as a unit of account may raise problems analogous to measuring things with a ruler, yardstick, or measuring rod, which themselves have a tendency to shrink and expand over time. Nevertheless, we still frequently measure, record, and report wealth and other financial variables in monetary increments and money typically serves in this financial role of numeraire.

Because the value of money does change over time (both in terms of other currencies, but also in terms of real goods and services), GDP numbers are frequently reported both in current (i.e., contemporaneous) currency units as well as in "constant" or "base year" currency units. As an example, the 2004 U.S. GDP was around 12,000,000,000,000 Dollars (in 2004 Dollars), but this translates to (i.e., these goods and services would have cost) only around 2,000,000,000,000 in 1955 Dollars. The implication is that a Dollar today just isn't the same as a Dollar last year (or 50 years ago). If you don't believe us, just ask your grandparents for confirmation of this fact.

Not only does the value of money change as time goes by, but (and this may be one of the reasons why) money itself has a tendency to grow over time (through the phenomenon of interest). Interest, as well as the fact that different countries have different rates of interest (not to mention different interest rate conventions), is a fundamental aspect of money that will be dealt with in detail in Chapter 3.

Finally, money serves as a **store of value**. Once civilization was able to generate an above-subsistence standard of living for the members of society, the question of what to do with the surplus arose. How can we save? What should we do with this production or these resources that we do not plan to consume today? Obviously we would like to put our wealth, our savings, our money to work, but, even if money paid no interest at all,[5] there are those who would hold it for a rainy day (that is, for insurance purposes), or for retirement (after one's actual productivity wanes), or as a diversifying asset (since its value would not necessarily move in lockstep with other assets), or as a commodity that might hold its value even if other financial assets crash.

It is interesting to note that, for their high-net-worth clients, banks have sometimes recommended holding currency in their portfolios. This is not simply advocating that wealthy individuals sit on cash or invest in liquid assets (e.g., a U.S. client maintaining a balance of U.S. Dollars or short-term Dollar-denominated money market instruments as one category of his/her holdings), but actually dedicating a portion of one's wealth to a "basket" of currencies as part of one's asset allocation decision-making process. This might involve a U.S. client holding some Euros, some Pounds Sterling, some Swiss Francs, and some Japanese Yen in his/her portfolio; the logic of this decision recognizes the return on currencies (interest) as well as the possible portfolio diversification benefits they may provide. Foreign exchange is not necessarily highly correlated with equities, fixed income, interest rates, commodities, or other assets such as real estate or fine art. While the notion of "foreign exchange as an asset class" may not yet be a universally accepted investment principle, it is certainly a reasonable and relatively interesting idea.

THE MAJOR CURRENCIES

Thus far we have talked mainly about U.S. currency, but what of the money of other countries? Which are the most important for the FX market? Does every country have its own currency? How many currencies are out there? Can you actually trade every currency? Do the prices of currencies move freely or are exchange rates "pegged" or "fixed"? For those floating exchange rates, how much do their prices fluctuate? We have a great deal to talk about.

Which currencies are important? The following list is not meant to slight any country (or any country's currency) as unimportant or insignificant, but is simply intended to identify those currencies that account for the vast majority of foreign exchange transactions and with which we shall spend most of our time. These currencies are

The United States Dollar

The Euro

The Japanese Yen

The Great Britain Pound

The Swiss Franc

Of course, Canadian Dollars, Australian Dollars, Swedish Krona, Brazilian Real, South African Rand, New Zealand Dollars, Mexican Pesos, Thai Baht, etc. trade hands every day, but in total they do not come close to accounting for the volume of trade involving any of the "big five" mentioned.

The British Pound goes by other names: the English Pound (perhaps meant to distinguish it from the Scottish Pound which, until relatively recently, for the one Pound denomination, appeared as a paper note as opposed to its southern relative, which, in that face amount, circulates only as a coin). The Great Britain Pound is also known as the Pound Sterling or, more simply, Sterling. This is one of the things you have to get used to in FX; there are a lot of nicknames floating around and you need to be able to speak the language. When quoting the exchange rate between British Pounds and U.S. Dollars, it is most commonly referred to as "Cable" in the professional market and, while its origins may be slightly obscure, it is probably easiest to keep this in mind by thinking of the transatlantic cable (which joins the U.S. and the U.K.). But is it quoted as Pounds per Dollar or Dollars per Pound? We return to that in Chapter 5.

As far as the identification of currencies and their quotation, a variety of conventions are employed in the financial press and by various institutions around the world (many of them undoubtedly and utterly confusing). For this reason, in this book, we will stick to the International Standards Organization Codes (ISO Codes), which are generally universally employed in the interbank or over-the-counter (OTC) market. ISO Codes use three letters to identify a currency. Usually, the first two letters refer to the country of origin and the third letter refers to the name of the primary currency unit. Therefore,

FIGURE 1.3 Ten Dollar Bill

USD = United States Dollar

See Figure 1.3.

The International Monetary Fund (IMF), contrarily, for example, uses the identification label: US$ or US $.

GBP = Great Britain Pound (United Kingdom Pound Sterling)

As a unit of currency, the term "Pound" originated from the value of a troy Pound of high quality silver known as "sterling silver." (See Figure 1.4.)

FIGURE 1.4 Ten Pound Note

FIGURE 1.5   One Thousand Yen Note

JPY = Japanese Yen

The word "Yen" derives from the Japanese term meaning "round," presumably used to refer to the gold coin of that shape which was first introduced in 1870. (Similarly, the Chinese currency is sometimes referred to as the "Yuan," which also translates as "round"—having first been introduced as a silver coin in the nineteenth century; the Yuan is also referred to as the "Renminbi," which translates as "the people's currency"). See Figure 1.5.

In the *Financial Times* (of London), GBP appears as "£" and JPY is identified using the symbol "¥".

CHF = Swiss Franc

What about CHF? Where does this come from? The official name for Switzerland is "Confederation Helvetica" (a Confederation of "Cantons," one of the founding constituents of which was Schwyz). Depending on where you are in this nation, an inhabitant of Switzerland may identify their country as Schweiz (if German-speaking) or Suisse (if French-speaking) or Svizzera (if Italian-speaking) or possibly even the Swiss Confederation (in English). One of the appealing aspects of using the Latin name, like many other things in Switzerland, is that it is neutral; it does not require the choice of any one of the primary languages spoken in that country.[6] See Figure 1.6.

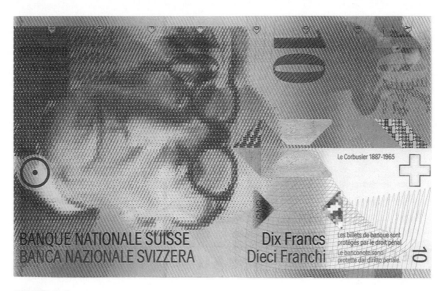

FIGURE 1.6 Ten Swiss Franc Note

Also in the London *Financial Times* (and elsewhere), Swiss Francs are denoted "SFr."

EUR = Euro

What is EUR? EUR refers to the currency of the EuroZone (the combined countries that use the Euro as their money). (See Figure 1.7.) This

FIGURE 1.7 Ten Euro Note

is obviously an exception to the convention previously indicated where, with XYZ, *XY* indicates the country and *Z* the name of the currency. Over the years, I have said that if someone were to write The Foreign Exchange Rule Book—something far more ambitious than we have attempted here—then it would be a really fat book, the reason being there are always exceptions to the rule in foreign exchange.

Of course, almost every other country has its own currency. What would you guess is the ISO code for Canadian Dollar? Right, CAD. How about Mexican Peso? Of course, MXP sounds reasonable, but it is identified as MXN. Why? It refers to the Mexican Nuevo Peso (the New Peso) and so actually does, in a not-so-obvious way, follow the rule. Having seen it, one can probably remember that KRW is used for the South Korean Won, but may find it a bit tougher to remember SEK for Swedish Krona. We have compiled a fairly exhaustive (and at the time of publication, up to date) list of currencies in the appendix to this chapter (including legacy currencies that you may run into if you are reading any older books or journal articles).

For those who may want to follow the foreign exchange markets in the press, there are a number of sources of information that might prove helpful. The *Wall Street Journal* regularly publishes a table identifying the value of the (U.S.) Dollar against many of the world's currencies. (See Figure 1.8.) The *Journal* also publishes a daily matrix of reciprocal foreign exchange prices for the most important ("key") currencies. (See Figure 1.9.)

Moreover, the *Financial Times* publishes FX rates showing both the European and American perspectives. (See Figure 1.10.)

Finally, a number of news services, such as Bloomberg, offer FX quotes; the accuracy, frequency of updating, and other measures of informational quality may depend on the level of service to which you subscribe. (See Figures 1.11 and 1.12.)

SOME INTERESTING QUESTIONS

Having identified the most important currencies (USD, EUR, JPY, GBP, and CHF) and recognizing these as important because they are acknowledged as constituting the bulk of the trade in the FX market (and are those with which we spend most of our time in this book), we can return and answer some of our earlier questions.

Currencies

U.S. dollar foreign-exchange rates in late New York trading

Country/currency	Friday In US$	Per US$	US$ against each currency Last week	Year-to-date	Country/currency	Friday In US$	Per US$	US$ against each currency Last week	Year-to-date
Argentina peso-a	0.3438	2.9087	...	-2.2%	Mexico peso-a	0.0930	10.7573	-0.7%	-3.4%
Australia dollar	0.7627	1.3111	-0.7%	2.6	New Zealand dollar	0.6920	1.4451	-0.6	3.8
Bahrain dinar	2.6525	0.3770	...	...	Norway krone	0.1527	6.5488	1.1	7.9
Brazil real	0.4484	2.2302	-1.5	-16.0	Pakistan rupee	0.0168	59.702	-0.2	0.5
Canada dollar	0.8603	1.1624	-0.8	-3.1	Peru new sol	0.2991	3.3434	0.9	2.0
1-month forward	0.8610	1.1614	-0.8	-3.2	Philippines peso	0.0178	56.085	-0.3	-0.1
3-months forward	0.8626	1.1593	-0.8	-3.4	Poland zloty	0.3066	3.2616	1.5	8.3
6-months forward	0.8648	1.1563	-0.8	-3.6	Russia ruble-d	0.03508	28.506	0.1	2.9
Chile peso	0.001888	529.66	-1.5	-4.7	Saudi Arabia riyal	0.2665	3.7523	...	...
China yuan	0.1236	8.0922	0.1	-2.2	Singapore dollar	0.5910	1.6920	0.4	3.7
Colombia peso	0.0004372	2287.28	-0.1	-2.8	Slovakia koruna	0.03096	32.2997	0.7	13.1
Czech. Rep. koruna-b	0.0406	24.625	0.7	10.0	South Africa rand	0.1572	6.3613	-0.2	12.3
Denmark krone	0.1611	6.2073	0.2	13.2	South Korea won	0.0009583	1043.51	1.3	0.8
Ecuador US dollar	1	1	...	...	Sweden krona	0.1290	7.7519	-0.5	16.7
Egypt pound-a	0.1736	5.7600	...	-5.1	Switzerland franc	0.7726	1.2943	0.2	13.5
Euro area euro	1.2021	0.8319	0.2	12.9	1-month forward	0.7746	1.2910	0.2	13.4
Hong Kong dollar	0.1289	7.7574	...	-0.2	3-months forward	0.7790	1.2837	0.2	13.1
Hungary forint	0.004814	207.73	0.8	14.9	6-months forward	0.7857	1.2728	0.1	12.8
India rupee	0.0228	43.956	0.2	1.6	Taiwan dollar	0.03013	33.190	...	4.4
Indonesia rupiah	0.0000971	10299	0.7	10.9	Thailand baht	0.02436	41.051	-0.1	5.6
Israel shekel	0.2176	4.5956	-0.1	6.4	Turkey new lira-d	0.7427	1.3465	-0.2	-0.4
Japan yen	0.008809	113.52	1.0	10.9	U.K. pound sterling	1.7638	0.5670	0.8	8.8
1-month forward	0.008838	113.15	1.0	10.7	1-month forward	1.7628	0.5673	0.8	8.6
3-months forward	0.008900	112.36	0.9	10.4	3-months forward	1.7618	0.5676	0.8	8.3
6-months forward	0.008997	111.15	0.9	10.0	6-months forward	1.7618	0.5676	0.7	7.8
Jordan dinar	1.4100	0.7092	0.1	...	United Arab Emirates dirham	0.2723	3.6724	...	...
Kuwait dinar	3.4247	0.2920	...	-0.9	Uruguay peso-e	0.0415	24.096	0.2	-8.7
Lebanon pound	0.0006651	1503.53	...	-0.7	Venezuela bolivar	0.000466	2145.92	...	11.8
Malaysia ringgit-c	0.2653	3.7693	...	-0.8					
Malta lira	2.8000	0.3571	1.4	11.6	SDR-f	1.4495	0.6899	0.5	6.8

a-floating rate b-commercial rate c-government rate d-Russian Central Bank rate e-financial f-Special Drawing Rights (SDR); from the International Monetary Fund; based on exchange rates for U.S., British, and Japanese currencies.
Note: Based on trading among banks in amounts of $1 million and more, as quoted at 4 P.M. ET by Reuters.

FIGURE 1.8   WSJ World Value Currency Table
Source: Wall Street Journal. © 2006 Reuters. Reprinted with permission from Reuters.

Key Currency Cross Rates   Late New York Trading Wednesday, September 28, 2005

	Dollar	Euro	Pound	SFranc	Peso	Yen	CdnDlr
Canada	1.1729	1.4119	2.0733	0.9072	.10806	.01037	...
Japan	113.15	136.21	200.01	87.520	10.424	...	96.470
Mexico	10.8542	13.0663	19.187	8.3957	...	.09593	9.2543
Switzerland	1.2928	1.5563	2.2853	...	.11911	.01143	1.1023
U.K.	.56570	.6810	...	.4376	.05212	.00500	.48232
Euro	.83070	...	1.4684	.64255	.07653	.00734	.70826
U.S.	...	1.2038	1.7677	.77350	.09213	.00884	.85260

Source: Reuters

FIGURE 1.9   WSJ World Key Currency Cross Rates
Source: Wall Street Journal. © 2006 Reuters. Reprinted with permission from Reuters.

FIGURE 1.10   FT Daily FX Quotes
Source: Financial Times of London. © 2006 Reuters. Reprinted with permission from Reuters.

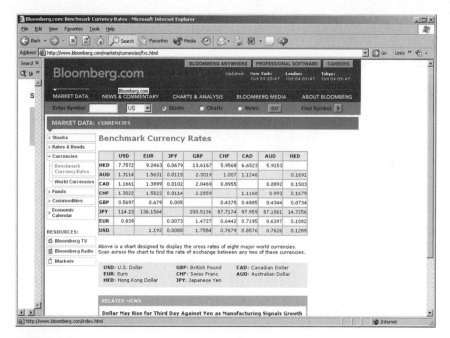

FIGURE 1.11   FX Page
Source: www.bloomberg.com. © 2006 Bloomberg LP. All rights reserved. Reprinted by permission.

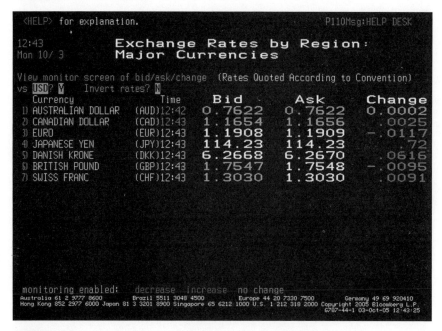

FIGURE 1.12   Exchange Rates by Region: Major Currencies
Source: © 2006 Bloomberg LP. All rights reserved. Reprinted by permission.

Does Every Country Have Its Own Currency?

No. Because of the lack of confidence in a currency (for example, because a government may have indulged in the excessive printing and spending of their national currency, effectively debasing their money and often leading to hyperinflation), some countries (such as Ecuador, starting on September 11, 2000) abandoned their currency (which, in this instance, was called the "Sucre") and adopted the money of another country (in Ecuador's case, the United States Dollar) as their official currency. Other examples include East Timor and El Salvador. Panama has used the U.S. Dollar as its official currency since 1904. Although the use of one country's money by another country could involve any of the more stable currencies, this situation has typically come to be called "dollarization" because of the frequency of relying on the U.S. Dollar as the external currency of choice.

Other countries, instead of switching from their own money to that of another nation, have simply "pegged" their currency to the U.S. Dollar, such as Bermuda, Bahamas, and Hong Kong (successfully) and Argentina (unsuccessfully). Having said that, the vast majority of countries have their own currency, with the exception of (1) the EuroZone, (2) a group of island nations in the Caribbean, (3) some formerly-French-colonial Central African countries, and (4) some former United Nations (UN) and/or U.S. territories (such as Palau, the Federated States of Micronesia, and the Marshall Islands).

How Many Currencies Are There?

There are slightly more than 200 currencies used around the world today including money that was issued and may still have value (even though it has been officially retired) such as some of the legacy Euro currencies (e.g., German Deutsche Marks, Italian Lira, Spanish Peseta, French Francs). As mentioned above, most countries have their own currency. While the UN recognizes 191 countries as Member States of the United Nations, their list is not exhaustive (as there are countries that the UN simply does not recognize) and the number of countries is continually changing. Some 30 new countries have emerged in the past 15 years alone.[7] And there are even some examples, such as Taiwan and East Timor, whose status as an independent country is sometimes the subject of debate.[8]

For the most part, currency today takes the form of either notes or coins (when other than maintained in electronic form). The characteristics that are viewed as advantageous in a country's money include portability, durability, divisibility, ease of creation (if not abused by the government), and properties of recognition/verification (the other side of that coin being difficulty in counterfeiting).[9] Paper currency was first issued in China over a thousand years ago serving, among other purposes, as a convenient vehicle for making wage payments to the military. Marco Polo, in the late thirteenth century, wrote of the wonders of this invention. Paper money in Europe first appeared in Sweden in the seventeenth century. In both China and Sweden, the paper notes were backed by, and convertible into, precious metal at the discretion of the holder. In Canada, also in the late seventeenth century, because of a lack of coins and precious metal, the French colonial government issued playing card money (actual playing cards cut into quarters on which had been added hand-inscribed monetary denominations, the signature of the colonial governor, and the seal of the treasurer). It is interesting that the phrase "paper money" continues to be used even though, in many cases, it is technically inappropriate. U.S. notes are essentially "cloth" (being made of about 25% linen and 75% cotton and laced with colored fibers) while Australian bank notes are literally plastic (being made of a synthetic polymer).

Most countries take great pride in their currency, gracing the notes and coins with historical figures and political leaders of singular significance, local landmarks, native fauna and flora, and other motifs and designs that reflect national identity and patriotic pride.[10] (See Figure 1.13.)

FIGURE 1.13 Notable Figures

It was for this reason (not the abdication of the ability to engage in autonomous monetary policy) that led many (including the author) to believe that the Euro—at the time, the proposed common currency for several of the most powerful economic countries in the world—would fail to become a reality. Interestingly, the Euro coins do allow for a degree of nationalism, as their backs (or "reverses," to use the proper numismatic expression) display symbols idiosyncratic to the issuing country. (See Figure 1.14.)

Of course, merchants in France, for example, are required to honor (i.e., accept) German-stamped Euro.

Citizens of the United States may not be aware that, while U.S. currency is recognized and generally accepted around the world, it is also frequently ridiculed—for two reasons: the bills are all the same color (with recent advances only marginally tempering this criticism) and they are all the same size!

Can You Trade Every Currency?

No. Some countries limit or restrict trade in their money. When this occurs, the currency is said to be "controlled." Currencies that fall into this cate-

FIGURE 1.14   The Euro Coins

gory include the Russian Ruble and the Chinese Renminbi or Yuan. Although there may be restrictions placed on the ownership and transport of a country's money, it sometimes is possible for one wishing to hedge against a change in the price of one of these currencies to enter into a contract (one example of which would be a nondeliverable forward or NDF, to be discussed later) in which payment (i.e., compensation) occurs in another, unrestricted currency.

There have also been occasions when countries have wished or sought to discourage trading in their currency. In 1987, an FX trader in New York named Andy Krieger aggressively sold (or shorted, i.e., bet against) the New Zealand Dollar or "Kiwi" as it's known to foreign exchange market professionals. Presumably, Krieger sold, "more Kiwis than the entire money supply of New Zealand." It's further been alleged that "New Zealand's finance minister telephoned Bankers Trust (his employer) to complain and beg for mercy."[11]

Central banks have available a couple of tools that they can employ to discourage speculation in their currency such as raising the overnight rate of interest on their currency to 500%, and, although trading is nominally permitted, there are some significant reasons to avoid doing so and some clear dangers in risking one's financial capital, essentially betting against a government.

Currency Pegs, Bands, Intervention, and Floating Exchange Rates

In the past, some countries have decided to fix or "peg" the exchange rate between their currency and that of another country. A relatively recent example was Argentina, via their Currency Board (an institution through which every Argentinian Peso was presumably backed by the possession of one U.S. Dollar on the part of the Central Bank of Argentina), fixing the exchange rate at a ratio of one-to-one; this system was in place from 1991 until 2002. An important feature of such a regime is the convertibility of money and the willingness on the part of the government to actively enforce this fixed conversion rate of exchange.

On January 6, 2002, the system broke down and the Argentinian Peso devalued and floated—from 1 Peso per Dollar to over 3 Pesos per Dollar in April 2002—spiking at around 3.87 Pesos per Dollar in June of that year. Since then, the exchange rate has fluctuated around 2.90 Argentinian Pesos per Dollar. While there are real economic implications from the collapse of a currency board, this fixed exchange rate system lasted successfully for 10 years and had been acknowledged as having brought economic benefits and financial confidence to a country that had a less-than-stellar prior track record of currency stability and a history of periodic hyperinflation. In recent history, Hong Kong, Bulgaria, and Bosnia have all had currency boards.

Other currencies are formally pegged without the seemingly negative consequences that have recently attended the Argentinian Peso. For example, from 1955 through 1975, the Mexican Peso was maintained at a fixed level relative to the U.S. Dollar. Furthermore, starting in 1983, Hong Kong also pegged its currency to the U.S. Dollar (at a rate of 7.80 Hong Kong Dollar to USD 1). Until just recently, the Malaysian Ringgit had been fixed at 3.80 Ringgit per Dollar (starting in 1997). The U.S. Dollar is not the only currency to which others are or have been tied. After becoming free of the former Soviet Union, Estonia, in 1991, chose to link its new currency, the Kroon, to the German Deutsche Mark. Some countries have been less adamant on insisting that the exchange rate be a single number, but rather simply required that its currency move within a (typically tight) range or band about a central level. We will see this idea later in our discussion of the Exchange Rate Mechanism between the major European currencies in Chapter 4.

Still other countries informally peg their currency. The People's Republic of China, from the mid-1990s through the middle of 2005, systematically kept the exchange rate at right around 8.28 Renminbi (or Yuan) per Dollar, despite the repeated protestations of the United States (in particular, as reflected in the statements of the U.S. Secretary of the Treasury John W. Snow, starting in September 2003). In July 2005, in what was considered a significant event in the world of foreign exchange, China allowed the exchange rate to drift down toward 8 Yuan (or Renminbi) per Dollar and some other pegged Asian currencies followed suit. Since that time, the number of Yuan per Dollar has slowly slipped further.

Many of the countries that hope to join the Euro community in the near future either have pegged their currency to the Euro or have decided to maintain the value of their currency within a tight band until their conversion to the Euro has been completed.

Finally, some countries, usually through their central banks, have occasionally directly intervened in the foreign exchange markets, that is, traded with the intention of either moving the exchange rate in a specific direction or sometimes with the goal of keeping it from moving. This is just one additional way in which the foreign exchange market differs from the markets for other financial assets, which, with the exception of sovereign debt markets, do not generally experience direct governmental involvement on such a scale.[12] While most exchange rates today are determined by market forces, intervention by central banks may serve to generate, mitigate, accelerate, or truncate directional movements in their currency. The expression "dirty float" has been used to refer to a nominally market-determined exchange rate while recognizing that it is not purely or freely floating due to periodic or discretionary sovereign or governmental interference.

As a rule, most economists believe that fixing prices usually results in some sort of market inefficiency. We return later to discuss the pros and cons of fixed versus floating exchange rate regimes when we look at the economics of exchange rate determination in Chapter 11.

Before going into the specifics of transacting in foreign exchange (starting with the spot market in Chapter 5), we would like to provide a framework for thinking about markets in general (in Chapter 2) and then give some color and perspective on the historical development of the global currency markets (in Chapter 4) that has resulted in the framework, conventions, and institutions that we have today.

APPENDIX: Countries, Currencies, and ISO Codes

ISO Codes (including legacy currencies and countries that share a common currency)

Country	Currency Used/Name	ISO Code	(Numeric Code)
A			
Afghanistan	Afghani	AFA	(971)
Albania	Lek	ALL	(008)
Algeria	Algerian Dinar	DZD	(012)
American Samoa	U.S. Dollar	USD	(840)
Andorra	Euro	EUR	(978)
	(formerly Andorran Franc)	ADF	
	(formerly Andorran Peseta)	ADP	
Angola	New Kwanza	AON	(973)
Anguilla	East Caribbean Dollar	XCD	(951)

(Continued)

Country	Currency Used/Name	ISO Code	(Numeric Code)
Antarctica	(No universal currency)		
Antigua and Barbuda	East Caribbean Dollar	XCD	(951)
Argentina	Argentinean or Argentine Peso	ARS	(032)
		(ARP, ARG)	
Armenia	Armenian Dram	AMD	(051)
Aruba	Aruban Guilder/Florin	AWG	(533)
Australia	Australian Dollar	AUD	(036)
Austria	Euro	EUR	(978)
	(formerly Austrian Schilling)	ATS	
Azerbaijan	Azerbaijanian Manat	AZM	(031)
B			
Bahamas	Bahamian Dollar	BSD	(044)
Bahrain	Bahraini Dinar	BHD	(048)
Bangladesh	Taka	BDT	(050)
Barbados	Barbados Dollar	BBD	(052)
Belarus	Belarussian Ruble	BYR	(974)
Belgium	Euro	EUR	(978)
	(formerly Belgium Franc)	BEF	
Belize	Belize Dollar	BZD	(084)
Benin	Central French African Franc	XOF	(952)
Bermuda	Bermudian (Bermuda) Dollar	BMD	(060)
Bhutan	Indian Rupee	BTN	(064)
Bolivia	Boliviano	BOB	(068)
	Mvdol	BOV	(984)
Bosnia and Herzegovina	Convertible Marks/Dinar	BAM	(977)
Botswana	Pula	BWP	(072)
Bouvet Island	Norwegian Krone	NOK	(578)
Brazil	Brazilian Real	BRL	(986)
Britain (see United Kingdom)	Great Britain Pound	GBP	(826)
British Indian Ocean Terr.	US Dollar	USD	(840)
Brunei Darussalam	Brunei Dollar	BND	(096)
Bulgaria	Bulgarian Lev	BGN	(975)
Bundesrepublik Deutscheland (see Germany)			

Country	Currency Used/Name	ISO Code	(Numeric Code)
Burkina Faso	Central French African Franc	XOF	(952)
Burma (see Myanmar)			
Burundi	Burundi Franc	BIF	(108)
C			
Cambodia	Riel	KHR	(116)
Cameroon	Central French African Franc	XAF	(950)
Canada	Canadian Dollar	CAD	(124)
Cape Verde	Escudo Caboverdiano	CVE	(132)
Cayman Islands	Cayman Islands Dollar	KYD	(136)
Central African Republic	Central French African Franc	XAF	(950)
Chad	Central French African Franc	XAF	(950)
Chile	Chilean Peso	CLP	(152)
	Unidades de Formento	CLF	(990)
China	Renminbi Yuan	CNY (RMB)	(156)
Christmas Island	Australian Dollar	AUD	(036)
Cocos (Keeling) Islands	Australian Dollar	AUD	(036)
Colombia	Colombian Peso	COP	(170)
	Unidad de Valor Real	COU	(970)
Comoros	Comorian Franc	KMF	(174)
Confederation Helvetica	C.H. Franc/Swiss Franc	CHF	(756)
Congo	Central French African Franc	XAF	(950)
Democratic Republic of Congo	Franc Congolais/New Zaire	CDF	(976)
Cook Islands	New Zealand Dollar	NZD	(554)
Costa Rica	Costa Rican Colon	CRC	(188)
Cote D'Ivoire (Ivory Coast)	Central French African Franc	XOF	(952)
Croatia	Croatian Kuna	HRK	(191)
Cuba	Cuban Peso	CUP	(192)

(Continued)

Country	Currency Used/Name	ISO Code	(Numeric Code)
Cyprus	Cyprus Pound (in a holding pattern for the Euro)	CYP	(196)
Czech Republic	Czech Koruna (in a holding pattern for the Euro)	CZK	(203)

D

Country	Currency Used/Name	ISO Code	(Numeric Code)
Denmark	Danish Krone	DKK	(208)
Deutscheland	Euro (formerly Deutsche Mark)	EUR DEM	(978)
Djibouti	Djibouti Franc	DJF	(262)
Dominica	East Caribbean Dollar	XCD	(951)
Dominican Republic	Dominican (Republic) Peso	DOP	(214)

E

Country	Currency Used/Name	ISO Code	(Numeric Code)
Ecuador	US Dollar (formerly Ecuador Sucre)	USD ECS	(840)
Egypt	Egyptian Pound	EGP	(818)
El Salvador	El Salvador Colon	SVC	(222)
	US Dollar	USD	(840)
England (see United Kingdom)	Great Britain Pound	GBP	(826)
Equatorial Guinea	Central French African Franc	XAF	(950)
Eritrea	Nakfa	ERN	(232)
Estonia	Kroon (in a holding pattern for the Euro)	EEK	(233)
Ethiopia	Ethiopian Birr	ETB	(230)
Europe/EuroZone	Euro	EUR	(978)

F

Country	Currency Used/Name	ISO Code	(Numeric Code)
Falkland Islands	Falkland Islands Pound	FKP	(238)
Faroe Islands	Danish Krone	DKK	(208)
Federated States of Micronesia (see Micronesia)			
Fiji	Fiji Dollar	FJD	(242)
Finland	Euro (formerly Finnish Markka)	EUR FIM	(978)

Country	Currency Used/Name	ISO Code	(Numeric Code)
France	Euro	EUR	(978)
	(formerly French Franc)	FRF	
French Guiana	Euro	EUR	(978)
French Polynesia	CFP Franc	XAF	(953)
French Southern Territory	Euro	EUR	(978)
G			
Gabon	Central French African Franc	XAF	(950)
Gambia	Dalasi	GMD	(270)
Georgia	Lari	GEL	(981)
Germany	Euro	EUR	(978)
	(formerly Deutsche Mark)	DEM	
Ghana	Cedi	GHC	(288)
Gibraltar	Gibraltar Pound	GIP	(292)
Great Britain (see United Kingdom)	Great Britain Pound	GBP	(826)
Greece	Euro	EUR	(978)
	(formerly Greek Drachma)	GRD	
Greenland	Danish Krone	DKK	(208)
Grenada	East Caribbean Dollar	XCD	(951)
Guadeloupe	Euro	EUR	(978)
Guam	US Dollar	USD	(840)
Guatemala	Quetzal	GTQ	(320)
Guinea	Guinea Franc	GNF	(324)
Guinea-Bissau	Guinea-Bissau Peso	GWP	(624)
	Central French African Franc	XOF	(952)
Guyana	Guyanese Dollar	GYD	(328)
H			
Haiti	Gourde	HTG	(332)
	US Dollar	USD	(840)
Heard Islands and McDonald Islands	Australian Dollar	AUD	(036)
Hellas	Euro	EUR	(978)
	(formerly Greek Drachma)	GRD	

(Continued)

Country	Currency Used/Name	ISO Code	(Numeric Code)
Holland	Euro	EUR	(978)
(see Netherlands)	(formerly Dutch Guilder)	NLG	
Honduras	Lempira	HNL	(340)
Hong Kong	Hong Kong Dollar	HKD	(344)
Hungary	Forint	HUF	(348)
	(in a holding pattern for the Euro)		
I			
Iceland	Iceland Krona	ISK	(352)
India	Indian Rupee	INR	(356)
Indonesia	Rupiah	IDR	(360)
International Monetary Fund (IMF)	SDR	XDR	(960)
Iran, Islamic Republic of	Iranian Rial	IRR	(364)
Iraq	Iraqi Dinar	IQD	(368)
Ireland	Euro	EUR	(978)
	(formerly Irish Punt/Pound)	IEP	
Israel	New Israeli Sheqel (Shekel)	ILS	(376)
Italy	Euro	EUR	(978)
	(formerly Italian Lira)	ITL	
Ivory Coast	Central French African Franc	XOF	(952)
J			
Jamaica	Jamaican Dollar	JMD	(388)
Japan	Yen	JPY	(392)
Jordan	Jordanian Dinar	JOD	(400)
K			
Kazakhstan	Tenge	KZT	(398)
Kenya	Kenyan Shilling	KES	(404)
Kiribati	Australian Dollar	AUD	(036)
Korea, Democratic People's Republic of North	North Korean Won	KPW	(408)
Korea, Republic of	South Korean Won	KRW	(410)
Kuwait	Kuwaiti Dinar	KWD	(414)
Kyrgyzstan	Som	KGS	(417)

Country	Currency Used/Name	ISO Code	(Numeric Code)
L			
Laos, People's Democratic Republic of	Kip	LAK	(418)
Latvia	Latvian Lats (in a holding pattern for the Euro)	LVL	(428)
Lebanon	Lebanese Pound	LBP	(422)
Lesotho	Loti	LSL	(426)
	Rand	ZAR	(710)
Liberia	Liberian Dollar	LRD	(430)
Libyan Arab Jamahiriya	Libyan Dinar	LYD	(434)
Liechtenstein	C.H. Franc/Swiss Franc	CHF	(756)
Lithuania	Lithuanian Litas (in a holding pattern for the Euro)	LTL	(440)
Luxembourg	Euro (formerly Luxembourg Franc)	EUR LUF	(978)
M			
Macao	Pataca	MOP	(446)
Macedonia	Denar	MKD	(807)
Madagascar	Malagasy Franc	MGF	(450)
	Malagasy Ariary	MGA	(969)
Malawi	Kwacha	MWK	(454)
Malaysia	Malaysian Ringgit	MYR	(458)
Maldives	Rufiyaa	MVR	(462)
Mali	Central French African Franc	XOF	(952)
Malta	Maltese Lira (in a holding pattern for the Euro)	MTL	(470)
Malvinas	Falkland Islands Pound	FKP	(238)
Marshall Islands	US Dollar	USD	(840)
Martinique	Euro	EUR	(978)
Mauritania	Ouguiya	MRO	(478)
Mauritius	Mauritius Rupee	MUR	(480)
Mayotte	Euro	EUR	(978)
Mexico	Mexican (Nuevo) Peso	MXN	(484)
	Mexican Unidad de Inversion	MXV	(979)

(Continued)

Country	Currency Used/Name	ISO Code	(Numeric Code)
Micronesia, Federated States of	US Dollar	USD	(840)
Moldova, Republic of	Moldovan Leu	MDL	(498)
Monaco	Euro	EUR	(978)
Mongolia	Tugrik	MNT	(496)
Montserrat	East Caribbean Dollar	XCD	(951)
Morocco	Moroccan Dirham	MAD	(504)
Mozambique	Meticais	MZM	(508)
Myanmar	Kyat	MMK	(104)
N			
Namibia	Namibian Dollar	NAD	(516)
	Rand	ZAR	(710)
Nauru	Australian Dollar	AUD	(036)
Nepal	Nepalese Rupee	NPR	(524)
Netherlands	Euro	EUR	(978)
	(formerly Dutch Guilder)	NLG	
Netherlands Antilles	Netherlands Antillian Guilder	ANG	(532)
New Caledonia	CFP Franc	XPF	(953)
New Zealand	New Zealand Dollar	NZD	(554)
Nicaragua	Cordoba Oro	NIO	(558)
Niger	Central French African Franc	XOF	(952)
Nigeria	Naira	NGN	(566)
Nippon	Japanese Yen	JPY	(392}
Niue	New Zealand Dollar	NZD	(554)
Norfolk Island	Australian Dollar	AUD	(036)
North Korea	North Korean Won	KPW	(408)
Northern Mariana Islands	US Dollar	USD	(840)
Norway	Norwegian Krone	NOK	(578)
O			
Oman	Omani Rial	OMR	(512)
P			
Pakistan	Pakistan Rupee	PKR	(586)
Palau	US Dollar	USD	(840)
Panama	Balboa	PAB	(590)
	US Dollar	USD	(840)

Country	Currency Used/Name	ISO Code	(Numeric Code)
Papua New Guinea	Kina	PGK	(598)
Paraguay	Guarani	PYG	(600)
People's Republic of China	Renminbi Yuan	CNY	(156)
Peru	Nuevo Sol	PEN	(604)
Philippines	Philippine Peso	PHP	(608)
Pitcairn	New Zealand Dollar	NZD	(554)
Poland	Zloty (in a holding pattern for the Euro)	PLN	(985)
Portugal	Euro (formerly Portuguese Escudo)	EUR PTE	(978)
Puerto Rico	US Dollar	USD	(840)
Q			
Qatar	Qatari Rial	QAR	(634)
R			
Reunion	Euro	EUR	(978)
Romania	Lei	ROL	(642)
Russian Federation	Russian Ruble	RUB	(643)
Rwanda	Rwanda Franc	RWF	(646)
S			
Saint Helena	Saint Helena Pound	SHP	(654)
Saint Kitts and Nevis	East Caribbean Dollar	XCD	(951)
Saint Lucia	East Caribbean Dollar	XCD	(951)
Saint Pierre and Miquelon	Euro	EUR	(978)
Saint Vincent and The Grenadines	East Caribbean Dollar	XCD	(951)
Samoa	Tala	WST	(882)
San Marino	Euro	EUR	(978)
Sao Tome and Principe	Dobra	STD	(678)
Saudi Arabia	Saudi Riyal	SAR	(682)
Senegal	Central French African Franc	XOF	(952)
Serbia and Montenegro	Serbian Dinar (in Serbia) Euro (in Montenegro)	CSD EUR	(891) (978)
Seychelles	Seychelles Rupee	SCR	(690)

(Continued)

Country	Currency Used/Name	ISO Code	(Numeric Code)
Sierra Leone	Leone	SLL	(694)
Singapore	Singapore Dollar	SGD	(702)
Slovakia	Slovak Koruna (in a holding pattern for the Euro)	SKK	(703)
Slovenia	Tolar (in a holding pattern for the Euro)	SIT	(705)
Solomon Islands	Solomon Islands Dollar	SBD	(090)
Somalia	Somali Shilling	SOS	(706)
South Africa	Rand	ZAR	(710)
South Korea	South Korean Won	KRW	(410)
Spain	Euro (formerly Spanish Peseta)	EUR ESP	(978)
Sri Lanka	Sri Lanka Rupee	LKR	(144)
Sudan	Sudanese Dinar	SDD	(736)
	Sudanese Pound	SDP	
Suriname	Surinam Dollar	SRD	(968)
	Suriname Guilder	SRG	
Svalbard and Jan Mayen	Norwegian Krone	NOK	(578)
Swaziland	Lilangeni	SZL	(748)
Sweden	Swedish Krona	SEK	(752)
Switzerland	Swiss Franc/C.H. Franc	CHF	(756)
	WIR Euro	CHE	(947)
	WIR Franc	CHW	(948)
Syrian Arab Republic	Syrian Pound	SYP	(760)

T

Country	Currency Used/Name	ISO Code	(Numeric Code)
Taiwan	New Taiwan Dollar	TWD	(901)
Tajikistan	Somoni	TJS	(972)
Tanzania, United Republic of	Tanzanian Shilling	TZS	(834)
Thailand	Baht	THB	(764)
Timor-Leste	US Dollar	USD	(840)
Togo	Central French African Franc	XOF	(952)
Tokelau	New Zealand Dollar	NZD	(554)
Tonga	Pa'anga	TOP	(776)
Trinidad and Tobago	Trinidad and Tobago Dollar	TTD	(780)
Tunisia	Tunisian Dinar	TND	(788)
Turkey	Old Turkish Lira	TRL	(792)
	New Turkish Lira	TRY	(949)

Country	Currency Used/Name	ISO Code	(Numeric Code)
Turkmenistan	Manat	TMM	(795)
Turks and Caicos Islands	US Dollar	USD	(840)
Tuvalu	Australian Dollar	AUD	(036)
U			
Uganda	Uganda Shilling	UGS	(800)
Ukraine	Hryvnia	UAH	(980)
United Arab Emirates	UAE Dirham	AED	(784)
United Kingdom	Pound Sterling	GBP	(826)
United States	US Dollar	USD	(840)
	(Next Day Delivery "T + 1")	USN	(997)
	(Same Day Delivery "T + 0")	USS	(998)
United States Minor Outlying Islands	US Dollar	USD	(840)
Uruguay	Uruguayan Peso	UYP	(858)
Uzbekistan	Uzbekistan Sum	UZS	(860)
V			
Vanuatu	Vatu	VUV	(548)
Vatican City	Euro	EUR	(978)
Venezuela	Bolivar	VEB	(862)
Viet Nam	Dong	VND	(704)
Virgin Islands (British)	US Dollar	USD	(840)
Virgin Islands (US)	US Dollar	USD	(840)
W			
Wallis and Futuna	CFP Franc	XPF	(953)
Western Sahara	Moroccan Dirham	MAD	(504)
Y			
Yemen	Yemeni Rial	YER	(886)
Yugoslavia	Yugoslav Dinar	YUN	
Z			
Zambia	Kwacha	ZMK	(894)
Zimbabwe	Zimbabwe Dollar	ZWD	(716)

Precious Metals

Gold	(AU from Latin "aurum" for "gold")	XAU	(959)
Palladium	(from Greek "Pallas")	XPD	(964)
Platinum	(from Spanish "platina" for "little silver")	XPT	(962)
Silver	(AG from Latin "argentum" for "silver")	XAG	(961)

Other Miscellaneous ISO Codes

European Monetary Unit (E.M.U.-6)	XBB	(956)
European Unit of Account 9 (E.U.A.-9)	XBC	(957)
European Unit of Account 17 (E.U.A.-17)	XBD	(958)
European Bond Markets Composite Unit (EURCO)	XBA	(955)
Transactions where no currency is involved	XXX	(999)
Reserved for testing purposes	XTS	(963)
Special Settlement Currencies:		
UIC—Franc	XFU	
Gold—Franc	XFO	

CHAPTER 2

Markets, Prices, and Marketmaking

WHAT IS A "MARKET"?

What is a "market"? The typical person off the street would probably say that a market is a place where trading occurs. While responding, that individual might have in the back of his/her mind visions of large, loud, and aggressive men in brightly colored jackets yelling and screaming at each other on traditional exchange floors. But does a market have to be a place? No. There are many types of markets: supermarkets (where you can purchase everything from food to flowers, detergent to DVDs), flea markets (where people buy and sell used items), black markets (in which illegal or illegally acquired commodities trade hands), stock markets, meat markets, money markets, and farmers markets. In short, there are many different institutions that we identify as a market. Nevertheless, when many of us think of a market, we tend to think of the organized financial markets and more explicitly, the trading floors of the securities exchanges.

Indeed, mention of "the" stock market brings to mind Wall Street and the New York Stock Exchange. (But did you know there are local stock exchanges around the United States: Philadelphia, Chicago, Boston—many of which are now electronic?) In the realm of equities (or stock), there is a distinction drawn between "listed" (as in "listed on the New York Stock Exchange" or "the Big Board") and "OTC" (as in over-the-counter). For many who work in equities, OTC refers to a NASDAQ stock (that is, a stock that is traded over the North American Securities Dealers Automated Quotation system—an electronic network aimed at getting buyers and sellers together without the use of a specialist system, broker network, or populated trading floor as is currently employed by the NYSE).[1] Where does the terminology OTC come from? Was there ever a counter over which transactions took place? As with most terminology, this expression likely has its origins grounded in fact. At one time, individuals engaged in the trading of (paper) security certificates out-of-doors over tabletops in lower Manhattan; no doubt, inclement weather is only one of the many reasons that the members of the American Curbside Brokers Association moved indoors, changed their name, and established the American Stock Exchange (AMEX)—a rival of the NYSE.

Though there once may have actually been a counter, nowadays OTC simply refers to trading which is either done over the telephone or done electronically (through an electronic communications network (ECN) or some other telecommunications or computer-based system).[2] The foreign exchange market today is almost exclusively done OTC. There are, as is almost always the case in foreign exchange, exceptions—such as the International Monetary Market (IMM) currency futures and the options written on those futures, which trade at the Merc (the Chicago Mercantile Exchange), the LIFFE (the London International Financial Futures Exchange), and the SIMEX (the Singapore International Monetary Exchange) and also foreign exchange options which trade on, of all places, the Philadelphia Stock Exchange, but these contracts constitute only a very, very small part of the volume in foreign exchange. A "market" is simply an institution that has, as its goal, bringing buyers and sellers together.

The foreign exchange markets are global, primarily over-the-counter, and relatively unregulated (compared to the securities markets).[3] As FX trading involves dealing in money and banks continue to serve as the warehouses of this commodity, these markets tend to be dominated by the large international money center banks.

WHAT IS A "PRICE"?

What is a "price"? Adam Smith (the real Adam Smith) once said,

> *The real price of everything, what everything really costs to the man who wants to acquire it, is the toil and trouble of acquiring it.*
> —Adam Smith, *An Inquiry into the Nature and Causes of the Wealth of Nations* (1776)

While I believe this to be true, it is not usually the way that I think about prices in my daily life. Ask yourself, "What is the price of a hamburger?" Unless you are a vegetarian, you probably have a number in mind, where that number depends on how upscale the hamburger joint is that you tend to frequent. For the sake of argument, let's say you respond with, "$4." That is, you say, "The price of a hamburger is 4 Dollars." This is fine. Usually when I ask this in the classroom, I tend to follow this question with another: "What is the price of a Dollar?" In all my years of teaching foreign exchange, only once has the response failed to be, "a Dollar." On that one exceptional occasion, I made the unfortunate choice of selecting a fellow whom I did not know was from Canada who responded, "1.36 Canadian." For many of us in the United States, the price of a Dollar is a Dollar (since Americans tend to think of prices in terms of our local U.S. currency units). This idea has even been reinforced over the years on U.S. currency, which has carried the phrase, "payable to the bearer on demand" and later "is redeemable for lawful money at the United States Treasury or any Federal Reserve Bank"—where, presumably, that redemption meant you could turn in a dirty old Dollar bill for a bright new one of the same denomination at your local bank (officially, through the Bureau of Engraving and Printing). According to the Treasury, the price of a Dollar really is a Dollar!

Let's try to think about prices differently. I believe that it is reasonable to think of the price of a hamburger as $4 (or, as we shall denote from this point on, "USD 4," which stands for "four U.S. Dollars"), but what this really means is that I will receive 1 hamburger for USD 4. These two numbers constitute an exchange or a "trade." In this sense, this price (and every price) can (and should) be thought of as a ratio of quantities:

$$\frac{\text{USD } 4}{1 \text{ hamburger}}$$

A Price Is a Ratio of Quantities

More precisely, what this indicates is that if I give up four USD, I will receive one hamburger. Though it may sound odd when articulated in this way, when we are buying hamburgers, we are selling Dollars, and the price identifies the rate of exchange. And though it may sound even stranger, McDonald's buys Dollars with hamburgers, though almost everyone would identify McDonald's typical daily activity as selling hamburgers.

Every time you buy one thing, you sell another thing (noting explicitly that this refers to one transaction, not two) and every time you sell something, you necessarily buy something else in exchange.

When looked at and summarized in this fashion, we clearly see that the price of 1 Dollar is $1/4$ of a hamburger.[4]

BUYERS AND SELLERS

Let's ask another question. For the sake of argument (even if it is counterfactual), assume you own a car; heck, as long as it's hypothetical, you may as well assume that you own an extremely nice car. Now my question is, "Would you like to buy another car just like yours?" Some of us may think that we do not "need" another car, but if I asked you whether you'd like to buy another car just like yours for USD 1, most people would immediately respond in the affirmative (if only because they would make such a purchase intending to resell that car in the near future at a higher price). If asked, "Would you be willing to sell your car?" some people might respond, "no" because they "need" their car, for example, to get to work, but, by the time I started offering USD 20,000,000, most people would tend to oblige. What is the point? Economists often talk about "the buyers" and "the sellers" as if they are well-defined groups of economic agents, but whether you are a buyer or a seller may very well depend on the price. Prices drive markets. This is no less true of the foreign exchange market than any other market, and, remember, it is best, especially in FX, to think of every price as a ratio of quantities.

MARKETMAKING

Most people say that the market went up because there were more buyers than sellers, but that need not be strictly true. One seller with a great deal of product to sell or "to go" may interface with a huge number of buyers, but the numerical superiority of the quantity of buyers may not be sufficient to keep the market price from plummeting as the seller goes about his/her business. Price behavior depends on the quantity being offered for sale, the quantity for which buyers are bidding, the time frame involved, the urgency of the two sides of the market, and a myriad of other factors that a well-known economist named John Maynard Keynes once characterized by the expression "animal spirits."

If you were to ask those individuals who perform financial transactions at a bank like UBS what they do for a living, many would respond, for example, to their acquaintances at a ball game, "We are traders" but if they were asked the same question at work with their manager looking over their shoulder, they would probably respond that they are "marketmakers." Of course, they do not make markets in the sense that they set up those institutions through which buyers and sellers interact; their occupation involves standing ready to buy if a client wishes to sell and standing ready to sell if a client wishes to buy. In essence, they agree to "be" the market to their client or counterparty. In return, for providing this liquidity to the market (and assuming the risks that such activities entail), the marketmaker is compensated by having the opportunity to buy low (quoting a low buying price or bid price or simply "bid") and to sell or offer high (charging a higher selling price or offer price, or asking price, or simply "offer" or "ask"). This bid–ask (or bid–offer) spread is one way that a marketmaker attempts to generate a profit and stay in business. The very best thing that could happen to a marketmaker is to experience a great deal of "two-sided flow" with, from the marketmaker's perspective, lots of buying on the bid and lots of selling at the offer. Being a marketmaker does not necessarily involve arbitrage or a certain profit, though, as an upward trending market may find a marketmaker selling throughout the day with no arbitrage profit (and a suitcase full of regret) to show for it on the close.

The rule of the marketmaker is

BUY LOW.

SELL HIGH.

The good news for the marketmaker is that their counterparty has to sell low and buy high. Counterparties (sometimes called "market takers") are said to have to "cross" the bid–ask spread.

The Bid–Ask or Bid–Offer Spread

To avoid the confusion associated with foreign exchange for now, let's think about gold. Gold is not foreign exchange—even if it has served, in many different forms, as money over time and, to this day, is sometimes used for international trade settlements. Gold is a very simple commodity (heck, it's more than just simple, it's an element: AU), and, as a fairly elementary product, it will allow some basic points to be made.

What might you want to know (or at least think about) if you were obliged to make a market in spot gold? There is a list of considerations most marketmakers would want to contemplate before sticking their necks out and making a two-sided market (that is, before providing a bid price and an ask price, on which an informed counterparty could deal). Some of the marketmaker's inquiries might include: At what price did the last trade take place? Where is the market going (up or down)? What is my position? Will any news be coming out that could impact the direction of the market? What is going on in related markets? What is "smart paper" doing? How wide can the bid–ask spread be? How volatile are gold prices?

Let's examine these in turn.

Where Was the Last Trade?

Unlike the formal securities exchanges, which record and report prices in an extremely timely and highly reliable fashion, the market for gold, like

40   FOREIGN EXCHANGE

foreign exchange, is predominantly OTC (and so there is no central repository of information into which all trade data flows, through which prices and quantities are organized, and from which these numbers are disseminated). Nevertheless, gold, like FX, is traded globally in a large, active, and relatively transparent market. It is usually easy to obtain a price for gold that one might be relatively confident reflects a very recent transaction. For the sake of argument, let's say that gold last traded at a spot price of S = USD 400 per ounce.[5] Are you ready to make a market? You might try the following: "375 bid, offered at 425" or more succinctly "375–425" (read "375 at 425"). This would indicate your willingness (as a marketmaker) to buy gold for USD 375 per ounce and your willingness to sell gold at USD 425 per ounce. If some counterparty were to "hit your bid" (which means to sell to you where you are willing to buy, i.e., 375) and another counterparty were, simultaneously, to "lift your offer" (which means to buy from you at the price at which you are willing to sell, i.e., 425), then you would "capture" the "bid–ask spread" of USD 50 with every matched pair of these transactions that you do.

Competitive forces, market convention, and sometimes even regulations impact the width of the bid–ask spread in financial markets. Other market participants, constantly trying to better the bid (i.e., bidding higher) or to better the offer (i.e., offering lower), will have the effect of pushing the market quotes toward 399–401.

If you were to ask most marketmakers whether they ever bid higher than the price reflected in the last trade (or offered to sell at a price less than the last trade price), they would almost surely answer in the affirmative. The reason I might bid 401 when the last trade took place at a price of S = 400 is because I think the market is going up; if the market price of gold were to go to S = 405, I would be very happy to have purchased it for 401 (or 404.50 for that matter). The point: Marketmakers have to think about where the market might be headed. The USD 64,000 question: How do you know whether the market price is going to go up or down?

Where Is the Market Headed?

There are two methods for gaining insight into where the market is going. The first goes by the name of **fundamental analysis** and the other is known by the blanket expression **technical analysis**. These are two very different approaches.

Fundamental analysis attempts to gain insight into market direction based on an examination of demand and supply—and the other economic factors that drive that particular market. It is possible to get very precise production (or supply) figures for gold. The U.S. Geological Survey reports

U.S. and world gold production figures and their data are published on a monthly basis. Given that the entire stock of gold ever taken from the ground, if consolidated into one location, would easily fit under the first level of the Eiffel Tower in Paris (or, put a little more scientifically, within a 30 meter cube), there really isn't that much gold in the world (that's been removed from the ground and refined, that is). What about demand? I once asked a class, "What country is the number one consumer of gold in the world?" and was corrected by someone from our Precious Metals desk who informed me that you don't really "consume" gold (except in minute quantities in some exotic desserts and off-beat liquors). The leading purchaser of gold, as a country, is India; there, it is turned into adornments, is used to plate dishes and servingware, is an extremely common wedding gift in many forms, is a traditional investment vehicle, and so on. The point is that things that impact the Indian economy (positively or negatively) are likely to impact the global market for gold.

Understanding the underlying economics of gold demand and supply (its importance and substitutability in electronics equipment, jewelry, dentistry; its attractiveness as an investment; world production figures; the fact that it is perceived as a hedge against inflation), one would think, should give a clue as to where the price of gold is headed. This sort of analysis is the meat-and-potatoes of the traditional economist.

Technical analysis, on the other hand, ignores such fundamentals and purports to be able to forecast market direction based largely (and often solely) on past price action or price behavior. By examining the historical record of gold prices, a technical analyst (or "technician") would analyze trends, waves or cycles, and other patterns in an attempt to gain some insights into where the price will be (usually) in the (relatively near-term) future. We will return to this topic later (in Chapter 13).

In any event, marketmakers have an obvious and deep-seated interest in gaining any possible insights into the direction of the market price.

What Is My Position?

As a marketmaker, you control only one thing: your position. You can be "long" gold, or "short" gold, or have no position at all.[6] Of course, in reality, marketmakers are constantly doing transactions, and therefore changing their inventory dynamically throughout the day. Now it is possible for you to influence your position as a marketmaker by the markets that you make (i.e., by the prices that you communicate to your clients). If you have purchased a great deal of gold as the day has evolved (i.e., you are very long), then, as a marketmaker, you are probably inclined to want to sell some of your inventory (since the larger your inventory, the greater the risk you have if the price of gold drops), and if you are short, you are probably inclined to want to buy back some of that gold (unless you are extremely confident the price will fall). A trader who is inclined to want to reduce a long position is said to be "better offered" (i.e., to be asking a lower selling price than the other traders), and someone is said to be "better bid" if they are conveying a higher proposed purchase price than the rest of the market.

Is Any News Coming Out That Will Impact the Market?

Some news is predictable, at least in terms of the timing of its dissemination. For example, gold mining production figures, as mentioned earlier, are reported monthly by the U.S. Geological Survey. In general, a great many financial and economic numbers, from unemployment data and new job figures, to GDP, international trade imbalances, measures of inflation (such as the Consumer Price Index), corporate earnings, housing starts and new home sales, survey results on consumer confidence, are all reported relatively regularly (although admittedly with a varying degree of reliability depending, for example, on whether the data are compiled from surveys or obtained from the population, on who reports the information, on whether the numbers are subject to frequent and/or significant revision). In short, although the number itself might be in question, there is no uncertainty about the timing of its release.

Other news is unpredictable in its timing. If the market were to hear that some disgruntled faction was blowing up the gold mines in South Africa or that a scientist had devised an economically feasible way to remove gold from sea water, one thing I would expect is that the price of gold would move violently. In this sense, news can be likened to the punch line of a good joke; the more unexpected it is, the greater the impact that it will have. And while there is little a marketmaker can do to prepare for the "unknown" news,[7] at least having some feel for the market's expectations of the data/figures/numbers that the market is anticipating (i.e., the market's consensus) can ensure a trader's proper reaction to the news, once transmitted or communicated.

What Is Smart Paper Doing?

Marketmakers, traders, broker/dealers, and many market participants refer to better informed agents as "smart paper" in reference to the paper tickets that once formed the foundation of market order flow. In some situations, a marketmaker is not allowed to inquire (of the broker executing a customer order) whether that customer is buying or selling; the responsibility of a marketmaker is to quote a two-sided market—as the knowledge of what a customer wishes to do (that is, buy or sell) presumably would allow an unscrupulous marketmaker to skew their price up or down and thus take advantage of that customer. Securities regulations are very strict in ensuring investors fair prices and orderly execution. Having said that, because the FX market is not encumbered by many of the rules and regulations of the securities laws (foreign exchange is not a security), in principle there is no reason why a marketmaker could not ask a client what they wanted to do (i.e., buy or sell). Practically, though, it is generally considered unprofessional to inquire on any reasonable size market order. Then again, on a particularly large order, one might hear an FX marketmaker ask, "Full amount?" By this they are asking if the entire order is being placed with them or if a basket of similar orders are simultaneously being launched to every other marketmaker. It might make a difference to a trader (in terms of taking on a large position, in terms of their anticipated ability to lay off some of that inventory with other market professionals, and in terms of managing their overall portfolio risk) who might otherwise be able to slowly "work their way out" of a large trade without the market knowing what trades they would like to or have to do. Finally, there are instances in which a client, wishing to place an order in a particularly illiquid currency pair or difficult-to-hedge exotic option (to be discussed later), might be asked, "Do you want to buy it or do you want to sell it (possibly with additional inquiries about the magnitude of the proposed transaction)?" because the legitimate width of the bid–ask spread might be (justifiably, but uncomfortably) rather wide in those instances.

In terms of who is "smart," it is fair to say that many counterparties to the marketmaking firms (who might be hedge funds, other banks, institutional funds, active corporate treasurers, financial advisors) are presumed to be well informed traders/investors (and therefore, might have a good sense of the direction of the market, in part because it's their job), whereas a dental firm that purchases gold for its clients' teeth or a university that periodically gilts the dome of one of its buildings would not be considered "smart paper" (in terms of having a particularly valuable insight into the direction of the market price of gold). As a rule, although marketmakers may acquire inventories (long and/or short), they are generally not investors and therefore are not as "smart" as their clients whose occupations involve knowing what to buy and when to buy it. Reinforcing this notion, one head of FX trading once told his traders, "If you don't have an opinion, don't have a position." In other words, be a marketmaker, not a speculator.

How Wide Can the Bid–Ask Spread Be?

Unlike the case in some of the other financial markets, there is no legislated maximum bid–ask spread in gold or FX, but the competitiveness of the gold and FX markets keeps the bid–offer range in these product areas as "tight" as anywhere (i.e., a very small bid–ask spread). Of course, this might also depend on the face or notional amount that one's counterparty wishes to trade. To put some perspective on the issue of bid–ask spreads, U.S. equities, until recently, traded in $1/8$ths and $1/16$ths of a Dollar; since decimalization (which arrived in the United States in 2000), prices have been quoted in cents (resulting in a reduction in the size of the quoted bid–offer spreads), with a typical bid–ask being a few cents wide. In FX, most currencies are quoted out to the fourth decimal place and markets are usually only a few "pips" wide (to be defined in Chapter 5). Of course, we should really look at bid–ask in terms of percentages (for this to be a legitimate comparison), but the extremely tight bid–ask spreads in the major currency pairs in FX generally reflect a very competitive and highly commoditized market. For the record, a typical bid–ask spread in gold on a typical day with last trade at S = 400.00 might be USD .40, or 399.80–400.20.

How Volatile Are Gold Prices?

Volatility, or the "jumpiness" of market prices, would matter to a marketmaker because if the price of gold tends to move up and down violently (which is what volatility is all about), then, to keep from being "run over" (that is, from being on the wrong side of an informed customer's trade), a marketmaker would want to widen out their bid–ask spread. For example, with the last trade at S = 400, a bid–ask of 399–401 might be in order if gold fluctuates only minimally each day, but a marketmaker might feel more comfortable quoting 397–403 if it was the case that gold frequently experienced two to three Dollar average daily price swings.

There are other things that a marketmaker might like to know as well:

What are the positions of the other market participants? In other words, Is the market (that is, "the rest of the market") long or short?

What's going on in related (i.e., stock and bond and other commodity) markets? We mentioned that a marketmaker would like to stay on top of what news is coming out.

How does the marketmaker's expectation of the forthcoming news announcement (i.e., his/her forecast) compare with the general market consensus for this number or data? And why?

Marketmakers should also have some sense of not only which way the market will move, but, also, how far. I have heard some successful traders claim to be right only about 40% of the time, but this statement appears far more credible if one realizes that they only put on trades that lose USD 1 if they are wrong but make USD 4 if they are right.

Finally, a marketmaker in gold might like to know something about interest rates for many reasons (as a bank account might be considered an alternative to investing in gold and also because forward prices (to be discussed in Chapter 6) have interest rates imbedded in their calculation and some market participants believe forward prices are closely related to spot prices).

EXAMPLE

A client calls a bank to trade spot gold. They hear (receive a market quote of) "398–402." They would like to buy 1,000 ounces.

Question: At what price will they deal and what flow will be generated by that transaction?

Answer: The client buys where the marketmaker is willing to sell. The marketmaker's offer here is 402 (or USD 402 per ounce of gold); multiplying this by 1,000, then, would identify the following flows:

The client gets 1,000 ounces of gold and pays USD 402,000.

The marketmaker at the bank will deliver 1,000 ounces of gold and receive USD 402,000.

MARKETS EXERCISES

Consider the market for spot platinum. You need to purchase 2,000 ounces to use in your business's production of thermocoupling units. As the assistant treasurer, you telephone your precious metals dealer and ask for a market in spot platinum. You hear, "974 at 976."

1. If the relevant price is acceptable, what will you say and do?
2. What considerations do you think might be relevant to a spot platinum marketmaker in quoting a two-sided market?

(Answers to exercises are found in the back of this book.)

SUMMARY

All too often, I have heard people blame marketmakers for manipulating market prices, and, while this has no doubt happened on occasion, for the most part, traders are facilitating their customers' orders and simply reacting and responding to the buying and selling that is going on in the market. An actual marketmaker once explained, "The prices you see are not set or determined by us. We reflect, like a thermometer, what the supply and demand are. That final price you see up on the board is representative of what the entire world feels that commodity is worth at that time and place."[8]

While being a marketmaker can be an interesting, exciting, and rewarding occupation, it can also be stressful, challenging, boring, and occasionally very frustrating. Banks/brokers/dealers, like UBS, interact with seasoned portfolio managers, brilliant hedge fund operators, and outstanding corporate treasurers. The difficulty is that these individuals are usually looking to buy assets that are going up in price and to sell assets that are going down in price—and, as a rule, they are very good at their jobs. This means that a marketmaker tends to sell assets whose prices will go up and to buy assets whose prices will go down—not a good business model. The only mitigating aspect of a marketmaker's activities is that a marketmaker is able to incorporate a bid–offer spread into the price quotes that are shown to the clients/counterparties.

CHAPTER 3

Interest Rates

WHAT ARE "INTEREST RATES"?

An interest rate is the price of money. Economists may talk about interest as the reward that accrues to foregone consumption, which could be argued, I suppose, at some level, but, in the end, the interest rate is simply the cost of borrowing money or the return from investing or depositing money. The nice thing about defining the interest rate as the price of money is that you don't have to specify whether it is a rate for borrowing (a cost) or a rate for lending (a benefit), though, as with every price in the financial markets, you should be prepared to encounter a bid–ask spread in the world of interest rates as well.

In Chapter 2, we defined every price as a ratio of quantities. When I think of an interest rate, I usually think in terms of percentages. For example, we might say that the interest rate is 5.20%. Where does the notion of price as a ratio come into play here? Let's say you wanted to host a party for a group of your friends celebrating the recent successes of your favorite sports team. If you wanted to serve food and beverages, you'd need to spend some money. If you did not have any cash readily available, you could, in principle, go to the bank and borrow some money. The banker would ask you how much money you'd like, would check your credit rating, would ask you to fill out and sign several forms, and then would ultimately quote you a rate of interest, say, 5.20%. If you decide to borrow USD 100 today, then in one year's time you would be obliged to pay back USD 105.20. That ratio, USD 105.20/USD 100, reflects the interest rate. You would have to pay back the money you borrowed (the USD 100) as well as the interest on that money (the additional USD 5.20). Though it may sound odd, the price of USD 100 today is USD 105.20 in one year.

What if you only needed to borrow the money for a week (until your next paycheck)? The banker would still quote you a rate of interest like 5.20%. That is because interest rates are almost, almost always quoted on an annual or annualized or per annum basis. That being said, if you borrow USD 100 today at an interest rate of $r = 5.20\%$, then in one week you would pay back only USD 100.10. Where did this come from? You would have to scale the interest rate for the time period involved (and here I assume that one week is exactly 1/52 of a year). The math would look like this

$$FV = PV(1 + rt) \qquad\qquad (3.1)$$

where we use PV to refer to the Present Value or Principal
                    FV to refer to the Future Value
                      r to indicate the (annualized) interest rate
         and t to reflect the   time period over which the
                                       borrowing or lending takes place
                                       (measured in years)

For the example we just looked at

$$100.10 = 100(1 + (.0520)(1/52))$$

and, for our earlier example:

$$105.20 = 100(1 + (.0520)(1))$$

This convention is known as **simple interest** and, if the time frame under consideration is a year or less, this is one of the most common ways in which interest is calculated.

INFLATION

An influential economist named Irving Fisher identified an important property associated with interest rates and drew a distinction that we review here. **Inflation** is defined as *the general increase in the average level of prices in the economy; it is typically reported, like interest rates, on an annual or annualized basis.*[1] Of course, in any given year, the prices of some products will be rising while the prices of some other items will be falling, so we have to look at the average price level relative to some "standard" or some well-defined "bundle" of goods. One of the measures of inflation calculated relative to a representative basket of U.S. household consumption goods and services is known as the Consumer Price Index. There are other measures of inflation for different strata of the economy: the Producer Price Index, the Wholesale Price Index, and the GDP Deflator.

What Professor Fisher noted was that if one put one's money in the bank for a year and received a market rate of interest or nominal rate of interest or money rate of interest (these all mean the same) of $r = 5.20\%$, but inflation was 3.20% during that year, then one's "real" purchasing power would have grown only at around 2.00%. This idea is summarized in what has come to be known as the (simple) Fisher Equation:

$$r_{\text{NOMINAL}} - \text{Inflation} = r_{\text{REAL}}$$

or

$$r_{\text{NOMINAL}} = r_{\text{REAL}} + \text{Inflation} \tag{3.2}$$

The interesting thing is that Irving Fisher tested this relationship (collecting data on nominal interest rates, inflation, and real returns) and, while this relationship seems almost definitional, it didn't seem to hold. What went wrong? Fisher used the contemporaneous rate of inflation, but that is not what depositors are thinking about when they put their money in the bank at a fixed rate of interest. A depositor has to ask, "What do I think the rate of inflation is going to be over the next year (or whatever the future time period under consideration)?" In this sense, the correct Fisher relationship looks like this:

$$r_{\text{NOMINAL}} = r_{\text{REAL}} + \text{EXPECTED Inflation} \tag{3.3}$$

Because this perspective involves expectations, it highlights the importance of the fact that interest rates are, necessarily, forward looking prices. Different countries have different nominal rates of interest, and different rates of inflation (as well as different rates of expected inflation), not to mention possibly different real interest rates (for a variety of reasons). Many economists believe **inflation is always and everywhere a monetary phenomenon.** Expansion of the money supply (or, more precisely, the expansion of the money supply in excess of real economic growth) tends to cause consumers to bid up the prices of the available goods and services in the economy—leading to an increase in the aggregate level of prices (i.e., inflation). Because countries exercise different degrees of control over the expansion of their money supply (in the language of the economists, because countries have different monetary policies), inflation, and therefore nominal interest rates, tend to be very different around the world. There is a great deal that could be said about interest rates. Let me confine the remainder of this chapter to five topics: day count, compounding, discounting, different types of interest rates, and interest rates in the real world.

DAY COUNT OR DAY BASIS

If one were to drop off money at the bank at noon today and retrieve it at noon tomorrow, you might presume you are entitled to one day of interest (and, in general, you would be correct in that presumption). How is that one day of interest calculated? Great question. More importantly, what does "one day" mean in terms of a fraction of a year? You may not see the potential ambiguity, but there are many possible conventions used in the financial community for measuring time. This is not an existential, philosophical, or abstruse scientific point. Most of us would presume that one day is exactly 1/365 of a year (which it sometimes is—although almost never in the United States). What if it was a leap year (in which February has 29 days); then we might guess that one day is 1/366 of a year (which it occasionally is—but usually not). The U.S. money market convention (and the one followed in most countries except the United Kingdom and a few other places around the world, mainly British Commonwealth countries) is to treat each day as 1/360 of a year. There are a few implications of using this convention:

1. If one were to deposit USD 100 for a week (exactly 7 days) at a rate of interest of $r = 5.20\%$, then it would grow (as we indicated earlier) into a Future Value (FV) of

   $$FV = PV(1 + rt) \text{ but here } t = \text{"actual number of days/360"}$$

   Unlike the FV number we calculated earlier (borrowing for a week at 5.20%), here we get

   $$100.10111111 = 100(1 + (.0520)(7/360))$$

   You might think this isn't much to get excited about, but if you consider a deposit of USD 50,000,000 instead of USD 100, it starts to add up (and a USD 50,000,000 face or notional transaction isn't a particularly large trade in the FX market). The implication of using this rule is that if you leave your money in the bank for an entire (non-leap) year, you will get more than USD 5.20 per USD 100 deposit, as an entire calendar year, according to this convention, refers to a time span greater than one year (i.e., (365/360)). Strange, but true.

   $$105.27222222 = 100(1 + (.0520) (365/360))$$

2. We might enter into a trade (agree to make a deposit) today and "undo" it (agree to withdraw the funds) in a week (7 days later), but you have to be careful; the "trade date" (or "T") and the settlement

date or value date are frequently different in the financial world. In the case of U.S. Treasury securities, today would be the trade date (or "T"), but settlement typically occurs one good business day later ("T + 1"). By "good business days," we mean business days (not weekends) that are not holidays; foreign exchange is singularly problematic because in a Dollar-Yen trade, we have to avoid holidays in both the United States and Japan. Different assets have different settlement lags. In the United States, equity or stock is "T + 3," corporate bonds are "T + 2," gold is "T + 2," and foreign exchange is (usually) "T + 2." It is the settlement-to-settlement time span that must be used to determine the day count for use in our formula (after all, that reflects the actual time over which someone has the money).

3. There are various day count conventions used around the world. For the most part, the United States, the EuroZone, Japan, and Switzerland use what we call "actual/360" while the United Kingdom uses an "actual/365" convention. For completeness, we simply note that there are other conventions, like "30/360" (which is nice in that it makes each month exactly 1/12 of a year, regardless of the actual number of days in that month—whether 30, 31, 28, or 29) and "actual/actual" (which takes into account leap years and, in such a year, would calculate 7 days of interest using "7/366" as our "t" for a one week borrowing/lending period).

COMPOUNDING

When we are calculating interest for a fraction of a year, as mentioned earlier, the market typically uses simple interest; if one were to deposit USD 100 for 4 years at a quoted annual rate of interest of $r = 5.20\%$, you might conjecture that your Future Value (what you would receive back after those 4 years) would be

$$FV = PV(\,1 + rt\,)$$
$$120.80 = 100(1 + (.0520)(4))$$

The problem with this would be that you would not be getting interest on your interest. If you deposited USD 100 for 1 year at 5.20%, you would think it should (with the proper day count) grow into USD 105.20 after a year. If that becomes the deposit for the next year, your money would then grow, after two years, into USD 110.6704. Continuing with this logic, your money would grow into USD 116.4252608 after 3 years and into USD 122.4793743616 after 4 years. The difference between what we just calculated ($\approx$ 122.48) and the number reported using a simple interest convention (120.80) can be accounted for precisely because of the interest on your interest.

The mathematics of this **compound interest** is as shown:

$$FV = PV(1 + r)^t \qquad\qquad (3.4)$$
$$122.4793744 = 100(1 + (.0520))^4$$

Specifically, this computation, which involves calculating interest once a year, is known as annual compounding. Usually if the time period involves over a year, we tend to incorporate some sort of compounding. But there is no reason to stop at calculating interest once a year. Why not compound twice a year? This would be known as semiannual compounding and could be calculated in the following manner:

$$FV = PV(1 + [r/2])^{2t}$$

and, in this case, our deposit of USD 100—growing at 5.20%—and compounded semiannually would become

$$122.4793744 = 100(1 + [.0520/2])^8 = 100(1.026)^8$$

Note: For this 4 year deposit, there are 8 half-year compounding periods, but you only get half of the quoted interest rate per period.

In general, one could compound N times a year (where for annual compounding, $N = 1$; semiannual compounding, $N = 2$; quarterly compounding, $N = 4$; monthly compounding, $N = 12$; weekly compounding, $N = 52$, and so on). The mathematics would be as follows

$$FV = PV(1 + [r/N])^{Nt} \qquad\qquad (3.5)$$

With a quoted rate of 5.20% for 4 years ($t = 4$), and with a principal of PV = USD 100, you would get the following FVs or Future Values. (See Table 3.1.)

Note that as the compounding frequency increases, although the future values continue to rise, they seem to be doing so at a diminishing rate. We can ask, "What if we were to compound 'continuously'?"

TABLE 3.1 Compounding Example with Different Compounding Frequencies

$PV = 100, t = 4, r = 5.20\%$		FV
Annual Compounding	$(N = 1)$	USD 122.4793744
Semiannual Compounding	$(N = 2)$	USD 122.7944918
Quarterly Compounding	$(N = 4)$	USD 122.9563962
Monthly Compounding	$(N = 12)$	USD 123.0660005
Weekly Compounding	$(N = 52)$	USD 123.1085215

Believe it or not, this is not a real stretch mathematically from what we have done (although you probably had hoped never to see this again after high school). Continuous compounding involves the following mathematics

$$FV = PV \, e^{rt} \qquad (3.6)$$

For the record, e, like π, is a unique, nonrepeating number; it is the base of the natural logarithms. The value of e is approximately 2.718281828. . . . And using the numbers from our earlier example ($PV = 100$, $r = 5.20\%$, and $t = 4$ years)—and a properly equipped calculator:

$$123.1213170 = 100e^{(.0520)(4)}$$

Two things to note here. First, this convention harkens back to simple interest (where we also saw "$r \times t$" in our calculation). Second, we see that there is, practically, little difference between weekly and continuous interest. As we move from weekly to daily to hourly to compounding every minute, the one would converge to the other. We have included this for completeness (as I know of no real world instrument or bank that quotes continuous interest and I would simply note that the traders usually recognize the "e" buttons on their calculators—if they even have them—as the ones with the dust on them). The ulterior motive of introducing this now is because we will see this sort of notation again later when we get to options.

Just as interest rates are used to grow money from today into the future, they can also be used to present value or discount money in the future back to the present.

DISCOUNTING

How much would you pay today in order to receive USD 100 in 4 years? Obviously, the amount you'd be willing to pay now depends on the rate of interest relevant for this 4 year time horizon. If we assume that the annual interest rate is $r = 5.20\%$, then, finding the Present Value (PV) associated with a Future Value (FV) of USD 100 (using an annual compounding convention),

$$FV = PV(1 + r)^t$$

$$100 = PV(1.0520)^4$$

$$100 = PV(1.22479374)$$

$$PV = 81.64640005$$

The proper price today of USD 100 in four years time is approximately USD 81.6464.

In general, rearranging our earlier compounding relationships, we get Table 3.2.

TABLE 3.2 Discounting Conventions and Their Associated Compounding Conventions

	Compounding	Discounting
Simple	$FV = PV(1 + rt)$	$PV = FV/(1 + rt)$ or alternatively $PV = FV(1 - rt)$
Annual Compounding	$FV = PV(1 + r)^t$	$PV = FV/(1 + r)^t$ or $PV = FV(1 + r)^{-t}$
General Compounding	$FV = PV(1 + [r/N])^{Nt}$	$PV = FV/(1 + [r/N])^{Nt}$ or $PV = FV(1 + [r/N])^{-Nt}$
Continuous Compounding	$FV = PV\, e^{rt}$	$PV = FV/e^{rt} = FV\, e^{-rt}$

TYPES OF INTEREST RATES

There are many different types of interest rates. One distinction could hearken back to different day count conventions. Another distinction could be drawn between borrowing rates and lending rates. Yet another categorization might center on who is doing the borrowing or lending (e.g., the government, a global bank, or a start-up high risk biotech firm) and/or their credit quality/credit rating. We will return to the rates that are most relevant and that we observe quoted in the market in the final section of this chapter.

We would like to point out here that there are different types of rates used for, or applicable to, different contracts or market instruments. There are **zero rates** or spot rates or zero-coupon rates; these are the interest rates that are used either to grow money today (i.e., at "time zero") to some point in the future or to discount (or present value) a certain amount of money from some point in the future back to today (that is, back to the present or back to "time zero"). These are the rates we have been talking about thus far.

The price of one-year money does not have to be the same as the price of two-year money. This phenomenon is known as the "term structure of interest rates"; it is often depicted graphically as in Figure 3.1.

The usual shape for the term structure of interest rates is as shown. There are a few explanations for this shape, which often go by the name of different theories. One suggests that you require a premium (a higher interest rate) for tying up your money for a longer time frame (e.g., entering into a longer-term deposit). This recognizes that people

FIGURE 3.1   Term Structure of Interest Rates

prefer to have their money available (or liquid) and so is known as the "liquidity preference hypothesis." Another explanation focuses on the connection between interest rates and inflation. If inflation is particularly low (relative to historical levels)—as it has been in recent times in the United States—then the market's belief may be that inflation will likely return to a more typical higher level in the future, and so longer-term interest rates will reflect the higher expected rates of inflation (as mentioned previously through the Fisher relationship). This is called the "expectations theory." Finally, there is an explanation known as "segmented markets"; this simply acknowledges that the interest rate for any given point in the future (the price of money over time) is driven by demand and supply (that is, by borrowing and lending). The demand and supply for short-term financing can differ from the demand and supply for longer-term financing, so short-term interest rates can differ from long-term interest rates. Although none of these rationales fully explains the term structure of interest rates, they all highlight an aspect of the shape of this "curve," which can be observed every day in the media. Two examples of this curve are reproduced from the *Wall Street Journal* in Figure 3.2.

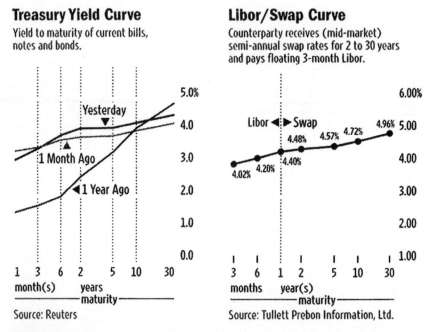

Treasury Yield Curve
Yield to maturity of current bills, notes and bonds.

Yesterday
▼
▲
1 Month Ago
◄ 1 Year Ago

5.0%
4.0
3.0
2.0
1.0
0.0

1 3 6   2   5 10   30
month(s) years
——————— maturity ———————
Source: Reuters

Libor/Swap Curve
Counterparty receives (mid-market) semi-annual swap rates for 2 to 30 years and pays floating 3-month Libor.

Libor ◄ ► Swap   4.48% 4.57% 4.72% 4.96%
4.02% 4.20% 4.40%

6.00%
5.00
4.00
3.00
2.00
1.00

3   6   1   2   5 10   30
months year(s)
——————— maturity ———————
Source: Tullett Prebon Information, Ltd.

FIGURE 3.2 Treasury Yield Curve and LIBOR/Swap Curve
Source: Wall Street Journal. Treasury Yield Curve data © 2006 Reuters. Reprinted with permission of Reuters. LIBOR/Swap Curve data © 2006 Tullett Prebon Information.

In addition to zero rates, there are also **forward rates** (referred to less frequently as future rates), which indicate the price of money for borrowing or lending associated with some time horizon—starting not today, but instead starting at some point in the future. For example, one might like to lock in a rate of interest rate for a deposit covering a one year time horizon—starting in three months. We might refer to that as a three month by fifteen month forward rate, denoted $r_{3 \times 15}$ = 5.25% (where the first subscripted term indicates the starting point in months and the second term indicates the ending point for that quote)—though others might use a different designation, such as a "three month by one year" or "three by twelve" rate (where the first term again indicates the start date in months but the second term identifies the tenor or time span that this rate covers).

Finally, there is an important contract known as an interest rate swap (involving the periodic exchange of interest payments at regular intervals for some predetermined time frame). The rates quoted for an interest rate swap are referred to, not surprisingly, as **swap rates**; these differ from both zero rates and forward rates.

While we have seen that different day count conventions generate different cash flows, they are all simply different "shades" of the same thing; in this sense, I think of different day counts the way I think of different apples: Some are red, some are yellow, and some are green, but they are all apples. The same could be said about different compounding conventions. When it comes to zero rates, forward rates, and swap rates, though, these are like apples, bananas, and coconuts. These are three very different (though ultimately related) interest rate concepts used for very different financial purposes.

INTEREST RATES IN THE REAL WORLD

There is an entire spectrum of interest rates reported every day, depending on the borrower/lender and depending on the financial instrument/contract. As a baseline, in many countries, the rate of interest relevant for the government (as the monopolist of the money) is often identified as "risk free" (because, in principle, they are able to simply print more, and therefore, one might think, should never default or fail to pay back on "borrowed money"). Consequently, the rate of interest that the government must pay on its debt is often referred to as the "risk free" rate. This designation should not be used lightly, though, and, for some sovereigns, it is clearly inappropriate.

In the earliest days of the United States, after gaining their independence from England, a genuine debate ensued about the debt that the colonies had accumulated in financing the Revolutionary War. Thomas Jefferson advocated repudiation (defaulting) so that the new nation could pursue its economic development unencumbered by what he considered to be staggering obligations. Alexander Hamilton, though, disagreed vehemently, insisting that this new country had to pay back what it had borrowed (including his recommendation that much of the debt of the individual colonies/states be assumed by the federal government)—calling this debt "the price of liberty." Hamilton (later Secretary of the Treasury) eventually prevailed, which may explain why he appears on the USD 10 note (as opposed to Jefferson who appears on the nickel or USD .05 coin). Though it has come close once or twice (due to technical political reasons), the United States (excluding the Confederate States of America) to date has never failed to pay on borrowed money. Similarly, Great Britain is recognized as having always honored its debt obligations, and therefore also deserves the designation "risk free." However, every country cannot claim that distinction. For example, in 1998, Russia simply chose not to pay on its bonds (denominated in Rubles); all Russia needed was paper and ink to redeem their debt, but they simply chose not to. Interestingly, many emerging market governments will issue bonds and other debt instruments denominated in another country's currency. Presumably that can make those instruments more attractive to a global investor base, but this practice also raises the question of whether that currency will be available on the payment and redemption dates.

At any rate, in just about every country, there is a government or sovereign debt market. In Singapore, even though the government does not need to borrow, they still issue national debt, which serves to provide a ("risk free") floor to the country's debt market and, in doing so, establishes a benchmark set of interest rates. The government, therefore, typically provides one "class" of interest rates.

Another extremely important category of interest rates comes from, and applies to, the banking sector. The interest rates to which a majority of over-the-counter interest rate contracts are indexed or tied is the London InterBank Offer Rate (LIBOR). LIBOR as such reflects the rate at which one bank, with solid credit, will lend to another, comparably credit-worthy bank. If I were in New York and heard that LIBOR just went up, I would presume that it referred to USD (Dollar) LIBOR. Of course, there is Yen LIBOR, Sterling LIBOR, Euro LIBOR or Euribor, and several others associated with the major currencies (Swiss Franc, Canadian Dollar, Australian Dollar, New Zealand Dollar, and Danish Krone).

In the spirit of the Olympics, the British Bankers Association (BBA) polls a number of banks in London (seeking their lending quotes on, for example, USD) and then proceeds to throw out the high and low (quartile) quotes—averaging the rest. In this way, the exact USD LIBOR number is viewed as less easily manipulated by a bank that might have an outstanding market exposure linked to the reported interest rate. The results of this process are made available shortly after 11:00 A.M. London time. You might ask, "Why do we ask London banks what U.S. interest rates are? Why don't we just ask banks in New York?" Good questions.[2]

The real reason that the BBA seeks U.S. Dollar quotes in London is that the major New York banks are all members of the Federal Reserve System (and as such, they are obliged to follow the recommendations of the Fed); Barclays (a U.K.-based bank) can offer its Dollars wherever they want; they are not so constrained from a regulatory point of view. In this sense, then, Barclays (and the other large banks in London) will provide a true, "free market" interest rate for Dollars outside the control of the Federal Reserve System. Because these Dollars are being held by a bank outside the United States, they are sometimes referred to as Eurodollars (and Eurodollar rates are generally viewed as being effectively synonymous with LIBOR).

When one thinks about either borrowing or lending money, it was noted that the interest rate (quoted annually) may be different for different time horizons. This phenomenon is reflected in the fact that the BBA reports a variety of tenors or time frames for USD LIBOR:

Overnight LIBOR

1 week LIBOR

2 week LIBOR

1 month LIBOR

2 month LIBOR

3 month LIBOR

6 month LIBOR

Out to 12 month LIBOR

Due to the dominance of the large (generally AA credit quality) money center banks in the FX markets, the presumption is that LIBOR indicates their correct cost of funding and so, in the calculations that follow throughout this book, we presume that the interest rate reflects the proper currency and time horizon for one of these LIBOR-based banks. (See Figure 3.3 for a USD-LIBOR "curve" and Figure 3.4 for a multiple currency LIBOR listing from Bloomberg.) After all, it is likely to be a bank's trading desk that takes advantage of an opportunity or arbitrage situation in FX (and less so that of a central bank or a subinvestment grade corporation).

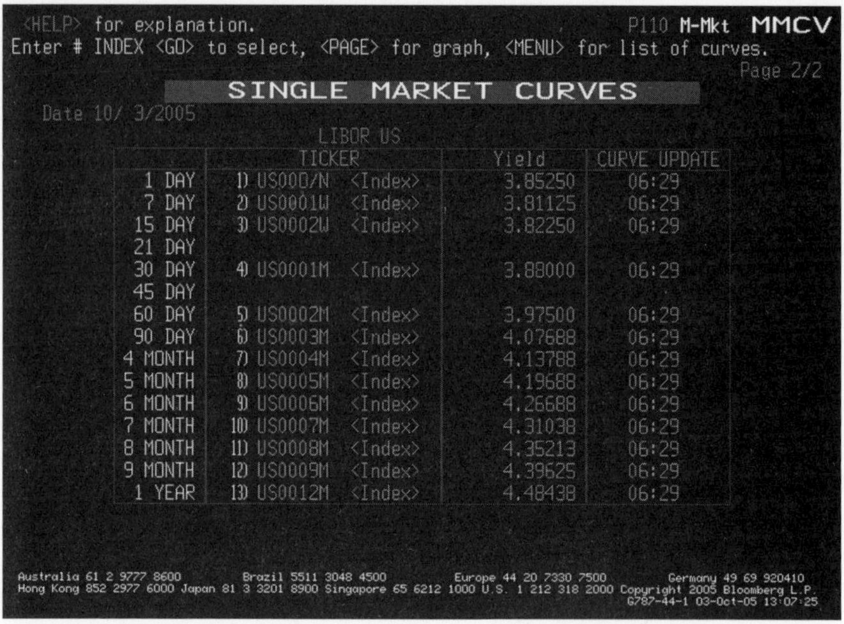

<HELP> for explanation. P110 M-Mkt **MMCV**
Enter # INDEX <GO> to select, <PAGE> for graph, <MENU> for list of curves.
Page 2/2

SINGLE MARKET CURVES

Date 10/ 3/2005

LIBOR US

	TICKER		Yield	CURVE UPDATE
1 DAY	1) US000/N	<Index>	3.85250	06:29
7 DAY	2) US0001W	<Index>	3.81125	06:29
15 DAY	3) US0002W	<Index>	3.82250	06:29
21 DAY				
30 DAY	4) US0001M	<Index>	3.88000	06:29
45 DAY				
60 DAY	5) US0002M	<Index>	3.97500	06:29
90 DAY	6) US0003M	<Index>	4.07688	06:29
4 MONTH	7) US0004M	<Index>	4.13788	06:29
5 MONTH	8) US0005M	<Index>	4.19688	06:29
6 MONTH	9) US0006M	<Index>	4.26688	06:29
7 MONTH	10) US0007M	<Index>	4.31038	06:29
8 MONTH	11) US0008M	<Index>	4.35213	06:29
9 MONTH	12) US0009M	<Index>	4.39625	06:29
1 YEAR	13) US0012M	<Index>	4.48438	06:29

Australia 61 2 9777 8600   Brazil 5511 3048 4500   Europe 44 20 7330 7500   Germany 49 69 920410
Hong Kong 852 2977 6000 Japan 81 3 3201 8900 Singapore 65 6212 1000 U.S. 1 212 318 2000 Copyright 2005 Bloomberg L.P.
G787-44-1 03-Oct-05 13:07:25

FIGURE 3.3 USD-LIBOR Curve
Source: © 2006 Bloomberg LP. All rights reserved. Reprinted by permission.

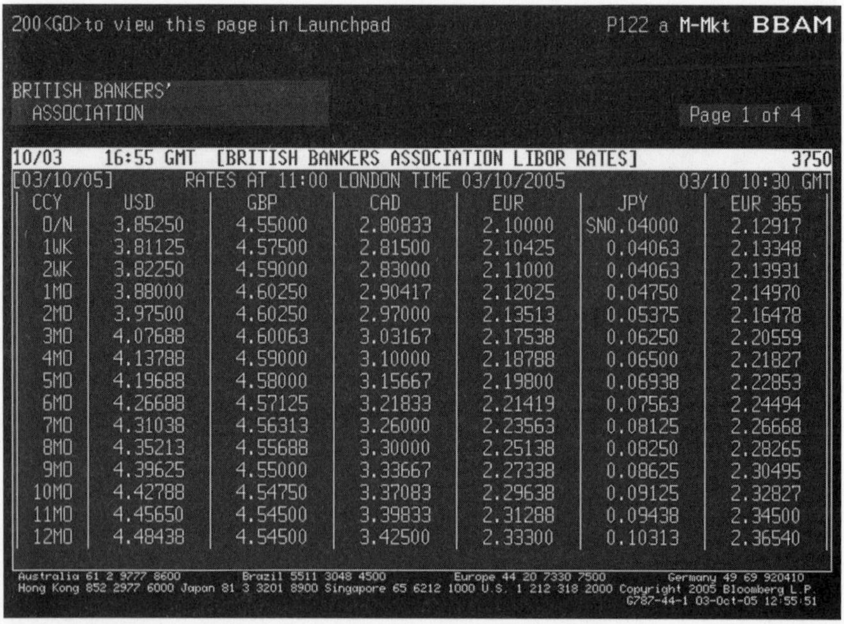

BRITISH BANKERS'
ASSOCIATION
Page 1 of 4

10/03   16:55 GMT [BRITISH BANKERS ASSOCIATION LIBOR RATES]   3750
[03/10/05]   RATES AT 11:00 LONDON TIME 03/10/2005   03/10 10:30 GMT

CCY	USD	GBP	CAD	EUR	JPY	EUR 365
O/N	3.85250	4.55000	2.80833	2.10000	SN0.04000	2.12917
1WK	3.81125	4.57500	2.81500	2.10425	0.04063	2.13348
2WK	3.82250	4.59000	2.83000	2.11000	0.04063	2.13931
1MO	3.88000	4.60250	2.90417	2.12025	0.04750	2.14970
2MO	3.97500	4.60250	2.97000	2.13513	0.05375	2.16478
3MO	4.07688	4.60063	3.03167	2.17538	0.06250	2.20559
4MO	4.13788	4.59000	3.10000	2.18788	0.06500	2.21827
5MO	4.19688	4.58000	3.15667	2.19800	0.06938	2.22853
6MO	4.26688	4.57125	3.21833	2.21419	0.07563	2.24494
7MO	4.31038	4.56313	3.26000	2.23563	0.08125	2.26668
8MO	4.35213	4.55688	3.30000	2.25138	0.08250	2.28265
9MO	4.39625	4.55000	3.33667	2.27338	0.08625	2.30495
10MO	4.42788	4.54750	3.37083	2.29638	0.09125	2.32827
11MO	4.45650	4.54500	3.39833	2.31288	0.09438	2.34500
12MO	4.48438	4.54500	3.42500	2.33300	0.10313	2.36540

Australia 61 2 9777 8600   Brazil 5511 3048 4500   Europe 44 20 7330 7500   Germany 49 69 920410
Hong Kong 852 2977 6000 Japan 81 3 3201 8900 Singapore 65 6212 1000 U.S. 1 212 318 2000 Copyright 2005 Bloomberg L.P.
G787-44-1 03-Oct-05 12:55:51

FIGURE 3.4 Composite Multiple Currency LIBOR Screen
Source: © 2006 Bloomberg LP. All rights reserved. Reprinted by permission.

For the record, all LIBORs are calculated using actual/360 day counts except GBP LIBOR, which uses an actual/365 day basis.

For the sake of completeness, we simply mention that there are a myriad of other types of interest rates as well. There are mortgage rates, prime rates, corporate bond yields, discount rates, deposit rates or "depos," repurchase rates, "repo rates," or simply "repos," and many, many more. (See Figure 3.5.)

Money Rates

Friday, September 30, 2005

The key U. S. and foreign annual interest rates below are a guide to general levels but don't always represent actual transactions.

Commercial Paper

Yields paid by corporations for short-term financing, typically for daily operation

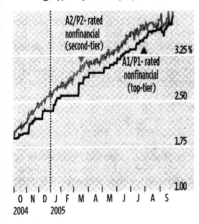

O N D J F M A M J J A S
2004   2005

Source: Federal Reserve

Prime Rate: 6.75% (effective 09/20/05). The base rate on corporate loans posted by at least 75% of the nation's 30 largest banks.
Discount Rate (Primary): 4.75% (effective 09/20/05).
Federal Funds: 4.063% high, 3.750% low, 3.875% near closing bid, 4.000% offered. Effective rate: 3.93%. Source: Tullett Prebon Information, Ltd. Federal-funds target rate: 3.750% (effective 09/20/05).
Call Money: 5.50% (effective 09/20/05).
Commercial Paper: Placed directly by General Electric Capital Corp.: 3.72% 30 to 34 days; 3.78% 35 to 59 days; 3.86% 60 to 89 days; 3.94% 90 to 119 days; 3.98% 120 to 149 days; 4.02% 150 to 179 days; 4.07% 180 to 209 days; 4.09% 210 to 239 days; 4.12% 240 to 265 days; 4.13% 266 to 270 days.

Euro Commercial Paper: Placed directly by General Electric Capital Corp.: 2.08% 30 days; 2.10% two months; 2.14% three months; 2.14% four months; 2.15% five months; 2.16% six months.
Dealer Commercial Paper: High-grade unsecured notes sold through dealers by major corporations: 3.79% 30 days; 3.90% 60 days; 4.00% 90 days.
Certificates of Deposit: 3.82% one month; 4.03% three months; 4.20% six months.
Bankers Acceptances: 3.82% 30 days; 3.92% 60 days; 4.01% 90 days; 4.08% 120 days; 4.14% 150 days; 4.19% 180 days. Source: Tullett Prebon Information, Ltd.
Eurodollars: 3.83% - 3.81% one month; 3.95% - 3.92% two months; 4.04% - 4.02% three months; 4.11% - 4.08% four months; 4.16% - 4.12% five months; 4.21% - 4.18% six months. Source: Tullett Prebon Information, Ltd.
London Interbank Offered Rates (Libor): 3.86375% one month; 4.0650% three months; 4.23063% six months; 4.4400% one year. Effective rate for contracts entered into two days from date appearing at top of this column.
Euro Libor: 2.12025% one month; 2.17388% three months; 2.20800% six months; 2.32025% one year. Effective rate for contracts entered into two days from date appearing at top of this column.
Euro Interbank Offered Rates (Euribor): 2.122% one month; 2.176% three months; 2.209% six months; 2.322% one year. Source: Reuters.
Foreign Prime Rates: Canada 4.50%; European Central Bank 2.00%; Japan 1.375%; Switzerland 2.63%; Britain 4.50%.
Treasury Bills: Results of the Monday, September 26, 2005, auction of short-term U.S. government bills, sold at a discount from face value in units of $1,000 to $1 million: 3.440% 13 weeks; 3.745% 26 weeks. Tuesday, September 27, 2005 auction: 3.150% 4 weeks.
Overnight Repurchase Rate: 3.40%. Source: Garban Intercapital.
Freddie Mac: Posted yields on 30-year mortgage commitments. Delivery within 30 days 5.72%, 60 days 5.76%, standard conventional fixed-rate mortgages: 3.375%, 2% rate capped one-year adjustable rate mortgages.
Fannie Mae: Posted yields on 30 year mortgage commitments (priced at par) for delivery within 30 days 5.853%, 60 days 5.891%, standard conventional fixed-rate mortgages. Constant Maturity Debt Index: 3.914% three months; 4.079% six months; 4.269% one year.
Merrill Lynch Ready Assets Trust: 2.94%.
Consumer Price Index: August, 196.4, up 3.6% from a year ago. Bureau of Labor Statistics.

FIGURE 3.5 Money Rates
Source: Wall Street Journal.

INTEREST RATE EXERCISES

1. Calculate the interest on USD 10,000,000 for 3 months (90 days) at $r = 4.80\%$ (where this rate is a simple actual/360 rate).
2. How many Euros would you receive if you deposited 40 million Euros for 12 years at a quarterly compounded rate of $r = 6.00\%$ (treating each quarter as exactly ¼ of a year).
3. What amount of Pounds Sterling today is equal to 20,000,000 Pounds in 200 days, if the relevant U.K. interest rate (quoted annually) is 8.20%?
4. How long will it take for your money to double? More concretely, if you are quoted a rate of interest of 6.00% (compounded annually), how long will it take for your money today (PV) to double (i.e., so that $FV = 2 \times PV$)?

CHAPTER 4

Brief History of Foreign Exchange

HISTORICAL BACKGROUND

Foreign exchange has been around as long as transactions have involved crossing country borders. No doubt, trade took place even before national boundaries and modern currencies existed. But once a country or region established a money of their own, then currency transactions became necessary. (Strictly speaking, this need not always have been the case if the two currencies were convertible. In other words, if two countries both used gold coins and the values of those coins were based entirely on the weights of the metal they contained, then there should have been a single exchange rate between those currencies).[1]

Although there are many interesting accounts of the early forms of money[2] (dealing primarily with the use of precious metal in the form of coins), the fundamental economic principle on this topic typically goes by the name of Gresham's Law. Thomas Gresham, in 1558, stated that bad money always drives out good money. What this means is that currency which has been debased (such as clipped or "sweated" coins or coins made of an inferior or lower precious metal content) tends to drive "better money" (whole coins or coins with a higher metal content) out of circulation (i.e., induce hoarding). When was the last time you saw a "real silver" U.S. dime, quarter, or half-dollar? John Kenneth Galbraith wrote, "It is perhaps the only economic law that has never been challenged."[3]

Prior to 1900, most national currencies were backed by gold and/or silver (and were, therefore, in a sense, immediately and directly comparable). Britain adopted a gold standard around 1820. Germany and France also moved to a gold standard for their currencies in 1871 and 1876, respectively. In China, they resisted a gold-backed currency because of the dominance of silver in that part of the world. On paper, the official gold standard in the United States set the value of one ounce of gold at USD 20.67—from 1834 through 1933. The United States, during the recovery after the Civil War, guaranteed that the Dollar could actually be converted into gold (but not silver) via the Coinage Act of 1873 (despite many political objections in the ensuing years); the most eloquent dissent was William Jennings Bryan's famous "Cross of Gold" speech (advocating "easy money," meaning currency not backed by the presence of ever scarce gold) delivered during his unsuccessful bid for the presidency in the Election of 1896). Bimetallism (the backing of fiat currency by silver and gold) was instituted soon thereafter in the United States, but the U.S. currency reverted to convertibility into gold alone in 1900.

It is important to note that prior to 1900, with some high profile exceptions (such as England, Spain, and Portugal), international trade was not a significant part of many countries' economic activity. Wheat was grown in a country, it was turned into flour in that country, it was baked into bread in that country, and that bread was consumed in that country. As transportation technology advanced (as well as the state of the art of preserving previously perishable products for extended conveyance), local specialization and the trade associated with it became increasingly important, and, consequently, more extensive economic interaction between geographies.

Following World War I, Germany was burdened with large reparation payments, so large in fact that some economists (including John Maynard Keynes of Keynesian Economics fame) thought them unrealistic and potentially debilitating. As Germany (whose currency was no longer backed by gold) expanded their money supply, in part in an effort to help meet their payment responsibilities, the economy spiraled out of control. One U.S. Dollar exchanged for around 8 Marks at the end of the World War I (1918–1919); by November 1923, at the peak of the hyperinflation, one Dollar was worth 4.2 trillion Marks. Workers were paid every day before noon and then raced to the stores to buy anything they could, aware that prices changed hourly. Eventually, political intervention (the Dawes Plan) and the introduction of a new currency (the Rentenmark, so named because of its backing by land and industrial plants) together helped somewhat to stabilize the German economy. Clearly the excessive growth of money in an economy can have negative effects.

Up until the global depression of the late 1920s and 1930s, most major currencies, with the exception of the German Mark, were freely traded and, as mentioned, via the gold standard, convertible into precious metal. The Great Depression changed all that. On April 5, 1933, with approximately 25% of the U.S. work force unemployed and with the world in the throes of a global depression, U.S. President Franklin Delano Roosevelt abandoned the gold standard, suspending the convertibility of Dollars into gold, and ordered all U.S. citizens to surrender their gold holdings. Milton Friedman and Anna Schwartz, in their classic *A Monetary History of the United States, 1867–1960*, assert that one of the primary causes of the Great Depression, and a significant factor in both the length and severity of that economic crisis, was the reduction in the supply of money in the economy; they estimate that the money supply fell by about a third between 1929 and 1933. In their words, the Great Depression was a "testimonial to the importance of monetary forces." If money serves to facilitate trade, obviously the scarcity of money can grind an economy to a halt. It appears as if, for an economy, too much money can be a bad thing and not enough money can be a bad thing as well.

Although the United States did abandon the gold standard, gold, nevertheless, did continue to be used as a settlement vehicle for international trade at the national/central bank level. In 1933, the United States officially reset the price of gold to USD 35 per ounce. This peg was maintained until 1971.

As Europe entered World War II, many large economic powers were forced off the gold standard. In the case of England, their gold reserves were depleted in an effort to arm themselves for the impending military conflict. As the war approached its conclusion (July 1944), a landmark event took place: the Bretton Woods Conference. This is recognized as the first attempt ever to institute an international monetary system. As a student of economics, I always envisioned this event as taking place on a smoky battlefield in France; Bretton Woods is actually a beautiful resort community in New Hampshire, U.S.A. and the sessions were held at the Mount Washington Hotel. At these meetings, attended by representatives from the Allied countries, there was a strong resolve to avoid the previous mistakes of past postwar settlements. John Maynard Keynes, the same prominent British economist who had misgivings over the World War I German reparations, was an active and vocal participant at this conference, and an important contributor to the ultimate results of this meeting.

Among other things, the Bretton Woods Agreement set up both the International Monetary Fund (IMF) and the International Bank for Reconstruction and Development, which later morphed into the World Bank, and resurrected the importance of the Bank for International Settlements (or BIS). More relevant for this book was the establishment of a fixed exchange rate system in which most of the major European currencies were pegged to the U.S. Dollar and, in an effort to provide even more stability to the new world economic order, the Dollar was pegged to gold (at the aforementioned rate of USD 35 per ounce).

These fixed exchange rates (sometimes referred to as "parity" values) were to be maintained (+/–1%—that is, within a "band") through the active market intervention of the governments and central banks of the ratifying countries. The supranational organizations mentioned above were to help facilitate these pegs. Of course, it was understood that there may be a need for a periodic adjustment of those par rates or par values (in the presence of serious international trade imbalances and with the permission of the IMF). The Bretton Woods Agreement effectively established the U.S. Dollar as the "reserve currency" of the world and, contrary to what many economists today would have conjectured, the Bretton Woods system worked quite well for about 25 years.

What was happening in the late 1960s (25 years or so later)? Well for one thing, in 1967, the British Pound was attacked and, for the first time since Bretton Woods, central bank intervention via currency market operations failed. More importantly, by 1968, the United States was deeply involved in the Viet Nam War and was financing it, in large part, through the printing press. There are only three ways for a government to get and spend money: taxation, borrowing, and printing. Of course, as the United States created money and spent it, there was pressure on the U.S. Dollar to weaken relative to other currencies. Eventually, it became clear that the lynchpin of the global monetary system was in trouble. On August 15, 1971, gold convertibility was suspended (at USD 35 per ounce); President Richard M. Nixon imposed wage and price controls. Something had to give. The U.S. Dollar was devalued later that year (reflected in a new gold peg of USD 38 per ounce) and further devalued (to USD 42 per ounce) in 1973.

Although the fixed exchange rate system seemed to be falling apart, the European Economic Community (EEC) recognized the difficulties that could result from a floating exchange rate system among the larger European currencies. For example, if one sold Italian shoes and handbags in Paris, then not knowing what the French Franc-Italian Lira exchange rate might be would tend to add potential risks, costs, and uncertainty to this international trade. As a result, in 1972, the EEC established tight "bands" between member country currencies; later that year, the "snake" (the name given to the exchange rate movements within the narrow permissible "band") died. The Deutsche Mark continued to strengthen, Italian Lira weakened, and the U.S. Dollar devalued by a full 10%. By the mid-1970s, we effectively had the beginning of floating exchange rates.

The European countries, though, continued to feel the need for some stability between their currencies. In 1978–1979, the European Monetary System (EMS) was established; this effectively maintained the exchange rates of the major European currencies relative to each other, through the support of the European central banks. The name for this new arrangement was the Exchange Rate Mechanism (ERM). Although there was occasional pressure, this system was effective for a number of years. Nevertheless, for several years, the U.S. Dollar continued to weaken (versus the European complex). By 1986, the Dollar was down 25% versus the major European currencies; because of the economic implications (which is explained in more detail in Chapter 11, but here we simply note that this was viewed unfavorably by the European community), many central banks coordinated their activities in a successful effort to halt the decline of the Dollar. Such intervention in a nominally floating exchange rate environment is sometimes called a "dirty float."

In 1992, an unprecedented event occurred. George Soros, who ran the Quantum Fund—a global macro hedge fund—took on some large positions in the FX markets. Specifically, he thought both the British Pound and the Italian Lira were overvalued in the market, so he sold them. Effectively, his actions (as well as the trading of others who may have taken on the same bet) served to undermine and ultimately undo the Exchange Rate Mechanism. England was forced to withdraw from the European Monetary System.

Later that year, the Maastricht Treaty replaced the old European Economic Community (EEC) with the new European Union (EU), but, in 1993, the bands were widened from 2.25% to 15% and so, there was effectively a floating exchange rate system in place among the important European currencies. It is the author's opinion that this, as much as any other political or economic factor, led to the introduction and acceptance of the Euro—the single European currency for the largest and most important European economies.

Although FX trading technology continued to advance steadily from the TELEX platform of the 1950s, with an obvious impetus for trading, hedging, and investment in the mid-1970s as fixed exchange rates were abandoned, volumes exploded and FX volatility created a new frontier for both proprietary ("prop") traders and marketmakers alike. There were some significant advances on this trading technology front in the early 1990s. At the time, much of the FX dealing was still done in the direct (over the phone, bank-to-bank) market or through the various voice brokers (that is, through the "squawk boxes" on every trading floor). The year 1993 is generally recognized as the birth of modern electronic FX trading; that year, the Electronic Brokering System (EBS), affectionately known as "the robot," brought a degree of transparency to the FX markets that had never existed before. EBS was founded by 15 member banks as a dealer-to-dealer trading tool. Many FX spot traders felt this served to drive out any remaining edge in their product area. In addition, other trading platforms, such as the Reuters Matching System, helped streamline trading in the interbank market. FX dealing systems, consortiums, and platforms continue to evolve.

In the early to mid-1990s, equity markets around the world were booming, but it seemed as if performance was particularly spectacular in the emerging markets of Southeast Asia. There was a flood of investment funds into Thailand, South Korea, Malaysia, and Indonesia; to foster this global trend and encourage those continued capital flows, many of these countries pegged their currencies to the U.S. Dollar. Preceded by a drop in the Japanese convertible bond market and exacerbated by an exodus from faltering returns in Thailand, the Asian bubble burst. As western investors attempted to flee the local instruments and to return their cash to more stable currencies, the Asian exchange rates crashed. Hedge funds only added to the frenzy. In 1997, currency crises in Asia were spreading across the region in a phenomenon that became known as the "Asian contagion." The explanations for this crisis are more complicated than simply identifying a speculative attack, but currency misalignments, interest rate issues, underlying economic factors, as well as the collapse of local stock markets all contributed to the FX crises.

The Euro arrived on the scene, literally if not physically, at the start of January 1999. This was a watershed event in the history of foreign exchange. The founding members of the Euro community included: Germany, Italy, France, Spain, Portugal, Ireland, Belgium, Netherlands, Luxembourg, Austria, and Finland. With the initial move from 11 major European currencies to the Euro, convergence required, at some point, fixing the exchange rates. This was done (except for Greece) prior to January 1, 1999 and became effective on that date. Greece was not one of the charter members, joining Euro membership on January 1, 2001; the Euro-Greek Drachma exchange rate was fixed on that date. A summary of the final fixed exchange rate conversions versus the Euro is seen in Table 4.1.

The European Central Bank (ECB) reflects an interesting mix of banking, politics, and finance. The home for the ECB is Frankfurt am Main, Germany (given its central location in continental Europe). The first ECB President, Willem F. Duisenberg, was something of a compromise candidate; someone quipped at the time that the Germans (known for their conservative monetary policy and aversion to inflation) did not want someone from France running the ECB; the French did not want a German; and no one wanted an Italian (although Italy, which had not been known for restraint in their monetary policy, often enjoying double-digit inflation over the years, was the first country to meet the relatively demanding economic requirements for Euro membership). So the role of the first president of the ECB fell to "Wim"

TABLE 4.1   Fixed Euro Conversion Rates versus the Legacy European Currencies*

(fixed January 1, 1999, except for Greek Drachma—fixed January 1, 2001)	
Austrian Schilling	€1 = ATS 13.760300 (Austrian Schillings)
Belgian Franc	€1 = BEF 40.339900 (Belgian Francs)
Finnish Markka	€1 = FIM 5.945730 (Finnish Markkas)
French Franc	€1 = FRF 6.559570 (French Francs)
German Deutsche Mark	€1 = DEM 1.955830 (Deutsche Marks)
Greek Drachma	€1 = GRD 340.750000 (Greek Drachmas)
Irish Punt	€1 = IEP 0.787564 (Irish Punts)
Italian Lira	€1 = ITL 1936.270000 (Italian Lire)
Luxembourg Franc	€1 = LUF 40.339900 (Luxembourg Francs)
Netherlands Guilder	€1 = NLG 2.203710 (Dutch Guilders)
Portuguese Escudo	€1 = PTE 200.482000 (Portuguese Escudos)
Spanish Peseta	€1 = ESP 166.386000 (Spanish Pesetas)

*For example, when the Euro was introduced and the German deutsche Mark (DEM) was first tied to the Euro at a fixed rate of exchange in anticipation of its retirement, this table indicates that 1.95583 Deutsche Marks were to be viewed as equivalent to 1 Euro and subsequently exchanged exclusively at this one rate.

The European Central Bank web site (www.ecb.int) designates the time frame that the various national central banks have set in terms of honoring the conversion of their legacy currencies. These range from unlimited conversion opportunities (offered by Germany, Ireland, Spain, and Austria on their notes and coins), to unlimited conversion on notes, but limitations on coin conversion (Belgium, Luxembourg), to limited coin and note conversion (France, Italy, Netherlands, Finland, Portugal, and Greece).

Duisenberg from the Netherlands. His involvement as the former head of a European central bank and one of the primary leaders of the European Monetary Institute (EMI), which transitioned into the ECB, recommended him highly for this role. Indeed, Wim was expected to step down soon after the Euro was "launched" (as an electronic book-entry unit of account), but he seemed to enjoy the role, ultimately wanting to see the birth, introduction, and distribution of the Euro in physical form (notes and coins) in January 2002. His prearranged successor, interestingly, was Jean-Claude Trichet; although Trichet is French, he possesses a very positive reputation among European central bankers and was acknowledged as an excellent succession candidate. Unfortunately, while he was waiting to succeed Duisenberg, he was charged with complicity in a French banking scandal and became embroiled in legal proceedings which delayed his assuming the reins of the ECB which (from which he was ultimately exonerated). All of this uncertainty did not serve the early performance of the Euro well. The Euro was introduced at a value of USD 1.1800 per Euro 1 (though one sees values of 1.2000 down to 1.1700 reported) and the Euro proceeded to plummet to USD .8252 per Euro 1 over the course of less than two years. The Euro became the sole legal tender in the EuroZone on March 1, 2002; all national currencies were to be retired by the end of March 2002; and Jean-Claude Trichet replaced Wim Duisenberg as the president of the European Central Bank toward the end of 2003.

Attributed largely to the immense U.S. trade imbalance (the United States is a significant net importer of goods and services, which implies that it is exporting U.S. Dollars all over the world with the concomitant implication that the value of the Dollar should fall, the Euro-Dollar exchange rate has risen to as high as USD 1.3633 per Euro on December 28, 2004, before subsequently coming back down. See Figure 4.1 for a graph of the exchange rate between the Euro and U.S. Dollars since its inception.

As of May 2004, 10 countries were admitted into a holding pattern for Euro membership. These are: Poland, Hungary, the Czech Republic, Slovakia, Slovenia, Estonia, Latvia, Lithuania, Malta, and Cyprus.

Incorporation into the EuroZone is likely to provide a significant eco-

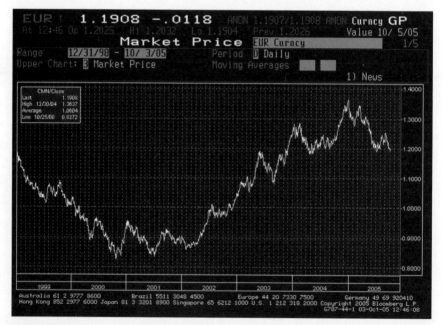

FIGURE 4.1   Bloomberg History of the Euro (Price)
Source: © 2006 Bloomberg LP. All rights reserved. Reprinted by permission.

nomic boost to these economies through the reduction of trade barriers and the possibility of freer pan-European investing, stimulating further development, growth, and industry in these burgeoning nations. There are economic criteria, though, that must first be met (as was the case with the earlier Euro members) including price stability or controlled inflation, sound fiscal circumstances or debt solvency, stable exchange rates, and the ability to have long-term interest rates converge to their Euro replacement.

Maybe more interesting than the list of who is in (and/or would like to be in), is the list of the European countries who have not adopted the Euro as their official currency. These countries include Great Britain, Switzerland, Denmark (which has repeatedly just marginally missed achieving the required majority vote in general elections), and the other Scandinavian countries (Sweden and Norway). It will certainly be interesting to watch.

One might think that the likelihood of currency crises would wane over time as international banking supervision, regulatory convergence, and financial media coverage advance, but, as mentioned earlier (in Note 4 of Chapter 1), the Turkish Lira experienced a devastating depreciation in 2001 following their forced abandonment of a fixed exchange rate regime. Media accounts at the time seemed more focused on the potential political fallout, the existence of local corruption, and the possible overthrow of the government rather than the financial consequences. The Argentinian Peso Crisis occurred the following year, in 2002, with the collapse of their Currency Board. Both these crises were driven by the inability to maintain the stated fixed exchange rate due to the lack of international reserves. We have probably not seen the last of the currency crises. More on crises in Chapter 12.

Where do we go from here?

To quote a prominent former foreign exchange dealer and distinguished author on FX markets, Claude Tygier:

> *There is no absolute way to know if the dollar will go up, down or sideways—it may well do all of these things. The only certainty is that it will move.*

THE FX MARKETS TODAY

The foreign exchange market is the world's largest financial market. Because of the lack of a central organizing body, the size and scope of the global foreign exchange markets are not known with exact precision, but the Bank for International Settlements (BIS),[4] which coordinates their fact finding with many central banks, conducts a triennial survey of the FX markets. Obviously they have many challenges not the least of which is dealing with the issue of double counting. (Recall that when one party buys Euros and sells Dollars, another party buys Dollars and sells Euros.) Nevertheless, the BIS statistics are generally viewed as fairly comprehensive and relatively reliable. We summarize their latest findings and identify the trends in this market as we address the development of this industry. (See Table 4.2.)

The dip from 1998 to 2001 can be explained by the introduction of the Euro [and the retirement of a number of the legacy European currencies (DEM, FRF, ITL, ESP)] that subsequently eliminated the need to trade the European crosses (which had not been an insignificant portion of annual FX trading volume).

To put this in perspective, average daily turnover in foreign exchange now exceeds USD 2 trillion in U.S. Dollar equivalent terms compared to an average daily turnover on the New York Stock Exchange (NYSE) of USD 40–50 billion. You could claim, rather justifiably, that this is not a fair comparison because the NYSE represents only a fraction of the U.S. (not global) equity market, but it does provide some sense as to the magnitude of daily FX volume.

Kenneth Froot and Richard Thaler cited the magnitude of FX trading volume in another illustrative manner.[5] They noted that daily U.S. GNP was approximately twice that of daily world trade in goods and services; more impressive was the fact that daily volume in FX at the time was approximately 20 times daily U.S. GNP. By their reckoning, FX trading volume was roughly around 40 times what the volume of international trade would warrant (and that assumes that all international trade transactions require a foreign exchange trade to unwind any currency risk, which clearly might not be true).

To put the magnitude of FX trading in perspective in one other way, the current volume of foreign exchange transactions corresponds

TABLE 4.2 Global Foreign Exchange Market Turnover (Daily Averages in April, in Billions of U.S. Dollars)

	1989	1992	1995	1998	2001	2004
Total Traditional Turnover	590	820	1,190	1,490	1,200	1,880

Source: "Triennial Central Bank Survey of Foreign Exchange and Derivatives Market Activity in April 2004," Monetary and Economic Department, Bank for International Settlements (September 2005).

to every person on the planet trading the equivalent of over USD 300 (PER DAY)!

Although the FX market has generally grown at an impressive pace, there has been a continued maturing and commoditization of this aspect of the financial industry. To give a few concrete examples of the evolution and consolidation of the FX market, the former Union Bank of Switzerland (UBS) and Swiss Bank Corporation (SBC) together employed around 300 FX spot traders in over 16 locations prior to their merger. Today, UBS (the new, merged entity) has less than 30 FX spot traders in three locations (Singapore, London, and Stamford, Connecticut) despite its 12+% market share. Another incredible fact is that, according to the BIS Survey, the number of FX dealing firms halved in the three years between 2001 and 2004. Possibly even more significant than the previous two facts, liquidity in the United States-versus-Europe exchange rate (as reflected by USD|DEM prior to the Euro and subsequently by EUR|USD)—indicative of the ability to obtain a dealable quote from the set of all marketmakers—has fallen by a factor of around 10 over the past 16 years or so.

Which currencies are traded? The breakdown in terms of the currencies making up the aforementioned volume is seen in Table 4.3.

TABLE 4.3 Selected Currency Distribution of Reported Foreign Exchange Market Turnover*

	1989	1992	1995	1998	2001	2004
U.S. Dollar (USD)	90%	82%	83%	87%	90%	89%
Euro (EUR)	—	—	—	—	38%	37%
German Deutsche Mark (DEM)	27%	40%	36%	30%	—	—
French Franc (FRF)	2%	4%	8%	5%	—	—
Other EMS currencies	4%	12%	16%	17%	—	—
Japanese Yen (JPY)	27%	23%	24%	20%	23%	20%
Pound Sterling (GBP)	15%	14%	9%	11%	13%	17%
Swiss Franc (CHF)	10%	8%	7%	7%	6%	6%
Australian Dollar (AUD)	2%	2%	3%	3%	4%	6%
Canadian Dollar (CAD)	1%	3%	3%	4%	5%	4%

*Note: Recalling that every trade involves one currency pair (two currencies), the complete columns (i.e., including every traded currency) should add to 200 percent.
Source: "Triennial Central Bank Survey of Foreign Exchange and Derivatives Market Activity in April 2004," Monetary and Economic Department, Bank for International Settlements (September 2005).

The Foreign Exchange Market Participants

Who are the market participants? Just about everybody! (See Table 4.4.)

Any corporation or company engaging in international business (either buying inputs abroad or selling their products/services "overseas") potentially has to deal with foreign exchange.

As the world shrinks, cross-border capital flows become more commonplace [e.g., U.S. investors putting their wealth into Swiss pharmaceutical stocks, Euro-denominated German bunds, Japanese government bonds (JGBs), or maybe even Australian commodities]; institutional fund managers who invest in assets denominated in other than their home currency must make an active decision either to hedge their currency risk or to leave their position open to (hopefully favorable) movements in foreign exchange rates. The process of entering into foreign exchange transactions on top of a traditional investment portfolio is often referred to as a "currency overlay" and the decision process that assesses the likelihood of the changes in value among the various classes of securities and commodities is called "asset allocation."

Hedge funds try to identify profitable opportunities in their attempt (1) to generate absolute returns of 10% to 15% per year regardless of the direction of market trends, (2) to achieve low portfolio or trading volatility—the "hedged" in hedge funds—and (3) to generate a low correlation with the traditional asset classes (equity, fixed income).

Banks are big in the FX markets. Both investment banks and commercial banks serve to facilitate their clients' foreign exchange transactions. Moreover, some central banks trade actively in these markets for a variety of reasons.

We even have seen participation on the part of high net worth individuals, and increasingly foreign exchange products are being packaged and distributed to retail clients (primarily in the form of structured notes and deposits).

In the textbooks, one sees reference to "hedgers" and "speculators"; while I'm not sure exactly who these are, on any given day, any one of the FX market participants might be engaging in either of these sorts of

TABLE 4.4 FX Market Participants

Investment Banks	Corporations
Institutional Investors (Mutual Funds, Pension Funds)	Hedge Funds
	Central Banks and Governments
Commercial Banks and Supranationals	Day Traders
High Net Worth Individuals	

trades. Presumably "hedging" involves offsetting risks that one has and "speculating" implies taking on risk in the hope of generating a positive return.

Institutional Information

Effectively, the foreign exchange markets are a (close to) 24-7 institution. To be precise, the FX markets open in Wellington, New Zealand, on (their) Monday at 7:00 A.M. and close on Friday evening in the United States when you can no longer get a dealable quote from any of the banks or broker/dealers. While this, in principle, leaves a little time gap (relative to a full 24-hour-a-day, 7-day-a-week continuously traded market), some FX market facilitators now provide nonstop, 24-hour a day, 7-day-a-week (usually electronic) coverage with live dealing capability, so the FX market today is both in theory and in fact a continuous market.

Furthermore, there has been a dramatic move to electronic execution over the past 10 years. At UBS in 2005, over 80% of all transactions ("tickets") are now being done electronically, while over 60% of the volume is made up of "e-trades." Prior to 1990, there was no electronic FX trading to speak of; by the mid-1990s, e-trades accounted for less than a third of the volume.

Drivers of the Foreign Exchange Market

What drives the FX markets? "Buyers and sellers" is the best and most correct (if rather simplistic) answer. What drives the buying and selling? International trade is considered an important determining factor, but so too are capital flows, foreign direct investment (which involves, for example, a Japanese investor allocating resources to a U.S. firm directly, not simply buying stock in that company), interest rates, monetary policy, expectations of inflation, and even rumors.

Unlike the market for a given stock (which is driven largely by the operations, performance, and competitive environment of that particular firm, possibly evaluated relative to its industry or sector), foreign exchange markets incorporate all the aspects of macroeconomic phenomenon directly into their pricing and trading. Having said that, FX also responds to political news and events. Moreover, as mentioned, governments sometimes become participants in these markets; this is often referred to as intervention.

On occasion, central banks have coordinated their behavior to arrive at an exchange rate level that they find mutually attractive.

THE REGULATORY ENVIRONMENT AND
CENTRAL BANK INTERVENTION

Regulations and Government Involvement

It has been noted that the FX markets are essentially unregulated, but, in the United States there is some oversight to these markets (as most central banks retain their authority to monitor, regulate, and intervene) and there are some restrictions (admittedly relatively nonbinding for most market participants). An example involves the effectively absolute U.S. embargo of Cuba (U.S. Department of the Treasury 31 C.F.R. Part 515—Cuban Assets Control Regulations and the U.S. Department of Commerce Export Administration Regulation 15 C.F.R. Parts 770-785 with its related implication for U.S. currency). Also, the control of U.S. bank notes (for which the Federal Reserve Bank estimates that between one-half and two-thirds of the supply of issued U.S. currency in circulation resides outside the United States) is, at least in principle, under the control of the Federal Reserve and the U.S. Treasury (as the sanctioned monopolist of U.S. currency). Further, oversight in the United States involves the Office of the Comptroller of the Currency (OCC[6]), which charters, regulates, and supervises all national banks, supervises the federal branches and agencies of foreign-based banks, and has connections with the Federal Deposit Insurance Corporation (FDIC). Finally, although not a significant part of the market, foreign exchange futures and options on those futures are listed on the International Monetary Market (IMM) and on the Chicago Mercantile Exchange (the Merc); because these are futures contracts, they are regulated by the Commodity Futures Trading Commission (CFTC).

One of the few hard and fast rules relating to foreign exchange involves the regulation regarding the conveyance of more than USD 10,000 (or foreign currency equivalent) in any form into or out of the United States (as seen on U.S. Customs and Border Protection Declaration 6059B, which is the form that one perfunctorily fills out with every international flight into the United States). (See Figure 4.2.) And even in this case, it is not automatically disallowed, but, as is often the case with regulation, simply requires the proper notification, reporting, and filing (involving, in this case, Report of International Transportation of Currency or Monetary Instruments—Customs Form 4790).

On a larger scale, the Basel Committee on Banking Supervision (of the BIS) has been a staunch advocate of improvements in risk management on the part of the international banking community, in particular the implementation of settlement risk reduction processes for FX trans-

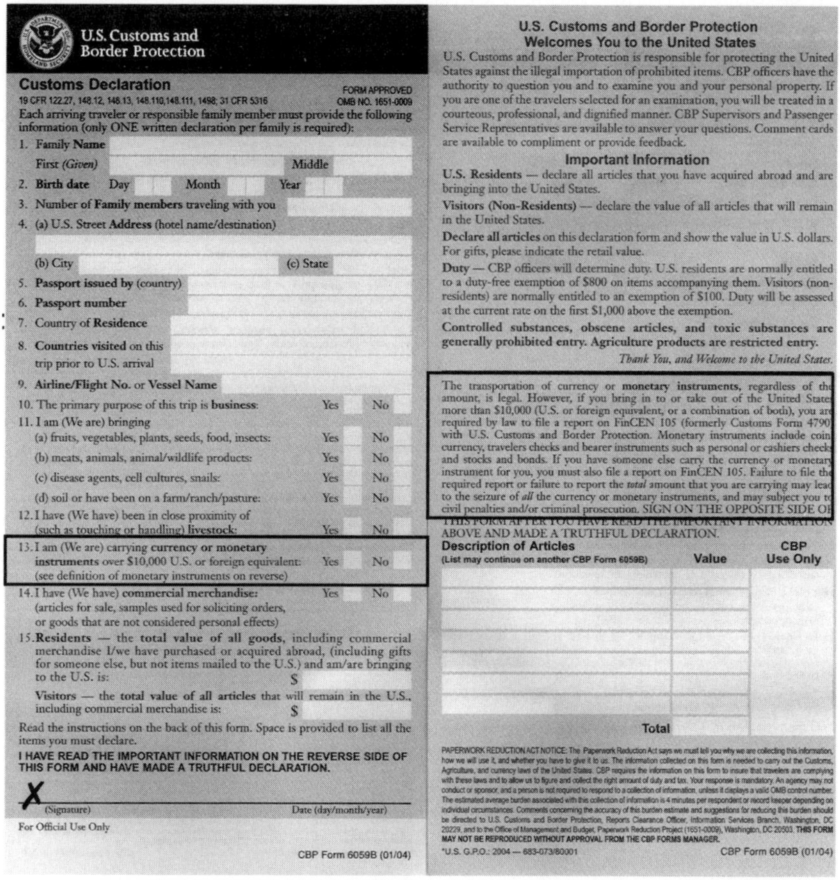

U.S. Customs and Border Protection

Customs Declaration

19 CFR 122.27, 148.12, 148.13, 148.110,148.111, 1498; 31 CFR 5316

FORM APPROVED OMB NO. 1651-0009

Each arriving traveler or responsible family member must provide the following information (only ONE written declaration per family is required):

1. **Family Name**
   First *(Given)* Middle
2. **Birth date** Day Month Year
3. Number of **Family members** traveling with you
4. (a) U.S. Street **Address** (hotel name/destination)
   (b) City (c) State
5. **Passport issued by** (country)
6. **Passport number**
7. Country of **Residence**
8. **Countries visited** on this trip prior to U.S. arrival
9. **Airline/Flight No.** or **Vessel Name**
10. The primary purpose of this trip is **business**: Yes No
11. I am (We are) bringing
    (a) fruits, vegetables, plants, seeds, food, insects: Yes No
    (b) meats, animals, animal/wildlife products: Yes No
    (c) disease agents, cell cultures, snails: Yes No
    (d) soil or have been on a farm/ranch/pasture: Yes No
12. I have (We have) been in close proximity of (such as touching or handling) **livestock**: Yes No
13. I am (We are) carrying **currency or monetary instruments** over $10,000 U.S. or foreign equivalent: Yes No (see definition of monetary instruments on reverse)
14. I have (We have) **commercial merchandise:** Yes No (articles for sale, samples used for soliciting orders, or goods that are not considered personal effects)
15. **Residents** — the **total value of all goods**, including commercial merchandise I/we have purchased or acquired abroad, (including gifts for someone else, but not items mailed to the U.S.) and am/are bringing to the U.S. is: $
    Visitors — the **total value of all articles** that will remain in the U.S., including commercial merchandise is: $

Read the instructions on the back of this form. Space is provided to list all the items you must declare.

I HAVE READ THE IMPORTANT INFORMATION ON THE REVERSE SIDE OF THIS FORM AND HAVE MADE A TRUTHFUL DECLARATION.

X (Signature) Date (day/month/year)

For Official Use Only

CBP Form 6059B (01/04)

U.S. Customs and Border Protection Welcomes You to the United States

U.S. Customs and Border Protection is responsible for protecting the United States against the illegal importation of prohibited items. CBP officers have the authority to question you and to examine you and your personal property. If you are one of the travelers selected for an examination, you will be treated in a courteous, professional, and dignified manner. CBP Supervisors and Passenger Service Representatives are available to answer your questions. Comment cards are available to compliment or provide feedback.

Important Information

U.S. Residents — declare all articles that you have acquired abroad and are bringing into the United States.

Visitors (Non-Residents) — declare the value of all articles that will remain in the United States.

Declare all articles on this declaration form and show the value in U.S. dollars. For gifts, please indicate the retail value.

Duty — CBP officers will determine duty. U.S. residents are normally entitled to a duty-free exemption of $800 on items accompanying them. Visitors (non-residents) are normally entitled to an exemption of $100. Duty will be assessed at the current rate on the first $1,000 above the exemption.

Controlled substances, obscene articles, and toxic substances are generally prohibited entry. Agriculture products are restricted entry.

Thank You, and Welcome to the United States.

The transportation of currency or **monetary instruments**, regardless of th amount, is legal. However, if you bring in to or take out of the United State more than $10,000 (U.S. or foreign equivalent, or a combination of both), you ar required by law to file a report on FinCEN 105 (formerly Customs Form 4790 with U.S. Customs and Border Protection. Monetary instruments include coin currency, travelers checks and bearer instruments such as personal or cashiers check and stocks and bonds. If you have someone else carry the currency or monetar instrument for you, you must also file a report on FinCEN 105. Failure to file th required report or failure to report the *total* amount that you are carrying may lea to the seizure of *all* the currency or monetary instruments, and may subject you t civil penalties and/or criminal prosecution. SIGN ON THE OPPOSITE SIDE O THIS FORM AFTER YOU HAVE READ THE IMPORTANT INFORMATION ABOVE AND MADE A TRUTHFUL DECLARATION.

Description of Articles (List may continue on another CBP Form 6059B)	Value	CBP Use Only
Total		

PAPERWORK REDUCTION ACT NOTICE: The Paperwork Reduction Act says we must tell you why we are collecting this information, how we will use it, and whether you have to give it to us. The information collected on this form is needed to carry out the Customs, Agriculture, and currency laws of the United States. CBP requires the information on this form to insure that travelers are complying with these laws and to allow us to figure and collect the right amount of duty and tax. Your response is mandatory. An agency may not conduct or sponsor, and a person is not required to respond to a collection of information, unless it displays a valid OMB control number. The estimated average burden associated with this collection of information is 4 minutes per respondent or record keeper depending on individual circumstances. Comments concerning the accuracy of this burden estimate and suggestions for reducing this burden should be directed to U.S. Customs and Border Protection, Reports Clearance Officer, Information Services Branch, Washington, DC 20229, and to the Office of Management and Budget, Paperwork Reduction Project (1651-0009), Washington, DC 20503. **THIS FORM MAY NOT BE REPRODUCED WITHOUT APPROVAL FROM THE CBP FORMS MANAGER.**

*U.S. G.P.O.: 2004 — 683-073/80001 CBP Form 6059B (01/04)

FIGURE 4.2 One of the Few Examples of FX Regulation
Source: U.S. Customs and Border Protection, U.S. Department of Homeland Security.

actions. And there may be required registration on the part of an FX dealer with the National Futures Association (NFA) or the CFTC, but it should be noted that such registration does not necessarily provide counterparty protection or a guarantee of contract performance. In the United Kingdom, a dealer's registration with the Financial Services Authority (FSA), based on their stricter regulatory and reporting requirements, would presumably carry greater weight, but, globally, there is no single dealer network or ubiquitous regulatory framework that covers every country.

In general, when a trader hears that a market is not regulated, they understand it to mean that transactions are not subject to past price movements (such as the up-tick rule in securities markets whereby, for a SHORT sale, the last directional movement in the price must have been up—U.S. Exchange Act Rule 10a-1 and NASD Rule 3350), reporting requirements (such as the 5% beneficiary ownership reporting rule with U.S. equities—Regulation 13D-G), limit moves, circuit breakers, or other interferences or hindrances to trade that, while they may have an issuer's or investor's best interest in mind, restrict their fundamental activity of buying and selling. In this sense, the sort of activities that involve the rules on information flow (keeping client names confidential, alerting others to central bank intervention, not front-running a customer's order, attempting to push a price in a certain direction, and so on), while possibly not illegal in the world of FX, could have a devastating impact and deleterious implications for a dealer's reputation. The self-regulation imposed as a result seems to have served this industry and its clients well to date.

Central Bank Intervention

Although not formally regulation, central banks have intervened (and sometimes still do intervene) in the foreign exchange markets. On some occasions, one central bank will enter the market and engage in transactions on behalf of another central bank. For example, the Fed in New York might trade USD|JPY on behalf of the Bank of Japan (the BoJ) during North American trading hours; interestingly, when the Fed has done this, they would claim NOT to have intervened, but simply to have executed an order or a series of orders for a fellow central bank.

At times in the past, the Fed has definitely actively traded foreign exchange with the intent of impacting exchange rates in a way consistent with U.S. economic policy. Although the Fed, the U.S. central bank, is probably one of the most autonomous central banks [that is, independent of political influence, one of the reasons that a full term of office for a Member of the Board of Governors lasts 14 years (i.e., long enough to provide effective insulation from any given president or Congress)], it lists among its objectives [aside from the implementation of monetary policy, its supervisory role for banking institutions, and its critical role in the payments (i.e., check clearing) system], "influencing the value of the Dollar in relation to foreign currencies, primarily with the goal of stabilizing disorderly market conditions."[7] More precisely, the Federal Reserve works in consultation with the U.S. Treasury in setting exchange rate policy and the Federal Reserve Bank of New York is responsible for executing the associated FX transactions.

The primary objectives identified by most of the major central banks (the European Central Bank, the Swiss National Bank, the Bank of England, the Bank of Japan, and the Fed) include many of the following:

- Monitoring and Managing Monetary and Credit Conditions (through Monetary Policy).
- The Pursuit of Full or Maximum or a High Level of Employment (or the Reduction of Unemployment).
- Maintaining Stable Prices (or Avoiding Inflation).
- Preserving the Purchasing Power of the Currency (or Reducing the Volatility of Exchange Rates).
- Issuing Bank Notes or Currency Consistent with Economic Policy.
- Encouraging Moderate Long-Term Interest Rates or Controlling the Money Supply.
- Promoting Real or Sustainable Economic Growth and Development.
- Improving the Welfare of its Citizens.
- Ensuring the Soundness and Stability of the Banking and Financial Systems.
- Providing Financial Services (to the Government, Banks, and other Financial Institutions).
- Supporting the Smooth Operation of the Payment System.

Over the years, assessment of the short-term and longer-term impact of foreign exchange intervention has met with mixed reviews. Lucio Sarno and Mark Taylor (2001) wrote an excellent survey article, "Official Intervention in the Foreign Exchange Market: Is It Effective and, If So, How Does It Work?,"[8] for anyone wishing to pursue this topic in greater detail. In several relatively recent articles, though, it is argued convincingly that central bank intervention has become slightly more effective in recent years than it has been in the past.

There have been two trends on the part of the U.S. central bank in recent years: increased transparency and severely diminished instances of their direct intervention. Approximately a month after each calendar quarter, the New York Fed issues a report to Congress documenting their foreign exchange dealings; this report is made public as "Treasury and Federal Reserve Foreign Exchange Operations." Officially (as of mid-year 2005), the Fed last intervened in the third quarter (Q3) of 2000 (and prior to that, one has to go back to 1998 to find documented confirmation of any intervention at all) (see Figure 4.3), whereas the European Central Bank (ECB) launched its first intervention on September 22, 2000 (less than two years after the introduction of the Euro).

This leads us to consider the positive (what has happened) and the

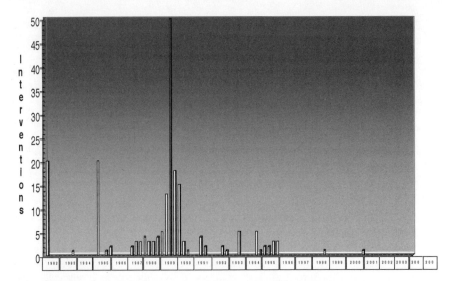

FIGURE 4.3 U.S. Foreign Exchange Intervention: 1982–2005
Source: New York Federal Reserve.

normative (what should happen from a policy perspective). As mentioned, empirically the United States has historically not been an active market agent of late when it comes to FX intervention, but that begs the question of whether they, or any and every central bank, should take a more proactive role in essentially influencing their global terms of trade. Given the experiences of those central banks who have made unsuccessful bids to influence their currency's market value, Jacob Frenkel has an unambiguous policy recommendation:

> *Foreign exchange intervention should only be done in very extreme cases and for the maintenance of orderly markets rather than for the determination of an exchange rate. First, you cannot do it. And, second, if you do it, you create moral hazard that will come back to haunt you."*
> —Jacob Frenkel in Overview from "New Challenges for Monetary Policy" Symposium Proceedings (1999), pp. 397–403

SUMMARY

The Foreign Exchange markets are much larger, more liquid, and less regulated than all of the other financial markets. As currencies have evolved from gold and silver coins, to notes backed by, and convertible into, precious metal, to today's fiat money, and as the world has gotten smaller (more globally interdependent), the trading of foreign exchange has grown—and grown rapidly. One of the most significant events for FX in recent years has been the introduction of the Euro. A number of countries are in a queue for consolidation into the EuroZone. The range of market participants in the FX markets is broad: institutional funds, corporations, banks, hedge funds, high net worth individuals, and even the periodic involvement of a central bank. How these markets will continue to develop is anyone's guess, but the trends suggest that the volume of trade in FX will continue to expand to accommodate the hedging and positioning done by these players, that there will be further exodus and/or consolidation on the part of the broker/dealers, and that the general movement toward electronic FX execution platforms will show no sign of slowing.

CHAPTER 5

The Foreign Exchange Spot Market

THE SPOT MARKET

The foreign exchange markets revolve around spot (that, is the FX spot market).

Confusion—Right from the Start

When I first walked onto our bank's trading floor in the United States (the floor on which FX transactions were carried out), I distinctly remember a large, rather animated man jump from his chair to his feet and yell out, seemingly to no one in particular, "I buy dollar yen!"—to which I naturally thought, "Well, . . . make up your mind." This is but one example of a foreign exchange spot dealer communicating in their unique vernacular. This leads us, first and foremost, to consider the quoting conventions associated with foreign exchange—one of the most confusing things around!

We said that the foreign exchange markets revolve around the FX spot market. Let's be more specific about this statement in two ways.

1. When we say "the foreign exchange markets" (an expression that appears in abbreviated form in the subtitle of this book), what do we mean? By identifying these as plural, we do not only mean to indicate the main geographic trading centers for the various time zones (more dispersed in AustralAsia: Wellington, New Zealand; Sydney, Australia; Singapore; Hong Kong; Tokyo and Osaka, Japan; more concentrated in Europe: London, Zurich, Frankfurt, Paris; and very concentrated in North America: Stamford, Connecticut, New York, and a couple of

other locations), but also the markets for different FX products (spot, forwards, futures, swaps, options, exotics—pretty much everything beside spot being labeled "a derivative").

2. Also, let's be explicit about what we mean by "the spot market in foreign exchange" and understand how prices are quoted in this context. Recall our earlier assertion that there are five major currencies: USD, EUR, JPY, GBP, and CHF. How are these quoted in the spot market?

SPOT FX QUOTING CONVENTIONS

For now, let's abstract from bid–ask spreads (to which we return later) and remember what we said earlier about prices: "Every price is a ratio of quantities." With this in mind, and recognizing that you have to quote the price of one currency in terms of another, the convention for quoting the spot exchange rate between, say, U.S. Dollars (USD) and Swiss Francs (CHF) is written USD|CHF (said "Dollar–Swiss") and identifies the number of Swiss Francs per Dollar. Sounds backward, doesn't it? USD|CHF or "Dollar-Swiss" means "Swiss per Dollar." Don't blame me; I didn't make this up! We sometimes see this as

USD|CHF 1.2500   or   USD|CHF S = 1.2500

Written differently, as an explicit ratio of quantities

$$\frac{CHF\ 1.2500}{USD\ 1}$$

When we quote USD|CHF (or any currency pair), we recognize the first currency, in this case the U.S. Dollar, as the "underlying" asset, that is, the thing that is being traded. The second currency, CHF, is the one that identifies the units in which the price of the underlying currency is being quoted; in other words, it indicates the number of units of that currency that is equal to (i.e., trades for) one unit of the underlying currency. In this example, Dollar-Swiss quotes the price of one USD in terms of CHF. In the professional or interbank market, to buy Dollar-Swiss (USD|CHF) means to buy Dollars with Swiss Francs (or more pedantically, to buy Dollars and pay for them with Swiss Francs or, said slightly differently, to buy Dollars and to sell Swiss Francs, which you recall, although it sounds like two trades, characterizes one single transaction).

Understanding this, then, informs us exactly what my colleague who was "buying Dollar-Yen" was doing. He was buying USD with JPY (or buying United States Dollars and selling Japanese Yen). Of course, you can buy Dollars with Yen, but you could also buy Dollars with Swiss Francs or any number of other currencies.

Returning to USD|CHF, someone on our FX desk once told me that you can think about any spot quote like "USD|CHF 1.2500" in the following way:

Separating the "USD|" from the "CHF 1.2500," replacing the "|" with a "1," and putting an "=" between the terms gives:

$$USD\ 1 = CHF\ 1.2500$$

Of course, there is no reason (other than convention) to quote this exchange rate in terms of "Swiss Francs per Dollar." As mentioned earlier, we could (although we generally don't in the interbank market) quote CHF|USD. This would simply be the reciprocal or multiplicative inverse of 1.2500, namely, .8000. If 1.25 Swiss Francs trade for 1 U.S. Dollar, then USD .8000 should trade for 1 Swiss Franc.

What would USD|JPY S = 111.00 mean? It would mean that 111 Japanese Yen trade for 1 U.S. Dollar. Put another way, it takes 111 Yen to buy 1 Dollar. Alternatively, 1 U.S. Dollar will buy 111.00 Japanese Yen.

There is already one point of possible confusion, that is, how far out (i.e., how many decimal places) should FX be quoted. With USD|CHF, we quoted out four decimal places, while with USD|JPY we quoted out only two decimal places. As a general guide, keep in mind the number 8. Between USD|CHF and CHF|USD, we would quote both out four decimal places (making a total of eight figures beyond the decimal points); by this gauge, when we quote USD|JPY, we go out only two decimal places, so, if we were to consider JPY|USD, we would have to go out six decimal places with this quote (again, making a total of eight numbers quoted beyond the decimal points). Yen is one of the primary exceptions, though; most currency pairs are quoted out four decimal places regardless. The fact that Japanese Yen is an exception, though, can come in handy for instructional purposes.

As a general rule of thumb, if you are looking at an unfamiliar page or table of FX quotes, start by locating the exchange rate between U.S. Dollars and Japanese Yen; this provides an excellent point of orientation. If the number is between, say, 80 and 300, you can bet that it's Yen per Dollar or

USD|JPY; on the other hand, if it starts with a .0-something, it's Dollars per Yen or JPY|USD.

The Major Spot Quotes

Given the five major currencies, we summarize their standard interbank quoting conventions with the four quotes below (accompanied by representative spot values):

USD|CHF	1.2500
USD|JPY	111.00

EUR|USD	1.2500
GBP|USD	1.8000

The first two quotes (USD|CHF and USD|JPY) are similar in some sense and the second two quotes (EUR|USD and GBP|USD) are similar in some sense. Let's stop for a minute and think about these.

One of these pairs is called an American quote and the other pair is considered a European quote. Take a minute and guess which is which. (For the record, conjectures on this are almost always wrong!)

The first two quotes have in common the fact that the underlying asset is the U.S. Dollar. The second pair of quotes have in common the fact that the prices are quoted in terms of U.S. Dollars. To keep these labels straight, ask yourself, in terms of what units are Americans used to seeing prices quoted? U.S. Dollars, of course. For that reason, the bottom pair (Euro-Dollar and Sterling-Dollar) are American quotes. EUR|USD 1.2500 means that Euro 1 = USD 1.2500 (or that the price of 1 Euro is 1.25 U.S. Dollars). GBP|USD 1.8000 means that Pound Sterling 1 = USD 1.8000 (or the price of 1 Pound is 1.80 U.S. Dollars).

An American who is contemplating taking a vacation to Rome or London would have to ask, "How many of my Dollars would I have to pay to get one of those Euros or to get one of those Pounds?" This is clearly viewed from the American perspective. Having said that, can we rationalize the first set of quotes above as European quotes? If a Swiss family were to plan a vacation to Disneyland (the real Disneyland—none of this Euro Disney stuff), they would have to ask themselves, "How many of our Swiss Francs will we need to buy Dollars?" To my knowledge, they do not take Swiss Francs in Disneyland. This is clearly the European perspective. What about USD|JPY? Obviously this currency pair has nothing to do with Europe (indicating the exchange rate between an Asian currency and a North American currency), but it is still referred to as a European quote. The logic behind the name of this convention (that is, the convention with the U.S. Dollar as the underlying currency) goes back to the end of World War II—after which most of the major European currencies (with the exception of the British Pound) were quoted in this manner versus the U.S. Dollar (e.g., USD|DEM or Dollar-Deutsche Mark, USD|ITL or Dollar-Italian Lira, USD|FRF or Dollar-French Franc, USD|ESP or Dollar-Spanish Peseta). USD|JPY follows the quoting convention that was used for most of the European currencies and is labeled accordingly. European quotes are also sometimes known as "banker's quotes" (as this, historically, was the interbank norm).

There are other designations for FX quotes, but they simply involve more jargon. You may hear people talk about base currency and counter or quote currency; with USD|CHF, the Dollar is the base and the Swiss Franc is the quote or countercurrency. You may also hear about "direct quotes" and "indirect quotes"; these require raising the issue of foreign and domestic (that I proposed to avoid at the start); I will not use this terminology at all, as I do not find it helpful and consider it confusing at best.

SPOT EXERCISE #1

1. What is the name of the exchange rate quoting convention (i.e., American or European) between U.S. Dollars and Canadian Dollars if we quote USD|CAD?
2. What would it mean if USD|CAD S = 1.2000
3. If USD|CAD S = 1.2000, what would CAD|USD S = ?
4. What is the name of the exchange rate quoting convention between Australian Dollars and U.S. Dollars if we quote AUD|USD?
5. What would it mean if AUD|USD S = .7500

Nicknames

Many of the currency pairs are referred to using nicknames. As mentioned, GBP|USD is known as "Cable"; USD|CHF is sometimes referred to as "Swissy"; AUD|USD is "Aussie"; NZD|USD is "Kiwi"; and so on. An entertaining site containing the nicknames in local vernacular for the Euro (with translations) can be found (under Slang Words) at http://en.wikipedia.org/wiki/Euro.

But Why?

A common question is, "Why are some currencies quoted one way and some the other way?" In an effort to provide both a rationale and some explanation for the conventions, I usually respond to this question (in the classroom) by asking, "Who is good at math and who is bad at math?" I then ask the person who is good at math to solve the following straightforward math problem (without the use of their calculator):

What is 1/2 + 1/3 + 1/4 + 1/5 + 1/6 + 1/7 ?

Having given a head start to the person who is good at math, I ask the other person (who claims to find math more problematic) the following problem:

What is 2 + 3 + 4 + 5 + 6 + 7 ?

To date, the person asked to solve the first problem has never beaten the person asked to solve the second.

What is the point? The point is that the math is easier with larger numbers. More precisely, it is easier to work with numbers bigger than one. As a rule-of-thumb, though not a hard-and-fast rule, currency pairs are quoted so that you work with a number greater than one. Historically, Japanese Yen have been small in value relative to a U.S. Dollar, so we quote Yen per Dollar or USD|JPY. Also, in recent times, a Swiss Franc has been worth less than a U.S. Dollar, so we quote Swiss Francs per Dollar, USD|CHF, or Dollar-Swiss. Having said that, the Great Britain Pound has historically been worth more than a U.S. Dollar, so we quote Dollars per Pound or GBP|USD or Sterling-Dollar. Interestingly, when the Euro first hit the scene at the start of 1999, it was quoted at USD 1.1800 per Euro 1 (or EUR|USD spot was 1.1800), which fit the pattern. Over the course of the next couple of years, it dropped below USD .8300 per Euro 1, that is, EUR|USD violated the "quote the exchange rate so the number is greater than 1" convention. In the last few years, though, the Euro has rebounded (topping USD 1.3500 per EUR 1), and it is currently trading around USD 1.2500 per EUR 1—so it again fits the rule.

As is always the case in FX, there are exceptions. The most common "standard" quotes that we see trading under parity (or under the number one) are EUR|GBP, AUD|USD, and NZD|USD. In deference to the Great Britain Pound and since the Queen was on their money, we presume there was an inclination to want to treat these latter two currency pairs in the same way that GBP|USD was quoted.

SPOT EXERCISE #2

How would you guess we would quote the exchange rate between Japanese Yen and Swiss Francs. How would you guess we quote the exchange rate between Euros and Swiss Francs? Many people would refer to these currency pairs as "cross rates." More on these soon.

In general, if we were to quote Ringgit|Peso or MYR|MXN at S = 2.8578, this would imply that 2.8578 Mexican Pesos currently trade for 1 Malaysian Ringgit.

If I see, for example, "USD/CHF" (with a slash) either in the paper or on a computer screen, I'm honestly not sure, a priori, what it means. But if presented with a table of FX quotes, as in Figure 1.9 from the *Wall Street Journal*. I can always orient myself (to any idiosyncratic quoting method), as previously mentioned, by checking the exchange rate between U.S. Dollars and Japanese Yen.

Pips and Big Figures

If USD|CHF starts the day at S = 1.2500 and an hour later it is at S = 1.2501, we would say that this price had gone up one "pip."

A "pip" is the smallest quoted unit of the spot price.

Similarly, a five-pip decline in EUR|USD would take you from S = 1.2500 to S = 1.2495. Of course, you have to be careful because a pip in USD|CHF is in terms of Swiss Francs and a pip in EUR|USD is in terms of U.S. Dollars (and so they are, in a sense, not the same). Your inclination at this point might be to think of a pip as the number .0001, but that is not always true. If we look at USD|JPY S = 111.00, then a one-pip change takes you to S = 111.01. Remember, a pip is the smallest quoted unit of the spot price.

If USD|CHF started the day at S = 1.2500 and ended the day at S = 1.2600, we would say that it went up 100 pips. There are two things to point out here. The first:

We refer to 100 pips as a "big figure."

If EUR|USD S = 1.2500 and it rose three big figures, it would go to S = 1.2800. An FX market professional would say, "Euro-Dollar is trading at one-twenty-eight 'the figure.'" With USD|JPY S = 111.00, what would an increase of three big figures mean? This would mean that S now equals 114.00 (remember, 100 pips is a big figure and a pip in USD|JPY = .01).

The second point:

A big figure often relates to (the smallest quoted) currency unit in that currency.

If USD|CHF rises from 1.2500 to 1.2600, it has gone up by one big figure; more precisely, the price of 1 USD has risen by .01 Swiss Francs, and .01 Swiss Francs is known as a rappen. At any rate, a big figure corresponds to a Swiss rappen or Swiss "penny." If EUR|USD rises from S = 1.2500 to 1.2600, the price of 1 Euro has just risen by .01 U.S. Dollars or a U.S. cent or penny (again, the connection to the smallest currency unit). If USD|JPY rises by one big figure from S = 111.00 to S = 112.00, the price of a Dollar has risen by one Yen (once again, the smallest currency unit).

ECONOMIC INTERPRETATION

More important than the jargon is the interpretation. If USD|CHF rises from S = 1.2500 to S = 1.2600, what has just happened? The price of 1 USD has just risen from 1.2500 Swiss Francs to 1.2600 Swiss Francs. We would say that the Dollar has **strengthened**. With, say, 1,000 U.S. Dollars, you can now buy more Swiss Francs (1,260) than you could before (1,250).

Everything in foreign exchange is relative.

If you think about this from the Swiss perspective, it implies that you used to be able to buy 1 Dollar with 1.25 Swiss Francs; now, with S = 1.2600, it takes more Swiss Francs than it used to in order to buy any given amount of Dollars. We would say that the Swiss Franc has **weakened**. If we inverted the exchange rate (and thought about it in terms of CHF|USD, with the Swiss Franc as the underlying asset), we'd have originally seen S = .8000 (1 Swiss Franc is trading for USD .80 or 80 U.S. cents) and then later S = .7937 (the Swiss Franc is cheaper or weaker). The price of a Swiss Franc fell; the Swiss Franc is weaker and the Dollar is stronger. Some people may use the words "appreciated" or "revalued" in place of "strengthened" and/or the words "depreciated" or "devalued" in place of "weakened," but I always think about revaluations and devaluations in the context of formal changes in a fixed exchange rate framework (and so avoid the employment of these terms in this way). What does it mean if somebody says, "The Dollar went up"? To tell you the truth, I don't exactly know; it probably means that the Dollar strengthened, but if it's the headline of an article in the financial press, I usually read on—just to be sure. (I have seen such a statement used to imply that EUR|USD just went up, that is, more Dollars per Euro, but this means that the Dollar has weakened. See the source of the ambiguity?)

SPOT EXERCISE #3

1. Could the price of a Dollar fall against the Swiss Franc but rise against the Japanese Yen? If so, what must have happened to the exchange rate between Swiss Francs and Japanese Yen? More specifically, will CHF|JPY have gone up or gone down?
2. Can you buy U.S. Dollars with Pounds Sterling?

SPOT EXERCISE #4

Complete the following table of foreign exchange (cross) rates:

	USD	EUR	JPY	GBP	CHF
USD	—	1.2500			
EUR		—			
JPY	110.00		—		96.00
GBP				—	
CHF				2.4000	—

(*Hint:* Look back at Figure 1.9. To get oriented, start with USD and JPY.)

What Is the Value of a Dollar?

Economists are always asking, "What are things worth?" What is a Dollar worth? How might we address the question of the "correct" or "true" value of a U.S. Dollar?

Trivia Question   *Question:* Do you know what currently appears on every piece of U.S. currency—every coin and every note?

> *Answer:* "In God We Trust" (because there is nothing behind USD any more other than "faith," that is, the full faith, credit, and trust of the U.S. government). (See Figure 5.1.)

FIGURE 5.1   "In God We Trust"

PURCHASING POWER PARITY

One approach that economists have developed to gauge the value of a currency is to observe what it can purchase. One would think that if a certain "basket" of goods costs USD 3,000 in New York and that same "basket" costs CHF 3,750 in Zurich, Switzerland, then the exchange rate ought to be USD|CHF S = 1.2500 (Figure 5.2). This is known as **purchasing power parity**, the notion that the exchange rate should reflect the relative purchasing power of the currencies under examination.

Of course, one might ask, "What's to be done (or more precisely, what is the arbitrage) if the foreign exchange rates are out of line?" In other words, if the basket of goods that costs USD 3,000 in New York were to trade at CHF 3,500 in Switzerland (with the USD|CHF exchange rate at S = 1.2500), then the Swiss basket looks cheap in CHF relative to the U.S. basket in Dollars. But would enterprising individuals find it profitable to buy the goods in Switzerland, fly them over to the United States, and sell these items out of their suitcase at J.F.K. Airport in New York at the current market prices? Clearly, this would be a bit impractical. And all this ignores tariffs, duties, taxes, import and export restrictions, . . . In short, although the exchange rate appears out of line given

= USD 3,000   = CHF 3,750

so USDICHF should = 1.2500

FIGURE 5.2   Purchasing Power Parity

the goods markets (or maybe the goods markets look out of line given the exchange rate), there is no market mechanism or set of trades that will necessarily force these back in line. Having said that, most economists believe purchasing power parity (or PPP) tends to hold (more or less) over the long run.

The Big Mac Index

The idea behind the comparison of identical (or closely comparable) international baskets of goods and services, priced in terms of their respective currencies (and notwithstanding the caveats about traded versus nontraded, tariffs and taxes) is intuitively appealing. Nevertheless, the logistics of arriving at the contents of that "ideal" basket, its periodic revision, the mathematical and economic theory of index numbers all serve to make the application of purchasing power parity rather daunting (if not inaccessible) to the layperson.

In 1986, the editor of the weekly business magazine *The Economist* introduced the Big Mac Index. Li Lian Ong tells us that this "tongue-in-cheek contribution to what is perhaps the most widely-researched and debated doctrine in international finance . . . is still going strong and is now widely cited and used by academics and practitioners alike."[1] In essence, instead of proposing a representative consumer basket of goods and services, this semiannual review compares the prices of a (presumably uniform) product in "local" currencies around the world—

with that "representative commodity" being a Big Mac hamburger sandwich. At first glance, this might appear to be little more than a curiosity, but the Big Mac may be a more representative commodity for the purposes of measuring international purchasing power than you might think. After all, what goes into a Big Mac? It is not only the big beefy patty, the lettuce and tomato, and the fluffy bun, but the cost of labor, the local rent, and the cost of energy (among other things). (See Figure 5.3.)

There is an apocryphal story of a university professor who started a fund whose investment philosophy was premised on purchasing power parity; legend has it that this vehicle did not fare well, reinforcing the belief that markets may be out of line—and may stay out of line— for some time, even if there is a tendency for them to drift back toward fair value.

Finance & Economics

The Economist's Big Mac Index

"Fast Food and Strong Currencies"

From The Economist
June 9, 2005

How much burger do you get for your euro, yuan, or Swiss franc?

The Economist's Big Mac Index seeks to make exchange-rate theory more digestible. It is arguably the world's most accurate financial indicator to be based on a fast-food item.

The hamburger standard

	Big Mac price in dollars*	Implied PPP of the dollar	Under (−)/ over (+) valuation against the dollar, %		Big Mac price in dollars*	Implied PPP of the dollar	Under (−)/ over (+) valuation against the dollar, %
United States†	3.06	—	—	Aruba	2.77	1.62	-10
Argentina	1.64	1.55	-46	Bulgaria	1.88	0.98	-39
Australia	2.50	1.06	-18	Colombia	2.79	2124	-9
Brazil	2.39	1.93	-22	Costa Rica	2.38	369	-22
Britain	3.44	1.63§	+12	Croatia	2.50	4.87	-18
Canada	2.63	1.07	-14	Dominican Rep	2.12	19.6	-31
Chile	2.53	490	-17	Estonia	2.31	9.64	-24
China	1.27	3.43	-59	Fiji	2.50	1.39	-18
Czech Republic	2.30	18.4	-25	Georgia	2.00	1.19	-34
Denmark	4.58	9.07	+50	Guatemala	2.20	5.47	-28
Egypt	1.55	2.94	-49	Honduras	1.91	11.7	-38
Euro area	3.58**	1.05††	+17	Iceland	6.67	143	+118
Hong Kong	1.54	3.92	-50	Jamaica	2.70	53.9	-12
Hungary	2.60	173	-15	Jordan	3.66	0.85	+19
Indonesia	1.53	4,771	-50	Latvia	1.92	0.36	-37
Japan	2.34	81.7	-23	Lebanon	2.85	1405	-7
Malaysia	1.38	1.72	-55	Lithuania	2.31	2.12	-24
Mexico	2.58	9.15	-16	Macau	1.40	3.66	-54
New Zealand	3.17	1.45	+4	Macedonia	1.90	31.0	-38
Peru	2.76	2.94	-10	Moldova	1.84	7.52	-40
Philippines	1.47	26.1	-52	Morocco	2.73	8.02	-11
Poland	1.96	2.12	-36	Nicaragua	2.11	11.3	-31
Russia	1.48	13.7	-52	Norway	6.06	12.7	+98
Singapore	2.17	1.18	-29	Pakistan	2.18	42.5	-29
South Africa	2.10	4.56	-31	Paraguay	1.44	2941	-53
South Korea	2.49	817	-19	Qatar	0.68	0.81	-78
Sweden	4.17	10.1	+36	Saudi Arabia	2.40	2.94	-22
Switzerland	5.05	2.06	+65	Serbia & Montenegro	2.08	45.8	-32
Taiwan	2.41	24.5	-21	Slovakia	2.09	21.6	-32
Thailand	1.48	19.6	-52	Slovenia	2.56	163	-16
Turkey	2.92	1.31	-5	Sri Lanka	1.75	57.2	-43
Venezuela	2.13	1,830	-30	Ukraine	1.43	2.37	-53
				UAE	2.45	2.94	-20
				Uruguay	1.82	14.4	-40

*At current exchange rates †Purchasing-power parity
†Average of New York, Chicago, San Francisco and Atlanta
§Dollars per pound **Weighted average of member countries
Sources: McDonald's; The Economist ††Dollars per euro

FIGURE 5.3 The Big Mac Index

Source: The Economist. © 2005 The Economist Newspaper Ltd. All rights reserved. Reprinted with permission. Further reproduction prohibited. www.economist.com.

CROSS RATES AND TRIANGULAR ARBITRAGE IN THE SPOT MARKET

Consider the two following spot FX quotes:

USD|CHF = 1.2500   and   EUR|USD = 1.2500

If we were to ask what the exchange rate between Euros and Swiss Francs should be, you might guess 1.0000 (as the exchange rates are the same), but you have to be careful. If you've ever taken a physics class, they are always reminding you to keep track of your units; in this case, writing these two currency quotes out (as ratios of quantities):

$$\frac{CHF\ 1.2500}{USD\ 1} \qquad \frac{USD\ 1.2500}{EUR\ 1}$$

Multiplying these out (with the USD units cancelling), we get

$$\frac{CHF\ 1.2500}{USD\ 1} \times \frac{USD\ 1.2500}{EUR\ 1} = \frac{CHF\ 1.5625}{EUR\ 1}$$

Thus, given the USD|CHF and EUR|USD quotes, the EUR|CHF spot price *should* = 1.5625.

If this is not the case (that is, if EUR|CHF does not equal 1.5625), there is a deterministic arbitrage that we could carry out that would result in a certain profit.

As an example, what if EUR|CHF S = 1.5500 (along with USD|CHF S = 1.2500 and EUR|USD S = 1.2500)? Something is "out of line" here, but, unlike that purchasing power parity situation mentioned earlier, here we can "do the arbitrage."

What trades would you propose? How do you get started? Given the first two spot prices, there is an implicit EUR|CHF spot price (of 1.5625). Since the EUR|CHF spot price in the market is different, there is an arbitrage. Remember, "Buy Low; Sell High." In this case, the market price (of a Euro) is too low (at 1.5500) when compared to the value as calculated by the other two quotes (1.5625), so you would want to BUY EURO. More specifically, you would want to BUY EUR and SELL CHF.

This approach is known as "triangular arbitrage" as there are three currencies involved. Let's say we start with USD 100,000,000. Given that we want to buy EUR with CHF, we need to get the CHF and then convert them into EUR. If one sets up a triangle with the three currency labels at the corners, it will facilitate the approach as shown in Figure 5.4.

Having determined that you want to Sell CHF and Buy EUR, this would imply a clock-wise movement of funds (shown in Figure 5.5)—having initially set up our triangle as in Figure 5.4. Now doing the FX conversions gives us Figure 5.6.

Three points. Your profits here are realized in USD as you carried the entire cash flow through to the end (i.e., back into USD). If we had wanted, we could have realized our profits in any one of the three currencies.

Also, I tell people that they should never get a triangular arbitrage problem wrong. If they go around the triangle and end up losing money (that is, they end up with less than they started), then they should just do the problem again going in the other direction. Of course, a trader doesn't have the luxury of utilizing this approach.

Finally, in FX, you should always ask yourself, "Does my answer make sense?" In this example, you made a profit of over USD 800,000, but is there a way to check that you've done it right? I like to call this a "reality check." To confirm our result, you can form the ratio of what you thought the EUR|CHF spot price should be (that is, 1.5625) to the price that you observed for EUR|CHF in the market (1.5500). The ratio is 1.008064516, which means that you should expect to make a little over .8% (which is exactly what you were able to make). Reassuring, isn't it?

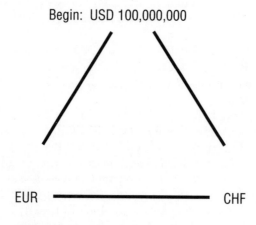

FIGURE 5.4 Triangular Arbitrage

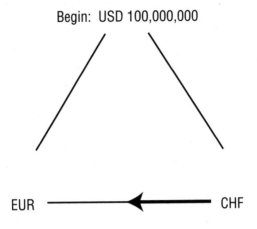

Begin: USD 100,000,000

EUR ⟵ CHF

FIGURE 5.5 Triangular Arbitrage: Sell CHF and Buy EURO

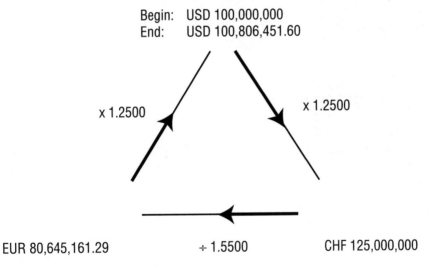

Begin: USD 100,000,000
End: USD 100,806,451.60

x 1.2500

x 1.2500

EUR 80,645,161.29   ÷ 1.5500   CHF 125,000,000

FIGURE 5.6 Triangular Arbitrage FX Conversions

SPOT TRIANGULAR ARBITRAGE EXERCISES #5

1. Given the following spot prices:
   USDIJPY 110.00
   USDICHF 1.2500
   and CHFIJPY 85.00

   do a triangular arbitrage starting with CHF 40,000,000, explicitly state your trades, realize your profit in CHF, and do a reality check to ensure your answer is correct.
2. Given the following spot quotes:
   EURIGBP .6850
   GBPIUSD 1.8420
   and EURIUSD 1.2500

   Do a triangular arbitrage starting with EUR 100,000,000; realize your profit in USD.

Somebody asked one of our FX spot dealers if they had ever done triangular arbitrage, and the trader, after a bit of thought responded, "Yes, I did . . . , once . . . , back in 1977." The FX markets are quite efficient and there are lots of people watching them, so trading opportunities like this do not happen very often (or remain around very long). The purpose of these exercises is not to teach you to make a living off the FX spot markets by identifying triangular arbitrage opportunities, but to give you a chance to practice working with exchange rates, converting currencies, and thinking about arbitrage.

THE BID–ASK SPREAD IN FOREIGN EXCHANGE

In the real world, when one trades, one will have to deal with a marketmaker, and, in so doing, will face a bid–ask spread. Unlike the equity markets where there is often a per share commission, in FX, there is only a bid–ask spread. Let's take the currency pair USDICHF and quote the bid-ask:

$$1.2540 - 1.2550.$$

The marketmaker will buy 1 Dollar for 1.2540 Swiss Francs and will sell 1 Dollar for 1.2550 Swiss Francs. Traders often assume market participants know the first part of the price quote (the "1.25" part, which is sometimes called the "handle") and, in the professional FX dealer market, would probably only quote the "40 at 50."

We said earlier that we could quote CHFIUSD. Presumably this would simply involve using the "1/x" button on our calculator. Doing so gives us:

$$.7974 - .7968.$$

Look at this quote. Wouldn't you (as a marketmaker) hate it when that happens? Your bid price is higher than your ask or offer price. One person to whom I pointed this out suggested that we "just turn them around" (in other words, make the bid .7968 and the ask .7974). What do you think? Believe it or not, that's the right thing to do. Recall, the USD|CHF bid was 1.2540, which was where the marketmaker BUYS Dollars and therefore SELLS Swiss Francs. Quoted the other way, this price (.7974), IS the ASK or OFFER for a Swiss Franc, which is why you should "turn the quotes around":

$$.7968–.7974.$$

What is a typical bid–ask spread in foreign exchange? The bid–ask spread is driven by the competitiveness of the marketplace, the liquidity of the underlying assets, historical precedent, sometimes regulations, and so on. It is, again, important to note that a 10-pip bid–ask spread in one currency pair (like USD|CHF) is not the same as a 10-pip bid–ask spread in another currency pair (like EUR|USD).

In the following screen shots, we reproduce an FX spot trading tool interface similar to what a market participant might use. Note the highlighted "pips" and the suppressed handle. (See Figure 5.7.) We also show a generic spot transaction as recorded on such a tool. (See Figure 5.8.)

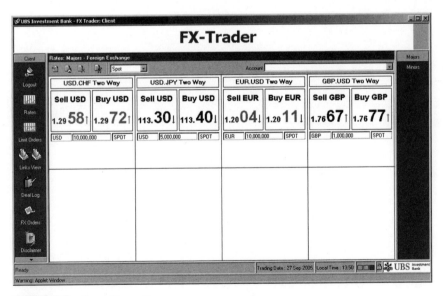

FIGURE 5.7 Spot Quote Screen
Source: © 2006 UBS Investment Bank. Reprinted by permission.

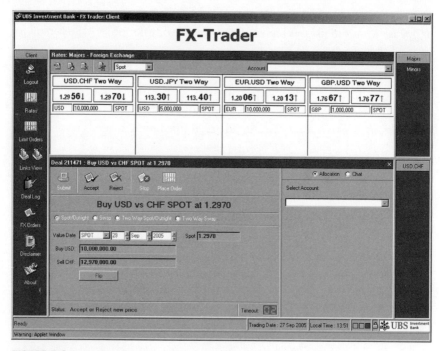

FIGURE 5.8 Spot Dealing Screen
Source: © 2006 UBS Investment Bank. Reprinted by permission.

TIMING

To most of us, "on the spot" means "right here and right now." In general, though, financial transactions which are entered into **today** (known as the "trade date" or "T") usually do not settle today; that is, the asset and the payment do not trade hands until some point in time in the near future (known as the "settlement date" or the "value date"). In the United States, most stock trades settle in three good business days (by "good business days," we mean three days not counting weekends or holidays); this convention is known as "T + 3." U.S. Treasury security trades settle one business day later ("T + 1"). Most corporate bond transactions settle two business days later ("T + 2"). Gold and other precious metal transactions are usually "T + 2." Spot foreign exchange transactions, for the most part,[2] settle on a two-good-business-day basis ("T + 2").

Interestingly, many of our FX traders and salespeople still have tradi-

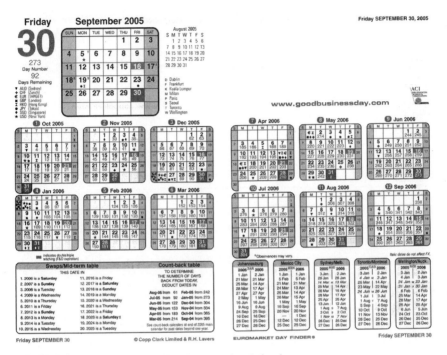

FIGURE 5.9 Typical Euromarket Day Finder Calendar
Source: Copp Clark Limited.

tional calendars on their desks. In Figure 5.9 we show a typical day on a Euromarket calendar (as would have been observed on September 28, 2005).[3] They are usually open to two good business days beyond that day's current date. Remember, in FX, everything revolves around spot.

SETTLEMENT

Although there are a large number of U.S. Dollars outside of the United States, this is more an exception than the norm when it comes to where a country's money tends to reside; most currencies remain within their national boundaries of origin. If you were, for example, to buy USD|CHF spot (with the associated two-good-business-day settlement), you will have to "pay" your Swiss Francs in two days into your counterparty's account in

Switzerland (into their "vostro" account—from the Latin for "your") and you should expect to "receive" the U.S. Dollars into your account in the United States (into your "nostro" account—from the Latin for "our"). Note that there can be a mismatch in terms of the timing of these currency flows and, unlike many other securities transactions today, is not necessarily "delivery versus payment" or "DVP." This has led to problems in the past that we discuss in a later chapter.

MARKET JARGON

FX professionals use a language all their own. I sometimes joke that one should never bet a Dollar with an FX person, because a Dollar means a million Dollars on an FX desk. A trade for 20 "bucks" or 20 Dollars is on a notional amount of USD 20,000,000. One sees "million" abbreviated in a variety of ways, as "Mil," "Mio," and "MM." You also might hear a quote for 5 "yard" of Yen; "yard" is short for "milliard" which means a billion.

If one is buying a currency, one would tend to express that with the words "mine" or "paid." If you are selling, you'd indicate that with "yours" or "given." There are a plethora of expressions used on FX desks; the jargon is half the battle.

Finally, there are a number of different types of orders that can be placed. A market order indicates an order to do a trade immediately at the best possible price currently available. There are limit orders, stop-loss orders, day orders, fill-or-kill, all-or-none, good-till-cancelled, stop-limit, trailing stop, order-cancels-order, and so on.

"THE BEST ARBITRAGE AROUND!"

In one of the weirder foreign exchange phenomena in recent times, it was discovered, soon after the Euro appeared in physical form, that the 10-Thai Baht coin (worth at the time about USD .23) was recognized by the vending machines in Europe as a two-Euro coin (worth around USD 1.73). Apparently people were flying back to Europe with bags of these 10-Baht coins. Talk about buying low and selling high! For the record, we are neither advocating nor condoning this sort of unethical behavior, but simply recognize a modern instance of Gresham's Law at work. (See Figure 5.10.)

Euro Suffers Thai Problem

[January 26, 2002 Posted: 6:39 AM EST (1139 GMT)]

BANGKOK, Thailand—Thai 10-baht coins are causing problems for Euro vending machines because they weigh the same as a two-euro coin but are worth eight times less.

The problem first surfaced in Spain but now European Union officials in Thailand have confirmed they are aware of the problem.

A EU spokesman in Bangkok said the European Central Bank was aware of the problem but Thailand had not been blamed for the confusion or asked to withdraw its coins.

"There are so many coins in circulation from different countries, that it's impossible for them all to be completely different," the spokesman told Reuters.

"If vending machine operators find foreign coins in their machines, it's up to them to change their software," he said.

Newer vending machines can measure metallic content and differentiate between the 10 baht and two euro, which contains zinc.

But older machines are fooled because both weigh 8.5 grammes and the Thai coin is just 0.25mm wider than the two euro.

Senior finance ministry official Thevan Vichitakul, quoted in the *Bangkok Post Daily*, said:
"The fact that our 10-baht coin is similar to the two-euro coin is the problem of the EU, not Thailand."

FIGURE 5.10 "The Best Arbitrage Around!"
Source: © 2002 Cable News Network LP, LLLP. An AOL Time Warner Company. All Rights Reserved.

CHAPTER 6

Foreign Exchange Forwards

Money often costs too much.

—Ralph Waldo Emerson

INTRODUCTION TO FORWARDS AND FORWARD PRICING

In some ways, the financial markets involve transactions that are similar to more mundane experiences. While on a trip, I may need a place to sleep. I could simply attempt to locate lodgings as my bedtime approaches, but that could prove problematic. I may not be able to find a vacancy, but, even if I could, I would have no idea what I would have to pay (and would probably feel like I was being taken advantage of, upon hearing that there are vacancies, but that I would have to pay $400 for that evening's stay). In short, many of us who travel tend to arrange for our hotel/motel accommodations in advance. That way, we are ensured that we can get what we would like—at a price that we feel is reasonable. A large number of foreign exchange trades are done in this fashion. If you arrange a currency trade, locking in a price (an exchange rate) and a quantity in advance, this is known as a "forward contract," a "forward transaction," a "forward trade," or, simply, a "forward."

There is no reason why you should expect the price in a forward trade to be the same as the price in a spot transaction. Would you expect the price of bananas to be the same in Helsinki as in Honduras? No. These prices would differ because the trades would occur at different points on the globe. An FX forward trade will generally involve a different price than a spot trade; these transactions take place at different points as well—different points in time (and, as you may have heard, time is money)!

Let me start this section by asking you a question or two (and, to try to make the point, let's get away from FX for the moment). Could I ever convince you to voluntarily agree to buy a stock today for S = USD 50 (a spot transaction) and simultaneously get you to agree to sell that stock in a week (a one-week forward transaction) for F = USD 48? Stop and think about it. It doesn't sound good, does it?

I would venture to say, though, that if I offered to make an additional side payment to you of USD 5, you might willingly agree to do both of these trades. (This brings up the notion of "payment" or "premium" and will be revisited when we talk about off-market forwards and options.) But what if I do not offer you any "side compensation"? Is it possible to envision a scenario under which you might still willingly agree to both of the trades mentioned above? Have you seen it yet?

What if the stock itself pays you something? Stocks have been known to pay dividends. A dividend is a payment from the company to the registered owner of the share(s). If the stock were to pay you a dividend of USD 5 per share over the course of this week, this pair of trades would now look relatively attractive.

Finally, what if I am not offering to pay you anything (on the side) and the stock doesn't pay any dividends. Could I convince you to buy the stock today in the spot market for S = USD 50 and to sell the stock in a week (sell the stock forward) at a price of **F = USD 50**? At least this looks a little better than our earlier numbers, but you shouldn't fall for it. What you would lose is the interest on your money. In general, if there is no benefit from owning and "carrying" an asset, you should insist on being compensated for tying up your money (with the result that you'd expect the forward price to be higher than the spot price). On the other hand, if the benefit of "carrying" the asset (in the earlier instance, the dividend) is large enough, you'd willingly agree to sell that asset in the future at a forward price that is lower than the current spot price. Forward pricing is all about costs and benefits!

In general, the forward price (F) will be based on the spot price (S) grossed up by "the cost of carry" (in our example, by the cost of money or the interest cost) and reduced by "the benefit of carrying the asset" (in our example, the dividend). Perhaps it is easier to write the following:

$$F = S + \text{Cost} - \text{Benefit} \tag{6.1}$$

Using a little notation, in this case of a dividend-paying stock, we could write

$$F = S + Srt - \text{Div} \tag{6.2}$$

Where F = the forward price
         S = the spot price
         r = the (annualized) interest rate
         t = the time (in years)
       Div = the dividend

FORWARD EXAMPLE

If a stock is trading at $S = 40.00$, interest rates are $r = 5.00\%$, we are thinking about a three-month time frame ($t = 1/4 = .25$), and, in two months and three and a half weeks, this stock will pay a (confirmed) dividend of Div = 1.50, where would you guess the three-month forward price would be quoted?

$$F = 40.00 + 40.00 \times (.05) \times (1/4) - (1.50) = 39.00$$

For simplicity, we sweep the couple of days of interest on the dividend under the rug (i.e., we will simply ignore it here).

FORWARD EXERCISE #1

If a stock is trading at $S = 100.00$, interest rates are $r = 4.00\%$, we are thinking about a one-year time frame ($t = 1$), and, over the course of the year, this stock will pay a quarterly dividend of Div = 0.25, where would the one-year forward price be quoted?

FOREIGN EXCHANGE FORWARDS AND FORWARD PRICING

Let's now attempt to bring this concept back to foreign exchange. It will be easiest to choose a currency pair, like USD|CHF, and think through what this spot–forward relationship would look like in FX. Assume USD|CHF S = 1.2500 (that is, USD 1 = CHF 1.2500). With this quote, the U.S. Dollar is the underlying asset, and the price of that asset is quoted in Swiss Francs. Let's start with the benefits. Are there benefits to buying and holding Dollars (the underlying asset)? Of course. Unless you put the USD in your pillowcase or a safety deposit box in a Swiss bank, you will receive interest on your Dollars. What about the cost? To answer that question, we have to think about perspective. From whose perspective is this price quoted? This is the Swiss (European) perspective. If a Swiss individual wanted to buy and carry USD 1 (because, perhaps, they want to go to Disneyland—again, the real Disneyland, not Euro Disney), they would either have to take their Swiss Francs out of their Swiss bank savings account (forgoing interest) or borrow the Swiss Francs (in order to purchase the Dollars). It will always be easier to think of the latter; in this case, there is an actual and explicit cost associated with borrowing CHF and buying USD; that cost is the Swiss interest rate incurred as a result of the borrowing. At this point, we might try to fit these elements into our earlier relationship (using USD 1 as the notional magnitude of our transaction):

$$F = S + S\, r_{CH}\, t - 1\, r_{US}\, t \qquad\qquad (6.3)$$

There's only one problem here. You're adding apples and oranges (or, really, Swiss Francs and Dollars). The cost of buying USD 1 is in Swiss Francs, but the benefit of "carrying one USD" is the interest you would re-ceive—presumably in Dollars. Putting units on these terms, we get:

$$^{CHF}F = {}^{CHF}S + {}^{CHF}S\, r_{CH}\, t - {}^{USD}1\, r_{US}\, t \qquad\qquad (6.4)$$

Since spot is quoted as CHF per USD 1, you would think the forward should be quoted in the same way, so the only problematic term here is the last one. If we want everything in terms of CHF (which makes sense, as that is how spot is quoted), one might propose multiplying the last term by the spot price. After all, that would convert those USD into CHF, would it not?

This would give us (using our earlier notation)

$$^{CHF}F = {}^{CHF}S + {}^{CHF}S\, r_{CH}\, t - {}^{CHF}S \times 1\, r_{US}\, t \qquad\qquad (6.5)$$

or more simply, now that everything is in Swiss Francs,

$$F = S + S\, r_{CH}\, t - S\, r_{US}\, t \qquad\qquad (6.6)$$

or

$$F = S + S\, (r_{CH} - r_{US})\, t \qquad\qquad (6.7)$$

If you ask almost anyone who works in foreign exchange why the spot price and the forward price differ, they will respond with these three words:

"interest rate differentials."

You can see it. If the costs and benefits are the same (that is, if Swiss in-terest rates and U.S. interest rates are equal), then the spot price and the forward price will be the same.

This is definitely the right intuition, but careful consideration might convince us that this isn't really right. After all, the interest that we would get on USD 1 would be realized only in the future, so, really, the spot price applied to the U.S. Dollar interest shouldn't be the spot price today; it seems as if it should actually be the spot price at the end of this time period (which, unfortunately, we do not know today). Sounds like we're back to square one, but not really. We could ask, "Is there a price that we can observe today at which we could exchange USD for CHF at some point in the future?" The answer, of course, is yes. That is the forward price. Returning to our relationship, it would now look like this

$$F = S + Sr_{CH}\, t - F 1\, r_{US}t$$

or

$$F = S(1 + r_{CH}\, t) - F\, r_{US}t$$

or

$$F(1 + r_{US}\, t) = S\,(1 + r_{CH}\, t)$$

or, finally,

$$F = \frac{S(1 + r_{CH}t)}{(1 + r_{US}t)} \tag{6.8}$$

This is the "correct" relationship.[1] It may seem odd (using F in our definition of the forward price—kind of like defining "constitutionality" as "of or relating to the Constitution"), but indeed this is the relationship that must hold—otherwise an arbitrage would exist.

FORWARD EXAMPLE

Currency pair (Dollar-Swiss): Spot USDICHF S = 1.2500

Using a one year (t = 1) time horizon with r_{US} = 5.00% and r_{CH} = 3.00%, calculate the one-year forward price.

The one-year USDICHF forward price should be F = 1.2500(1.03)/(1.05) = 1.2262 (rounded to the fourth decimal place).

FORWARD EXERCISE #2

If USDIJPY is trading in the spot market at S = 110.00, Japanese interest rates are r_j = 1.00%, U.S. rates are r_{US} = 5.00%, then where would you expect to see the one-year USDIJPY forward price quoted?

Let's try to arrive at this FX spot–forward relationship in another way: If USDICHF S = 1.2500, this means that CHF 1.2500 = USD 1 today in the spot market. These amounts of money are in some sense equal, or equivalent, or of the same value. Now if CHF 1.2500 today = USD 1 today, then, one would think that these would be expected to be equal at any given point in time in the future as well, but we can't forget that money grows over time. This would mean that, in one year, what was previously equal (USD 1 and CHF 1.2500) should still be equivalent, but USD 1 will have grown into USD 1.05 and CHF 1.2500 will have grown into CHF 1.2875. On a per Dollar basis, this implies USD 1 should = CHF 1.2262. This is most easily seen diagrammatically (see Figure 6.1).

Further, this can be depicted generically (again, using a European spot

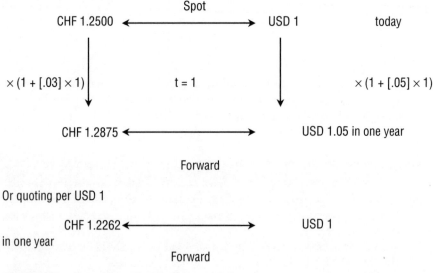

FIGURE 6.1   Example of Interest Rate Parity

In general, the relationship would diagrammatically look like this (quoting against the USD):

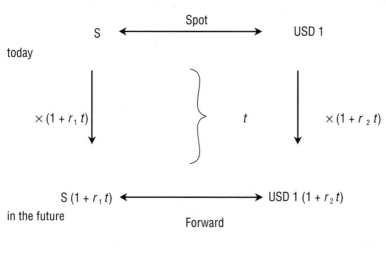

FIGURE 6.2   Generic Interest Rate Parity

quote). See Figure 6.2. This spot-forward FX relationship is known as *Interest Rate Parity*. Three technical points:

1. Rewriting the general spot-forward relationship in foreign exchange:

$$F = \frac{S(1+r_1 t)}{(1+r_2 t)} \qquad (6.9)$$

I am often asked, "Does the U.S. interest rate go on the top or the bottom?" Good question. Let me explain. In the case of USD|CHF, the spot price is quoted in terms of CHF. It therefore makes sense (does it not?) that the rate on top (in the numerator) should be the Swiss interest rate (the rate that goes with CHF). This next statement may sound hokey, but it always "works." In USD|CHF, the U.S. Dollar is the UNDERlying asset; for that reason, the U.S. Dollar interest rate goes UNDERneath (in the denominator). If we were to quote EUR|USD, the spot price is quoted in USD, so the U.S. interest rate goes on the top in our formula; the EUR is the UNDERlying asset, so the EUR interest rate goes UNDERneath. Possibly lame, but hopefully now easy to keep straight.[2]

2. For those strange individuals who would rather use continuous interest conventions, the spot–forward FX relationship would look like this

$$F = \frac{Se^{r_1 t}}{e^{r_2 t}} \quad \text{or} \quad F = Se^{(r_1 - r_2)t} \tag{6.10}$$

While mathematicians, "quants" (or quantitative analysts), and computers may like this interest convention, one has to be careful not to simply insert market interest rates (quoted annually using noncontinuous compounding) into this formula. The one nice thing is that we again see that if interest rates are the same in the two countries, the spot price and the forward price will be the same.

3. One might think we should consider compounding the interest (that is, using a compounding convention, as opposed to the simple interest convention, which we have built into Equation [6.9], but, in practice, the vast, vast majority of forward trades are done under a year (most under six months), and so it is appropriate to employ the money market convention of using simple interest.[3]

INTEREST RATE PARITY (COVERED INTEREST ARBITRAGE)

Before moving on, let's think once more about the intuition here—from an economist's perspective. Spot is spot. There is a price in the market today for USD 1 and it is CHF 1.2500. Interest rates differ in the United States and Switzerland. U.S. Dollars are growing at 5% and Swiss Francs are growing at 3%. In relative terms, USD are growing faster than CHF. They taught me in economics classes at the University of Chicago that when supply goes up, the price goes down. That is what is happening here. $S = 1.2500$ today and $F = 1.2262$ in one year. The price of a Dollar is expected to fall because the Dollars (compared to Swiss Francs) are becoming relatively more abundant. (See Figure 6.3.)

Let's take another stab at it. Why are interest rates in Switzerland different from interest rates in the United States? Both Switzerland and the United States have well-educated populaces; both have stable political and

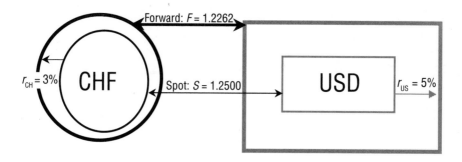

FIGURE 6.3 Interest Rate Parity: Graphical Explanation of Interest Rate Parity as a Special Case of Supply and Demand

financial systems; both have access to world-class technology; both have solid economic infrastructure. Why are interest rates different? The most likely reason that nominal or market interest rates differ is not because real interest rates differ (though they may), but because the two countries have different rates of inflation, which is primarily the result of their monetary policies. The nominal or market U.S. interest rate of 5% might be made up of a 2% real rate of interest (as described in Chapter 3) plus 3% (expected) inflation. The nominal or market Swiss interest rate might be composed of a 2% real rate of interest plus 1% (expected) inflation.

What is inflation? A general increase in the level of prices. What causes inflation? At the University of Chicago, as graduate students in the Department of Economics, we were taught to chant, "Inflation is always and everywhere a monetary phenomenon." In other words, prices rise if monetary growth exceeds the rate of growth in the real economy. Inflation is a direct result of the government printing and spending. In general, you will see inflation (or possibly even hyper-inflation) when a government simply prints and spends (again, to be precise, at a greater rate than the real rate of growth in the economy). Inflation is a particularly sneaky form of taxation; the government gets to spend the valuable currency before all the citizens realize that the money they are holding is worth less than it was a short time before, since there is now more of it around relative to the supply of goods and services. This explains the popularity of expansionary monetary policy. As the U.S. Dollar is being debased relative to (or printed faster than) the Swiss Franc, one would expect the relative value of the USD to fall. $S = 1.2500$ and $F = 1.2262$.

We have said that this pricing relationship is known as interest rate parity. Parity implies an equivalence or equality between two things. Obviously interest rates in the United States and Switzerland need not be the same (nor do they have to "converge" in any sense), but, if a wealthy Swiss individual thought about converting CHF today into USD (in order to capture the higher interest of 5% in the United States, relative to the Swiss rate of interest of 3%) and also attempted to convert those Dollars back into Swiss Francs using the forward market (because, after all, this person is Swiss), they would end up with the same amount of CHF as if they had simply invested it directly in their Swiss bank at a rate of interest of 3%. They also taught me at the University of Chicago that there's no such thing as a free lunch; interest rate parity is just another way of stating that fact.

Interest rate parity goes by other names. It is sometimes referred to as "covered interest arbitrage," which would suggest doing trades (e.g., selling forward and covering it by buying spot) if the markets are out of line in some sense. Let's consider spot-forward arbitrage in FX by showing the cash flows associated with an arbitrage situation.

FX SPOT–FORWARD ARBITRAGE

EXAMPLE

USD|CHF: $S = 1.2500$ $t = 1$ $r_{US} = 5.00\%$ $r_{CH} = 3.00\%$ and $F = 1.2000$

If these were all market quotes (i.e., we could buy or sell USD in the spot market for CHF 1.2500, we could borrow or lend U.S. Dollars for 1 year at 5%, we could borrow or lend CHF for 1 year at 3%, and we could buy or sell Dollars one year forward at CHF 1.2000), it would appear that something is wrong or out of line.

In the financial markets, "out of line" sounds like an arbitrage opportunity (and indeed there is one here). Earlier, we figured out that the 1-year USD|CHF forward should be quoted/trading around $F = 1.2262$. Here, the quoted forward price in the market is too low. Remembering perhaps the most important adage in the financial markets: "Buy Low, Sell High," what trades would you do? Think about it before reading on.

By comparing where the forward price IS quoted in the market ($F = 1.2000$) and the value at which you believe (based on interest rate parity) the forward SHOULD BE trading ($F = 1.2262$), it appears too low in the market. To be more precise, it seems as if the market price of a Dollar (quoted in terms of CHF) is too low in the forward market, so BUY USD FORWARD.

Once you have arrived at this point, the rest becomes mechanical.

If you are BUYING USD FORWARD, then you must be buying them with something. BUYING USD FORWARD = SELLING CHF FORWARD.

If you stop here, you are simply betting that the Dollar will strengthen, or at least not weaken below CHF 1.2000; this is not an arbitrage. You are doing these trades, though, because something is out of line. Spot–forward arbitrage requires that you do the opposite trade in the spot market. SELL USD SPOT = BUY CHF SPOT.

In order to see how to turn a profit, let's work out the cash flows. To begin, we must decide how big to play; in other words, you have to decide on a certain notional in one of the two currencies on which to base your cash flows. Let's do this on USD 100,000,000, which might sound like a large amount, but is certainly not unprecedented in FX trading.

In the spot market, we said you'd want to Sell USD and Buy CHF (remember, this is one trade). Where do we get the Dollars to sell? Let's assume we borrow them, and in this example, we are going to borrow USD 100,000,000 (for 1 year at a rate of 5%). Now you can Sell USD 100,000,000 and Buy CHF 125,000,000. Putting these CHF in a Swiss Franc account, you will receive 3% interest. Now what? Nothing, until a year goes by. At this point you will OWN CHF 128,750,000 and OWE USD 105,000,000. Where's the profit? Well, we have to close out these positions in the forward market to realize the gain associated with the opportunity we identified. Presumably we locked in the forward price of 1.2000 (allowing us to buy USD 1 by selling CHF 1.2000). If we convert all of the CHF that we OWN to USD (and doing so would result in our obtaining USD 107,291,666.67) and then pay back the USD we OWE (that is USD 105,000,000), we will end up with a profit of USD 2,291,666.67. Not bad for a couple of trades, huh? It may help to review these trades in diagrammatic form (see Figure 6.4) remembering our two legs:

BUY CHF SPOT = SELL USD SPOT
SELL CHF FORWARD = BUY USD FORWARD

and the notional size of the (spot) transaction: USD 100,000,000. Look familiar? It should. It is simply interest rate parity at work.

A number of questions.

1. What if you wanted to realize your profit in CHF? Could you do that? Of course. In this case, you would only want to convert enough of the CHF that you own in one year in order to cover the USD that you've borrowed (plus the interest on those Dollars, of course). Using our numbers, this would involve selling CHF 126,000,000, which at the forward price of $F = 1.2000$ would turn into USD 105,000,000. This would leave a profit in Swiss Francs of CHF 2,750,000.

Today

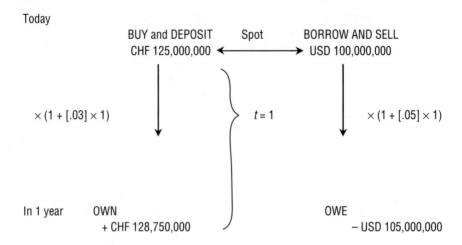

BUY and DEPOSIT   Spot   BORROW AND SELL
CHF 125,000,000 ⟷ USD 100,000,000

$\times (1 + [.03] \times 1)$ $t = 1$ $\times (1 + [.05] \times 1)$

In 1 year   OWN   OWE
+ CHF 128,750,000   − USD 105,000,000

And then SELLING CHF FORWARD (at the Forward Price of F = 1.2000)
= BUYING USD FORWARD

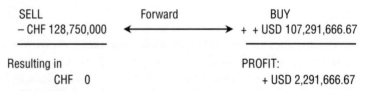

SELL   Forward   BUY
− CHF 128,750,000 ⟷ + + USD 107,291,666.67

Resulting in   PROFIT:
CHF   0   + USD 2,291,666.67

FIGURE 6.4   FX Spot-Forward Arbitrage

2. Does it matter how you choose to realize your profit? No and yes. A U.S. Dollar-based trader or institution might choose to realize their profit in USD; a Swiss bank might prefer to obtain their profits in CHF. A hedge fund might not care, unless, that is, they have a view on the future spot price (that is, USD|CHF in one year), if they thought that USD|CHF spot, because of the massive U.S. trade deficit, was going to be around 1.1600, then even if they are USD-based, they would prefer to realize their profit in CHF—with the expectation that these CHF will translate into even more USD in the spot market in 1 year than they might have been able to lock in if they had chosen up front to realize their profit in USD.

3. More importantly, though, when you enter into the forward contract, you agree to transact at the forward price (that is, you lock in the

price), but you also have to agree on a notional quantity. You can't just say, "I'd like to sell CHF = buy USD in 1 year at F = 1.2000." You have to say, "I'd like to buy USD 105,000,000 for the forward price of F = CHF 1.2000 per USD," which, of course, is the same as saying, "I'd like to sell CHF 128,750,000 in one year at the forward exchange rate of CHF 1.2000 per USD 1." In other words, when you enter into a forward, you have to agree on a forward price and a quantity (or face or notional) in at least one of the two currencies.

4. Trivial pursuit. Your profit in Dollars was USD 2,291,666.67. Your profit in Swiss Francs was CHF 2,750,000. If we were to form the ratio of CHF to USD, what do you think that number (or really, that exchange rate) would be? Try it. Not surprisingly, it is 1.2000 (the forward price), because that was the rate at which you exchanged CHF for USD in the future.

5. Could you have realized your profit today? The answer is yes. You could either spend some of the USD you borrowed today and still have everything work out nicely, with neither a profit nor a loss in one year or you could spend some of the CHF that you purchase today, with the same result. Why not try to figure out how many of your Dollars you could spend today and still have everything work out in one year's time?

6. Finally, does your profit figure look reasonable? As with our triangular arbitrage example in the spot market, it is good to do a reality check. In this case, we thought the forward *should* be quoted at F = 1.2262, whereas it was actually quoted in the market at F = 1.2000. The ratio of these two (1.2262/1.2000) gives us 1.0218333. How much did we expect to make? About 2.2%. How much did we make? Well, based on our original spot notional of USD 100,000,000, we made almost 2.3%. Close enough? Unlike spot triangular arbitrage, where our profit margin aligns exactly with our price-to-value ratio, here we are a little bit off because, when all is said and done (i.e., in one year), we didn't end up doing this trade on only USD 100,000,000. Nevertheless, as a quick and dirty check, we should find some comfort in the fact that we made a profit of a little more than 2%.

Hopefully this example has served to reinforce the notion that interest rate parity will generally hold in the market in a fairly hard and fast way, unlike purchasing power parity. Any significant deviation of the market forward price from the forward value as derived from interest rate parity (Equation [6.9]) and traders would quickly jump in and arbitrage any differences away.

One last point. In all of our forward calculations, we have input interest rates. Which interest rate should one use? Textbooks have sometimes suggested that one use the "risk free" rate of interest (e.g., the rate of interest relevant to a riskless or default-free market participant, such as the U.S. government), but this would be wrong. The U.S. government, while they may intervene in the FX market, is generally not in the business of turning an arbitrage profit. On the other hand, banks—and more precisely their FX trading desks—would pursue such low-risk trading opportunities. In this case, both the associated cash flow funding and forward valuation will involve the interest rates relevant to that particular institution (and the better money-center banks usually fund themselves at or around LIBOR). To the extent that the spread between the three-month U.S. Treasury rate versus the three-month U.K. government rate probably correlates well with the difference between three-month USD LIBOR and three-month GBP LIBOR, it may look as if the market is using these "risk free" rates, but it is *your* cost of money (if borrowing) and *your* return on money (if depositing), which would include a bid–ask spread in rates that you would have to consider before entering these trades.

At the end of this chapter, we give you the opportunity to try your hand at a foreign exchange spot-forward arbitrage problem on your own. As with spot triangular arbitrage, these are intended less as practice in how to profit from trading FX and more as exercises in working with FX forwards, in gaining a deeper understanding of the spot–forward relationship in FX, and in becoming familiar with the cash flows associated with these trades.

FX FORWARD PRICE QUOTES AND FORWARD POINTS

Now, how does it work in the real world?

With USD|CHF $S = 1.2500$, $t = 1$ year, $r_{US} = 5\%$, $r_{CH} = 3\%$, if you were to call an FX bank or dealer and ask for an indicative (midmarket) one-year forward quote (midmarket serving to set aside the bid–ask spread), you'd probably hear 238. What?

Let me briefly explain how forwards are quoted. If you were to request a forward outright or a forward outright price (which is what you probably had in mind a few seconds ago), a dealer/trader/salesperson might have said the following, "1.2262, no wait, 1.2260, just a second, 1.2265, no, no, . . . 1.2264, hold on, 1.2259, no, 1.2263, . . ."

What is that all about? Why is the forward price moving around like that? Because spot is moving around. A forward is a derivative and as such has a value that is derived from the underlying spot price. Every time the spot price moves, the forward moves. They are linked. How to avoid this when quoting forward prices? Dealers tend not to quote the forward price directly (or what we have referred to previously as the forward outright). They quote the difference between the forward price and the spot price (typically in pips, and often ignoring the numerical sign). It might sound confusing, but it really does make life easier.

In our previous example, recall that S = 1.2500 and F = 1.2262. Because $F < S$, some would say that the Dollar is trading at a discount (to the spot) in the forward market. If the forward price had been higher than the spot price, they would say that the Dollar is trading forward at a "premium." The difference between F and S is – .0238 or – 238 pips. And what is this difference? It is the difference between forward and spot or the "carry." It is driven by those interest rate differentials (and the time frame or time horizon under consideration). These are referred to as "forward points." Although the forward outright can change very quickly, the forward points might be good for the better part of the afternoon, and so quoting forward points gives marketmakers a way to provide a more stable (if somewhat convoluted) forward price quote to a counterparty.

Of course, once the client "deals" the forward, the spot is observed and the forward price is "locked in."

To see examples of forward points (without a bid–ask spread) in USD|JPY for a range of different maturities as well as for many of the major currencies (limited to one-month, three-month, and one-year maturities), look at Figures 6.5a and 6.5b.

In the professional interbank market, it is common when two banks do a forward trade, to see them do an accompanying, "offsetting" (i.e., opposite) spot transaction. In so doing, the banks are minimizing their FX risk and effectively "locking in" the "carry" or interest rates. This is typically referred to as an FX swap and explains why "forward points" are also known as "swap points." More on FX swaps in Chapter 8.

Some have joked that quoting conventions involving forward points is simply an attempt on the part of FX dealers to preserve their job security. FX dealers also often drop the negative sign from the forward point quote (assuming that the counterparty knows whether the forward is higher or lower than the spot price). This is just another instance of needing to know the language of foreign exchange.

When incorporating a bid–ask spread in both the spot price and the forward points, the market has tended to summarize the possibilities in the way shown in Figure 6.6.

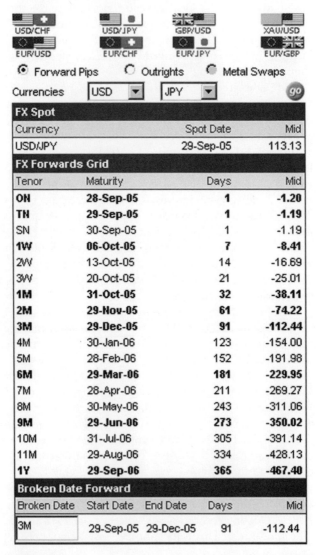

FIGURE 6.5a   Foreign Exchange Forward Points in USD|JPY
Source: © 2006 UBS Investment Bank. Reprinted by permission.

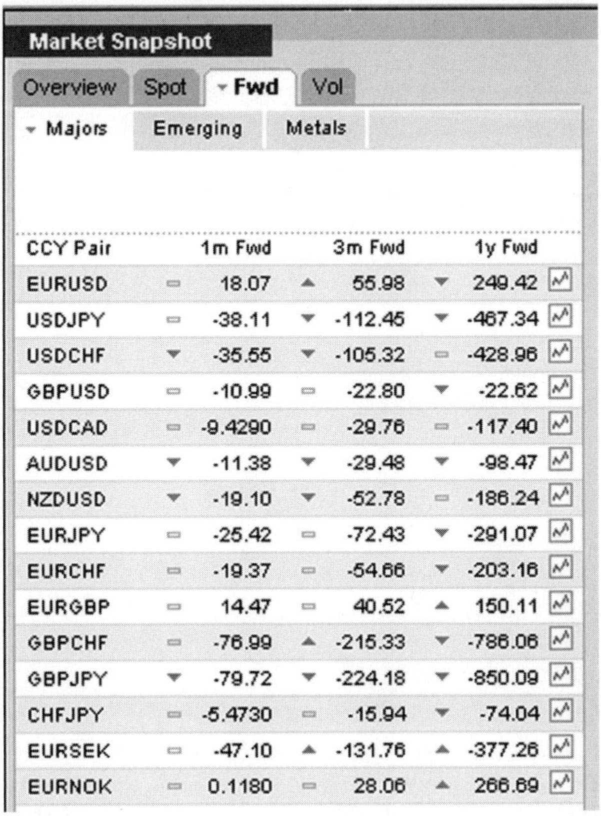

Market Snapshot

Overview | Spot | Fwd | Vol

Majors | Emerging | Metals

CCY Pair		1m Fwd		3m Fwd		1y Fwd
EURUSD	=	18.07	▲	55.98	▼	249.42
USDJPY	=	-38.11	▼	-112.45	▼	-467.34
USDCHF	▼	-35.55	▼	-105.32	=	-428.96
GBPUSD	=	-10.99	=	-22.80	▼	-22.62
USDCAD	=	-9.4290	=	-29.76	=	-117.40
AUDUSD	▼	-11.38	▼	-29.48	▼	-98.47
NZDUSD	▼	-19.10	▼	-52.78	=	-186.24
EURJPY	=	-25.42	=	-72.43	▼	-291.07
EURCHF	=	-19.37	=	-54.66	▼	-203.16
EURGBP	=	14.47	=	40.52	▲	150.11
GBPCHF	=	-76.99	▲	-215.33	▼	-786.06
GBPJPY	▼	-79.72	▼	-224.18	▼	-850.09
CHFJPY	=	-5.4730	=	-15.94	▼	-74.04
EURSEK	=	-47.10	▲	-131.76	▲	-377.26
EURNOK	=	0.1180	=	28.06	▲	266.69

FIGURE 6.5b Foreign Exchange Forward Points in the Majors
Source: © 2006 UBS Investment Bank. Reprinted by permission.

FIGURE 6.6 Generic FX Forward Point Screen

	Euro EUR|USD	Sterling GBP|USD	Swiss Franc USD|CHF	Japanese Yen USD|JPY
Spot	1.2500-05	1.8021-25	1.2498-04	112.49-57
T/N	0.21-0.25	0.33-0.30	0.98-0.95	1.65-1.61
S/N	0.15-0.19	0.275-0.24	0.95-0.93	1.67-1.64
1 WK.	5.55-5.60	2.10-1.90	6.95-6.85	11.75-11.60
2 WK.	10.05-10.10	4.15-3.85	13.90-13.65	22.50-22.10
1 MO.	20.15-20.45	9.80-9.30	27.25-26.75	49.00-48.00
2 MO.	40.90-41.50	18.85-18.10	61.30-60.70	102.00-100.75
3 MO.	62.00-63.00	28.90-28.00	91.00-90.25	153.00-151.50
6 MO.	120.75-122.00	59.00-56.50	193.00-191.75	310.00-308.00
1 YR.	256.00-258.00	118.00-115.00	408.00-406.00	624.50-622.00

FORWARD PRICE/FORWARD POINTS EXAMPLE

Using Figure 6.6, find the three-month EURIUSD forward market.

Start with EURIUSD spot: 1.2500-05   or   1.2500 – 1.2505.

Now, to get the forward quote, you line up the forward points (found in Figure 6.6) with the spot quote (remembering that these are pips):   1.2500 – 1.2505
                                                                                                      62.00   63.00

Now, to add or subtract? If the forward points are lined up lower-to-higher, one would then add to the spot price. If the forward points are lined up higher-to-lower, one would subtract them from the spot price. The FX traders have an expression they use to keep it straight:

Ascending, Add.
Descending, Deduct.

In this case, since the forward points are quoted   "62.00 – 23.00" and so are ascending, add them to the spot price to get the forward market: 1.2562 – 1.2568.

Does this make sense?

What was the bid–ask in spot? 5 pips.

What was the bid–ask in the forward points? 1 pip.

Do you think it's riskier to trade spot or forward? Forward.

So which bid–ask spread should be wider? The bid–ask in the forward will generally be wider than the bid–ask spread in the spot.

FORWARD PRICING/FORWARD POINT EXERCISES #3

Using Figure 6.6,

1. What is the one-year forward outright market in Cable (GBPIUSD)?
2. What is the six-month forward market in USDIJPY?
3. What is the one-month forward in USDICHF?
4. If you wanted to sell USD 10,000,000 in one month, how many CHF would you get?

TIMING

The extent of the subtlety associated with the timing of spot FX trades lies in recognizing that settlement dates do not coincide with trade dates and that generally settlement will take place on the spot date two good business days later ("T + 2").

Forward trades also have their own unique timing conventions, but they are a bit more convoluted. For the record, say today is Monday, August 1. This means that the spot date is Wednesday, August 3. Everything in FX revolves around spot. When would a one-week trade settle? The timing convention for "weekly" trades (one week, two weeks, three weeks) involves going from "day of the week" to "day of the week"—in our example, from Wednesday to Wednesday. In short, if we do a one-week forward trade on Monday, August 1, we'd expect that trade to settle on Wednesday, August 10. On the other hand, if one does a "monthly trade" (one month, two months, three months, six months), then the convention is that these trades involve going from "date" to "date." If you do a three-month forward trade on Monday, August 1, then spot is Wednesday, August 3, and that forward trade would involve settlement (the exchange of currency) on November 3 (assuming that day is not a holiday or a weekend, i.e, assuming the banks are open). In the event that this is not a good business day, the general rule of thumb is to roll that trade forward to the next good business day (unless this involves leaving the month, in which case you *usually* roll it back).

The most liquid forward quotes on any given day are usually the one-week, two-week, one-month, two-month, three-month, and six-month maturities. One can request a two-month, one-week, and four-day forward trade, but this would be relatively uncommon; this would be referred to as a "broken date." Since one-month forwards are traded every day, and since forwards often result in delivery, there are exchanges of currencies every day as a result of maturing forward contracts.

EXAMPLE OF AN FX FORWARD TRADE

As with a spot transaction, one must indicate the currency pair (say, USDICHF) and the size of the trade (in terms of one of the currencies, say, USD 10,000,000); with a forward, one must also specify a maturity (say, three months). Given this information (and armed with knowledge about the interest rates in the two countries), the forward price can be determined. Usually this is not done by hand. An example of an "e-tool" purchase of USD = sale of CHF in three months can be seen in Figure 6.7.

Although spot prices have historically been quoted in terms of pips or, in this case, four decimal places ($S = 1.2972$), note that here (and in general) the forward price is quoted out further ($F = 1.286792$).

Nondeliverable Forwards or NDFs

There are times when someone may like to trade a currency (whether for hedging purposes, to implement a speculative view, or as part of an

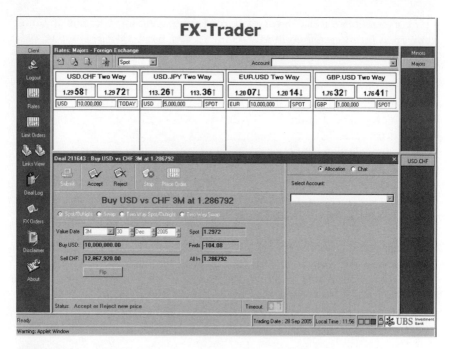

FIGURE 6.7   Example: Long Three-Month USD|CHF Forward Trade
Source: © 2006 UBS Investment Bank. Reprinted by permission.

investment strategy), but they cannot. Perhaps trading in that currency is restricted by the government, or perhaps they are not allowed (according to their fund's prospectus) to trade that currency. There are a number of reasons why a currency trade may not be permissible, but if one still wished to gain exposure to that currency, there are contracts through which one can acquire the economic exposure to the foreign exchange rate movement without the need of "physical delivery." One of these would be a nondeliverable forward (NDF).

As an example, let's say you believe the Russian Ruble will strengthen, but you are not allowed, for one reason or another, to trade the Ruble directly. You could agree to sell 10 million U.S. Dollars forward and buy Ruble forward (in 3 months) at a forward price of USD|RUB $F = 28.50$. Your view may be that Dollar-Ruble will, in three months time, be trading at a spot price of $S = 25.00$. This forward transaction would typically involve the following exchange of currencies in three months:

USD 10,000,000 out   and   RUB 285,000,000 in

but, with a nondeliverable forward, the exposure is simply cash-settled in a currency that is tradable. If you were exactly correct in your assessment of where USD|RUB was headed, then, at the settlement date of the forward, you would consider where this exchange should trade (with, in this example, $S = 25.00$):

$$\text{USD } 10,000,000 \quad \text{versus} \quad \text{RUB } 250,000,000$$

and effectively do an "unwind" so that there is no transfer of the Russian Ruble.

This should result in a "profit" of RUB 35,000,000, which, with a nondeliverable forward contract (and a spot exchange rate of $S = 25.00$) would terminate with a positive Dollar cash flow of USD 1,400,000 (= RUB 35,000,000/25.00).

In recent years, there's been a great deal of interest in nondeliverable forwards on Chinese Yuan/Renminbi. Spot USD|CNY is not "accessible," but there are many market participants with financial interests in the movement of this currency who've used NDFs. Of course, liquidity is always an issue with a controlled or restricted currency.[4] There are also nondeliverable options.

OFF-MARKET FORWARDS

Now that the pricing of FX forwards is hopefully clearly understood, I'd like to ask one further question. Let us use the numbers from our earlier USD|CHF example:

USD|CHF. $S = 1.2500$ $t = 1$ $r_{US} = 5.00\%$ $r_{CH} = 3.00\%$ and so $F = 1.2262$

As a forward marketmaker, what would you say to a client who telephoned and said, "I would like to purchase USD one-year forward at a price of $F = $ CHF 1.1000." You might be inclined to respond, "So would I!" because clearly that price is too low. If the client persisted, you might say, "Okay, I will sell you USD in one year at a forward price of $F = $ CHF 1.1000 but only if you do something." What would you ask your client to do?

Since this price is too low, you might ask your client to make a payment to you to compensate you for that difference. More precisely, you would probably want to be paid before you handed over such a forward contract involving too low a purchase price for your client. How much would you need to be paid and when would that payment take place? Let's say we would like to know the magnitude of the required payment today. The difference between the correct forward value (1.2262 for a transaction in one year) and the wrong or off-market forward (1.1000 for a transaction in one year) is CHF .1262 (in one year). Presumably if the client agreed to pay you that amount (per USD 1) in one year, this would effectively make this an "on-market" forward. More likely, the client would be asked to pay the present value of that amount today (properly discounted at the Swiss interest rate) = CHF .1225 per USD 1. If the client wanted to buy this off-market forward on USD 20,000,000, the up-front payment would be around CHF 2,450,000.

In general, off-market forwards are not traded often in the market, but as a transition topic, we simply note that if you understand FX forwards (especially off-market forwards), then you are halfway to understanding FX options.

FOREIGN EXCHANGE FORWARDS IN THE REAL WORLD

With a firm grasp of the issues involved in the valuation of forward contracts, I ask one last question. What do you think would happen to, say, the three-month USD|CHF forward price today if the Federal Reserve Bank were to raise U.S. interest rates today?

If the spot price and Swiss interest rates are unchanged, then, mechanically, we know that the three-month U.S. interest rate would go in the denominator of this currency quote

$$F = \frac{S(1 + r_{CH}t)}{(1 + r_{US}t)}$$

and we would expect the three-month USD|CHF forward to fall. But there is a huge presumption here, namely that spot will not change. If everyone expected the Federal Reserve to raise interest rates by 25 basis points (.25%) and that is what the Fed does, then that new higher return associated with the U.S. Dollar will have already been priced into the spot price, the spot price should not jump, and the three-month forward will probably fall. On the other hand, if the Fed raised rates by more (more precisely, by more than the market anticipated), the return from holding U.S. Dollars will be unexpectedly higher, and we would expect to see the spot price go up (as people bid up the price of the Dollar given its new, more attractive interest rate return). In this case, the ultimate effect on the three-month USD|CHF forward is not certain, and, depending on expectations, it may very well go up. For better or worse, the real world FX forward price quotes may not move in a perfunctory manner, given changes in the interest rates that drive them.

FOREIGN EXCHANGE FORWARD EXERCISES #4

1. Undertake a spot-forward arbitrage in the following circumstances:

   EURIUSD $S = 1.2940$ $t = 1$ year $r_{US} = 3.00\%$ and $r_{EU} = 4.00\%$

   and the one-year EURIUSD $F = 1.2750$

   Do this on a spot notional of EUR 100,000,000 and check your answer.

2. What could you say about Turkish interest rates versus U.S. interest rates if the forward points in USDITRY are positive?

3. What can you say about the forward points for USDICHF if the respective (zero) interest rate curves in the respective countries' currencies look like this (Figure 6.8):

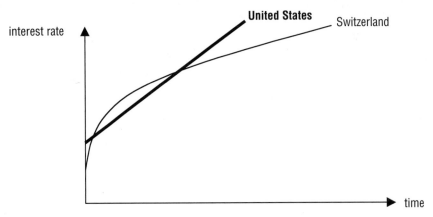

FIGURE 6.8   U.S. and Swiss Zero Interest Rate Curves

4. If GBPIUSD three-month forward is $F = 1.7568$, U.S. interest rates are 4.00%, U.K. interest rates 7.00%, and we assume three months involves 91 days, then

   ■ What is the GBPIUSD spot price?
   ■ What do you think would happen to this forward price if the Bank of England raises interest rates?
   ■ How much would you have to pay (today) for a three-month off-market forward of $F = 1.7200$ on a notional of GBP 10,000,000?

CHAPTER 7

Foreign Exchange Futures

BACKGROUND

Leo Melamed, former chairman of the Chicago Mercantile Exchange (CME), has documented, in two fascinating accounts, the beginnings and development of the market for foreign exchange futures contracts.[1] In the late 1960s, there was pressure on the fixed exchange rate system of Bretton Woods and an anticipation of the impending floating foreign exchange environment. Milton Friedman, at the invitation of the CME, published a paper in 1971 advocating a "futures market in foreign currencies"—"as broad, as deep, as resilient" as possible "in order to facilitate foreign trade and investment."[2] With the additional endorsement of government, which Melamed noted was surely desirable though not legally necessary, the CME set up the International Monetary Market (IMM) as a separate entity and it was within its markets that FX futures first traded. Foreign exchange currency futures contracts emerged as a trading vehicle on May 16, 1972—the date identified as the birth of FX futures. Merton Miller, a distinguished finance professor at the University of Chicago, later praised futures contracts as "the most significant financial innovation of the last twenty years" and stated in 1986, this was, and is, singularly high praise indeed. The CME Clearing House currently processes more than 80% of all futures (not just FX futures) traded in the United States.

Just as an FX forward contract involves an agreement to buy/sell a certain amount of a certain currency for a previously-agreed-upon amount of another currency (where this ratio, properly quoted, is known as the forward price) at some well-defined point in the future, so too does an FX future contract involve an agreement to buy/sell a certain amount of a certain currency (in exchange for another currency) for a predetermined price (known as the future price) at some point later in time (known as the maturity date).

FUTURES VERSUS FORWARDS

There are four primary differences between forward contracts (or simply
forwards) and future contracts (or simply futures).

1. The first has to do with **where they trade** (and this expression is used
   loosely); forwards are, by definition, over-the-counter (OTC) contracts, whereas futures are, by definition, "exchange-traded" contracts
   or exchange-traded derivatives (ETDs).
2. Forwards are **individually negotiated agreements** between two counterparties. As such they may be tailored in any way that the two parties see fit. This means that they may (and actually must) specify the
   amount (or notional or face), the (forward) price, the type, nature,
   quality of the underlying, the mechanism for delivery (timing, location), and possibly some additional features as part of the contract. Futures contracts are **standardized** contracts; that is, they specify the
   amount, typically quote the price in certain minimum increments,
   identify the nature or quality of the deliverable asset, have set maturities and delivery dates (or delivery windows), and well-defined delivery
   processes. Some exchanges have attempted to mitigate the replacement
   of their exchange-traded contracts with the more flexible OTC contracts, which might better suit the end users' financial, economic, or
   accounting needs by allowing some relaxation of the standardized features of the exchange-listed contracts especially when it comes to exchange-listed options contracts: these are sometimes identified as
   "flex" contracts. As an example, a flex contract might allow for end-
   of-month settlement (to accommodate financial statement reporting
   considerations) as opposed to the exchange convention, which does
   not coincide with the final day of the calendar month. Another variation might involve physically settling a cash-settled contract.
3. The third difference between forwards and futures has to do with **cash
   flows.** When one buys or sells a future, the transaction is actually done
   between members of the exchange. These may involve brokers acting
   on behalf of customers, locals trading their own financial capital, or
   any of the members of the exchange (which could represent larger
   banks and broker/dealers). Once a transaction is agreed upon, executed, and confirmed, though, the exchanges and clearing houses act
   as the counterparties to both sides of the trade. In the words of the
   Chicago Mercantile Exchange,

   > *Although many different customers trade at CME, all trades
   > are ultimately conducted between CME and a clearing mem-*

ber. **CME serves as the buyer to every seller and the seller to
every buyer,** *with a clearing member assuming the opposite
side of each trade. In so doing, clearing members essentially
vouch that the financial obligation will be met for all trades
matched and executed in CME facilities.*[3]

What this means is that the buyer of the future contract (that is,
the individual who has agreed to buy the underlying asset at some
point in the future) is effectively long the asset from the exchange, and
the seller of the future (the individual who has agreed to sell the underlying asset in the future) is short the asset to the exchange. The implication is that, once the trade is done ("I thought I bought it; you
thought you sold it—for a specific asset, for a specific time in the future and at a specific price"), the exchange takes on the role of the
counterparty to both sides of the transaction. The attractiveness of this
feature is that the exchange and clearing houses assume the counterparty or credit risk associated with every trade and ensure the performance for that agreed upon transaction. Because the exchange and the
clearing houses don't trust either of the counterparties to the trade,
though, they ask both the buyer and seller to "post margin"; **margin** is
simply a collateral deposit (of cash and sometimes, in part, negotiable
securities), which provides a buffer should the future's buyer or seller
disappear (as in "go bankrupt," fail to deliver/purchase, etc.). Forward
contracts, while some broker/dealers may request "collateral," especially from leveraged money clients (i.e., hedge funds), do not necessarily require "marking-to-market."[4] We go into more detail on margin
later.[5]

4. The fourth difference between forwards and futures is an empirical
one; while, for the most part, both forwards and futures are agreements to purchase/sell an underlying asset in the future, the majority of
forward contracts actually result in **delivery** while the majority of the
futures contracts that trade (over 95%) are closed out prior to the settlement date and, therefore, do not result in physical delivery.

These differences between forwards and futures are summarized in
Table 7.1.
Are there any significant differences between forward prices and futures prices? There have been numerous academic studies on this topic
and, in the case of foreign exchange, the general consensus is no.[6] A statistically significant difference between forward prices and futures prices does
not seem to exist for many products, like gold, commodities, and FX, but
there are well-understood and well-documented differences for interest-

TABLE 7.1   Forwards versus Futures

Forwards	Futures
Over-The-Counter (OTC)	Exchange-Traded Derivative (ETD)
Individually Tailored	Standardized Terms
No Cash Flows	Marked-To-Market Daily
Usually Result in Delivery	Vast Majority Do Not Result in Delivery
Counterparty Exposure	Exchange and Clearing House Exposure

rate-related forward contracts (such as OTC forward (interest) rate agreements or FRAs) and their exchange-traded counterparts, such as EuroDollar future contracts.[7] And even where there are a differences, as the time frame becomes small (one month, one week, one day), the differences tend to disappear.

FOREIGN EXCHANGE FUTURES CONTRACT SPECIFICATIONS

The International Monetary Market, a division of the Chicago Mercantile Exchange, lists futures contracts on 16 non-USD currencies (Euro, Japanese Yen, British Pound, Swiss Franc, Canadian Dollar, Australian Dollar, New Zealand Dollar, Mexican Peso, Brazilian Real, South African Rand, Swedish Krona, Norwegian Krone, Polish Zloty, Czech Koruna, Hungarian Florint, and Russian Ruble), a USD Index, and a number of Cross (Exchange) Rate Contracts (such as Euro-Japanese Yen).

Most of these contracts "mature" on the second business day before the third Wednesday of the month. Note, we use the words "mature" and "maturity" to refer to the termination and the longevity of a future contract, but we will use the words "expire" and "expiration" for options. With the exception of the crosses, on the Merc, all prices are quoted in U.S. Dollars (what we referred to earlier as American quotes). For the most part, these are quarterly contracts that settle in March (H), June (M), September (U), and December (Z). The mnemonic used by some floor traders is marcH, juMe, septUmber, and deZember. At any given time, there are usually six of these futures contracts listed and trading. The majority of these contracts are physically settled; that is, unless the trade is "reversed," or "closed out," or "unwound" prior to maturity, then these futures will result in the delivery of the underlying currency. As always in foreign exchange, there are exceptions. The Russian Ruble future contract, which, at

TABLE 7.2   Chicago Mercantile Exchange Futures Contract Specifications for Some of the Major Currency Futures

Currency	Ticker Symbol	Trade Unit (Contract Size)	Price Information
British Pound	BP	62,500 Pounds Sterling	1 point = USD.0001 per Pound = USD 6.25 per contract
Euro	EC	125,000 Euro	1 point = USD.0001 per Euro = USD 12.50 per contract
Japanese Yen	JY	12,500,000 Japanese Yen	1 point = USD.000001 per Yen = USD 12.50 per contract
Swiss Francs	SF	125,000 Swiss Francs	1 point = USD.0001 per Franc = USD 12.50 per contract
Australian Dollars	AD	100,000 Australian Dollars	1 point = USD.0001 per A. Dollar = USD 10.00 per contract
Canadian Dollars	CD	100,000 Canadian Dollars	1 point = USD.0001 per C. Dollar = USD 10.00 per contract

All of these futures contracts are physically delivered.
All of these futures contracts have six quarterly contracts listed (H, M, U, Z).
All of these futures contracts mature on the second business day before the third Wednesday of the settlement month (except Canadian Dollars, which mature on the day before the third Wednesday of the month).

any given time, is only listed out four quarters is "cash settled"—resulting, not in a delivery of Rubles, but in the U.S. Dollar equivalent of the Ruble payoff that would otherwise have been associated with that future. Another exception is the Brazilian Real, which, along with Mexican Peso and South African Rand, has monthly futures contracts listed—as opposed to quarterly contracts—and is also cash settled.

The contract specifications for the major non-U.S. Dollar currencies are summarized in Table 7.2.

A typical day's currency futures price quotes as seen in the *Wall Street Journal* are shown in Figure 7.1.

MARGIN

Every traded future requires that "margin" be posted by the two counterparties to that transaction in order to ensure the performance of the agreement inherent in the future contract. Margin is an expression used in a variety of ways in the financial community and on the exchanges.

FUTURES

Wednesday, September 28, 2005

Currency Futures

	OPEN	HIGH	LOW	SETTLE	CHG	LIFETIME HIGH	LIFETIME LOW	OPEN INT
Japanese Yen (CME)-¥12,500,000; $ per 100¥								
Dec	.8908	.8940	.8892	.8916	.0008	1.0084	.8887	138,020
Canadian Dollar (CME)-CAD 100,000; $ per CAD								
Dec	.8509	.8550	.8480	.8532	.0017	.8625	.7480	108,466
Mr06	.8509	.8569	.8500	.8555	.0017	.8642	.7927	1,361
British Pound (CME)-£62,500; $ per £								
Dec	1.7651	1.7698	1.7585	1.7639	-.0005	1.9090	1.7227	77,302
Mr06	1.7571	1.7677	1.7556	1.7620	-.0004	1.8550	1.7335	136
Swiss Franc (CME)-CHF 125,000; $ per CHF								
Dec	.7774	.7804	.7759	.7785	.0012	.8922	.7745	76,602
Mr06	.7839	.7856	.7827	.7848	.0012	.8888	.7815	58
Australian Dollar (CME)-AUD 100,000; $ per AUD								
Dec	.7533	.7573	.7519	.7559	.0028	.7835	.6664	63,148
Mr06	.7525	.7541	.7520	.7534	.0028	.7675	.6920	11
Mexican Peso (CME)-MXN 500,000; $ per 10MXN								
Oct	...	...	...	.91875	.00350	.93550	.91200	35
Dec	.90750	.91200	.90500	.91000	.00350	.93200	.82400	78,834
Euro (CME)-€125,000; $ per €								
Dec	1.2066	1.2106	1.2043	1.2075	.0012	1.3740	1.1944	133,749
Mr06	1.2123	1.2162	1.2103	1.2132	.0012	1.3789	1.2038	1,496

FIGURE 7.1 *Wall Street Journal* Currency Futures
Source: Wall Street Journal.

What was once described as "a good faith deposit" is now officially identified as a "performance bond" on the Merc's web site. Two brief things to note: First, the margin requirements are different depending on whether your position is (1) "naked" or "speculative" or (2) "an offset against another position" or a "hedge." Second, there are two margin numbers reported by the exchange: "initial" and "maintenance." The first is what must be placed with the clearing house (working with the futures exchange) once a position (long or short) is taken on. The second is the level which must be maintained given the daily "adjustments" (or variation margin) for the movements in the futures price(s). The futures clearing house in conjunction with the exchange monitors all trades and "marks the position to market" daily. This involves tracking all outstanding positions and crediting or debiting the margin accounts based on the daily price movements in the future contracts. Most futures contracts are "marked" at the end of the trading day; some futures contracts and other futures exchanges, though, may require marking-to-market a couple of times during the trading day.

Three of the most common questions about margin:

1. "What happens if my account drops below the maintenance level?"
2. "If my margin account is in excess of the minimum required, can I take the excess cash out?"
3. "Do I get interest on my money?"

The answers actually depend on the particular exchange. For many futures exchanges, if your margin account falls below the maintenance margin level, you must replenish it by depositing or wiring additional money into your account to satisfy the margin requirement, which, most commonly, involves returning the margin balance to the original level. Bank accounts are established to facilitate this process, which is a necessary part of doing business on a futures exchange. The notion of a "margin call" for a delinquent margin account, if not properly resolved, will generally result in the termination of one's position by the exchange. Often, margin balances over the initial level can be withdrawn. At one time, getting interest on the cash in your margin account was the exception as opposed to the rule. Nowadays, the exchanges offer interest earning facilities (IEFs), sweep accounts, and similar cash management arrangements, which do afford some return on your money. Interest is less an issue if one realizes that a number of high quality securities (like Treasury bills), letters of credit, and so on may be (and generally are) used to satisfy a portion of one's margin requirement, with an appropriate discount or "haircut" in recognition of the fact that the market value of the acceptable securities can themselves change. Also, for the record, the exchange reserves the right to revise these performance bond requirements as they see fit at any time, depending principally on the price level at which the underlying is trading and the historical volatility of that underlying price and to mark positions intraday given unusual market circumstances. One last point about margin: The performance bond required by the exchange of the clearing house may be less than that required by the clearing house of its clearing members, which may differ from what they require of their brokers, which in turn may differ from what brokers may impose on the ultimate end user or customer.

As an example of how futures' margining works, assume a member of the exchange purchases 20 Swiss Franc futures contracts at a future price of $F = USD .8000$ (per Swiss Franc) for a delivery in three months. One must post the required initial margin, which, if speculative, is USD 1,890 per contract for a total initial margin requirement of USD 37,800. Let's say that the trade occurred at a price of $F = USD .8000$ and that the future closed that day at the same price. Then there would not be a need for a daily adjustment to the initial margin in the account at the end of the day. If the next day the future closed at $F =$ USD .8010, then this contract has moved USD .0010 per Swiss Franc (which translates into a cash flow of USD .0010 × CHF 125,000 per contract × 20 contracts = USD 2,500 or more simply + 10 points × USD 12.50 per point (from Table 7.2) × 20 contracts. This cash would appear in the margin account of the trader who bought these futures (for a new total margin deposit of USD 40,300). Where does this money come from? It comes out of the account(s) of the member(s) who sold these contracts. Assume that on the next day, the future closes at $F =$ .7995. This is a one-day drop of 15 points (and so – .0015 × 125,000 × 20 = – USD 3,750 for a running margin balance to the futures purchaser of USD 36,550). This process continues through the last day of trading. If the member who bought these futures was not required to post any additional margin between the trade date and the maturity or delivery date, and if the future closes on the final day of trading at, say, $F =$ .8012, then that person's margin account should contain USD 40,800 (the initial margin of USD 37,800 and the net USD .0012 per Swiss Franc × 125,000 Swiss Francs per contract × 20 contracts = USD 3,000).

When delivery is made, the purchaser of the Swiss Franc futures will receive the CHF 2,500,000 (CHF 125,000 per contract × 20 contracts) and pay USD 2,003,000 [CHF 125,000 × F, (which, at maturity = USD .8012) × 20]. Hey, wait a minute! Didn't the future buyer agree to pay a price of F = USD .8000 per CHF? So shouldn't the buyer be paying USD 2,000,000? The answer is "Yes, sort of." Indeed, we agreed to buy CHF 2,500,000 at a price of USD .8000 per Swiss Franc for a total of USD 2,000,000. Why are we paying USD 2,003,000? Because, when the futures contract matures, we no longer need to have money in our margin account, and so can take home both our initial margin (USD 37,800) and the accumulated variation margin (USD 3,000). In effect we pay USD .8000, but the cumulative daily movements in the futures price have been accounted for in the margin account, so, when we actually pay USD 2,003,000 and get back our initial margin plus USD 3, 000, we effectively realize the trade price of USD .8000 per CHF 1.

The most important question here is, "What is USD .8012?" If we recall our spot-forward pricing relationship (Equation [6.8]), then on the final day (when $t = 0$), the futures price (F) should equal the spot price (S). And, **in effect**, what happens when there is a futures delivery is that there is a spot transaction at the current spot price. Through the process of daily marking-to-market, the exchange and clearing houses have reduced their counterparty exposure to a one-day window.

WHY USE FUTURES?

Although the pricing of FX forwards and FX futures is similar, some reasons have been postulated to explain a possible preference on the part of an individual or institution for FX futures contracts (as opposed to FX forwards).

- A fund's prospectus may allow for the use of futures but not forwards.
- A market participant's creditworthiness may preclude their ability to enter into OTC contracts, whereas, given sufficient margin, they can trade futures.
- The individual or institution may be unwilling or unable to take the credit/counterparty risk associated with forwards (whether this reluctance is justified for every possible counterparty or not).
- The transparency of the futures markets (with readily available daily closing prices) might be highly valued (though, again, liquidity in the OTC market and the access to marks has never been greater, given the explosion in the availability of market data—OTC and otherwise).

George Stigler, one of my professors at the University of Chicago, was always inclined to turn to the market itself to assess the value attached to any given product or contract; the market in FX forwards is significantly larger than the volume traded via FX futures.

OPTIONS ON FX FUTURES

Although we discuss options in Chapter 9, we simply note here that there are options on many of the FX futures traded on the exchanges. These option contracts, like the underlying futures, have standardized features (premium quotes, expiration dates, listed strike prices, and contract sizes—where each option typically "covers" one future). Also, exchange-traded options on FX futures typically involve American-style exercise, which allows the option buyer the opportunity to exercise the option at any point in time. Note, though, that this results in a long or short FX futures position, not in the acquisition or delivery of the underlying currency. To some market participants, options are viewed as an alternative to forwards or futures.

CURRENCY FUTURES EXERCISES

1. If a U.S. corporation had a firm commitment of two billion in Japanese Yen receivables arriving in December of that year

   What futures contracts could they use to "hedge"?
   Would they buy or sell them?
   How many would they want to trade?

2. In what ways do FX futures contracts differ from FX forward contracts?

SUMMARY

In essence, although we have emphasized the difference between FX forwards and futures and the idiosyncrasies of the futures contracts, they are very similar in that they both afford opportunities to buy or sell currency at some point in the future at a previously agreed upon (i.e., "locked in") price. Differences involve where they trade (OTC versus exchange), whether they are individually tailored versus standardized, the nature of the cash flow associated with these trading vehicles (possibly none versus daily—or even intraday—marking-to-market through a margin account), and, empirically, the likelihood of delivery. Volume in the OTC FX forward market greatly exceeds volume traded through FX futures, but the latter can provide a useful source of market data, which explains the number of academic studies that have utilized the available information on these exchange-traded instruments. There is one additional difference between futures and forwards: Currency futures trading is overseen by the Commodity Futures Trading Commission (versus the relatively unregulated OTC FX forward market). Finally, as mentioned, there are options on FX futures, typically traded side-by-side with the underlying futures contracts (on CFTC-regulated exchanges in the United States).

Foreign Exchange Swaps or Cross-Currency Swaps or Cross-Currency Interest Rate Swaps or . . .

INTRODUCTION

There are several different types of swaps. There are interest rate swaps, equity swaps, volatility swaps, baseball card swaps, and, of course, foreign exchange swaps. As a matter of fact, there is more than one type of FX swap, and, as we have come to expect, several different names for these.

For the record, swaps are OTC contracts, so we are leaving the exchange-traded world of Chapter 7). Also, most swaps involve terminology and documentation that have been "standardized" by the International Swaps and Derivatives Association (ISDA) and require having a "master ISDA" in place prior to dealing.

FX SPOT-FORWARD SWAPS

For many who work in foreign exchange, an FX swap is interpreted as a spot-forward swap. What this means is that, unlike a "forward outright" (or standalone forward trade), the two counterparties agree to a forward trade (on a notional amount of one of the two currencies) and an offsetting (opposite) spot transaction (typically on the same notional amount of that currency). Since the forward trade changes the FX risk for the quoting bank, the associated (opposite and offsetting) spot trade reduces risk for the marketmaker to basis risk or carry risk (i.e., interest rate risk). In essence, this FX forward trade is turned into an interest rate trade, and often FX forwards and FX swaps are managed by the "cash" or interest rate desks at the banks that make markets in this area.

Assume USD|CHF spot is trading at $S = 1.2500$, the one-year Swiss interest rate is $r_{CH} = 3.00\%$, and the one-year U.S. interest rate is $r_{US} = 5.00\%$. Now, if one were to do a one-year forward transaction—more specifically, if one were to buy USD 10,000,000 one-year forward versus the Swiss Franc—what would the resulting currency flows look like? We know (from Chapter 6) that the one-year forward will be quoted (with a bid–ask spread) around $F = 1.2262$. A forward outright would involve currency flows as pictured in Figure 8.1a. An FX spot-forward swap would involve currency flows as pictured in Figure 8.1b. Note that the notional amount in USD, in this case, is identical for the two "legs" of this swap, but since there is a spot-forward price difference, the other currency (CHF) "legs" will have to differ. It was once the case that the FX bank may have given a tighter bid–ask spread to a counterparty doing the offsetting spot transaction as seen in Figure 8.1.b since reducing the nature of their risk from spot price movements and interest rate risk to interest rate risk alone. The competitiveness of the FX markets combined with the liquidity in the spot market for most of the major currencies generally does not result in significantly different pricing between FX forward outrights and FX spot-forward swaps today.

What we have described here is little more than a fairly simple and straightforward variation on an FX forward transaction. Let's look at a more interesting type of FX swap.

CROSS-CURRENCY SWAPS OR FX CROSS-CURRENCY INTEREST RATE SWAPS OR FX BOND SWAPS

When a corporation wishes to borrow money, whether to build a new factory in a country in which they have not done business in the past or simply to obtain cheap funding, they may consider raising that financial capital in other than their primary country of operation (the company might say, in other than their "reporting currency").

I have often asked individuals in our classes, "What do issuers issue?" Usually the responses involve the words "stocks" and "bonds," but, in general, I believe the correct answer is that "Issuers issue what investors want." Typically issuers are looking for "cheap money" and issuers (like our corporation in search of operating funds) can get money "cheaply" if they are willing to give investors what they want. Don't issuers have to worry about their capital structure or their view on interest rates? Of course, but nowadays issuers can switch or "swap" out of the exposure

Note: Boxes above the horizontal axis represent currency that you receive (money in) and boxes below represent money out.

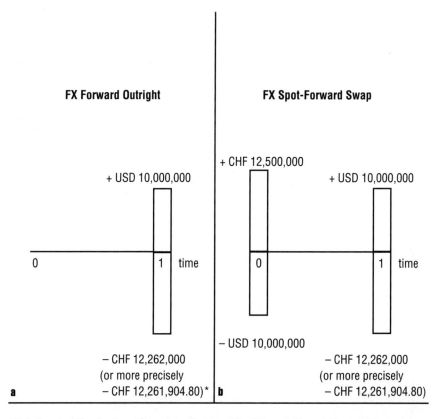

*Note: In calculating the 1-year forward, we have used $F = S(1 + r_1 t)/(1 + r_2 t)$. Three points.
1. Doing the math precisely (i.e., not rounding), this one-year forward price quote should be $F = 1.2500$ $(1.03)/(1.05) = 1.22619048$.
2. While the convention in the spot market (for USDICHF) is to quote the spot price out four decimal places, the convention in the forward market allows for quoting more decimal places (as alluded to in Chapter 6, Figure 6.6).
3. For currency flows beyond a year, simple interest (i.e., the fomula above) will not be appropriate, as we should allow for interest compounding.

FIGURE 8.1   FX Forward Outright versus FX Spot-Forward Swap

inherent in any financial product or contract by going to a bank and doing an appropriate swap transaction.

Let's try to be a little more concrete here. Say there is a large U.S.-based multinational corporation that is looking for funds, and, for the record, let's say they really would like USD—"cheap" USD. Where does FX come into play? While this company may be able to access the lenders in the United States—borrowing, for example, for five years at, say, either LIBOR or 5.00%—perhaps non-USD-based investors know this company, like their name and credit, and are willing to hold their "paper" at an over-all lower cost to the company. In that case, the corporation may issue (for example, fixed income instruments or bonds) abroad, where the securities are denominated, say, in Swiss Francs. And, although they may issue these bonds denominated in USD, it is much more common (and often more appealing, in this case, to the Swiss investor) to issue in the "local" currency (in this example, CHF).

While many companies might like to borrow money on a long-term floating rate basis (because that suits their asset–liability circumstances), investors seem to continue to value the certainty of cash flows associated with fixed coupon bonds, as opposed to floating rate notes (which are nothing more than variable coupon bonds, where the coupon is determined by some market interest rate, referred to as the "index"). For simplicity, let's presume that the company wants fixed rate liabilities (i.e., fixed coupon payments) and that the investors want fixed income assets. The only hitch, then, is that the company wants to pay USD but the Swiss investors want to receive CHF. How to deal with this?

As a numerical example, let's assume USD|CHF spot is trading at $S = 1.2500$. Further, let's assume that Swiss interest rates are $r_{CH} = 3.00\%$ for every maturity. This assumption (that the term structure of interest rates is flat), while generally not true, will simplify the discussion here because, in this special case, the zero (or spot) interest rates will be equal to the swap rates or par coupon rates (or par yields) to any given maturity. Let's similarly assume that the U.S. yield curve or interest rate term structure is flat at $r_{US} = 5.00\%$. Finally, we have to specify a magnitude or notional amount. Let's assume this USD-based company wishes to borrow USD 100,000,000 for five years.

What are the alternatives? We said that they may be able to borrow at LIBOR (floating) or at 5.00% (fixed); presumably these were both U.S. Dollar quotes. But what if they were able to issue a five-year 2.50% fixed (annually paid) coupon bond, denominated in CHF? Would that be appealing? The answer is Yes! Let's explain.

The liabilities associated with the CHF-denominated 2.50% annual coupon five-year bond would be as shown in Figure 8.2. In this picture,

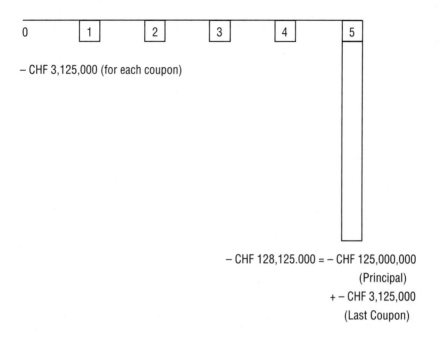

– CHF 3,125,000 (for each coupon)

– CHF 128,125.000 = – CHF 125,000,000
(Principal)
+ – CHF 3,125,000
(Last Coupon)

FIGURE 8.2   U.S. Corporate-Issued CHF Bond Liabilities

note that boxes below the horizontal axis indicate money that is (or will be) paid out.

Recall, the corporation wanted to raise USD 100,000,000. This requires them to raise CHF 125,000,000 today (with USD|CHF S = 1.2500). And the 2.50% annual coupon on the CHF 125,000,000 results in an annual CHF coupon of CHF 3,125,000. If this is all that the corporation does, it is taking on FX risk, and, if the Swiss Franc strengthens, they could seriously regret not having borrowed at 5.00% in USD. But just as an FX forward contract can eliminate FX price risk, so too can a cross-currency swap.

A cross-currency swap involves exchanging the cash flows (coupon and principal) associated with what appear to be two respective bonds (one in CHF and the other in USD). For the U.S.-based corporation, it would like to receive CHF (in order to pay off its CHF debt obligations) although ultimately, it would like to pay USD, but at a lower rate than that to which they had access in the U.S. market. This is shown in Figure 8.3.

In the end, the ultimate cost of funding to the U.S. corporation involves a cash flow lower than the market rate that they could otherwise have obtained in their home market, solely because investors outside their

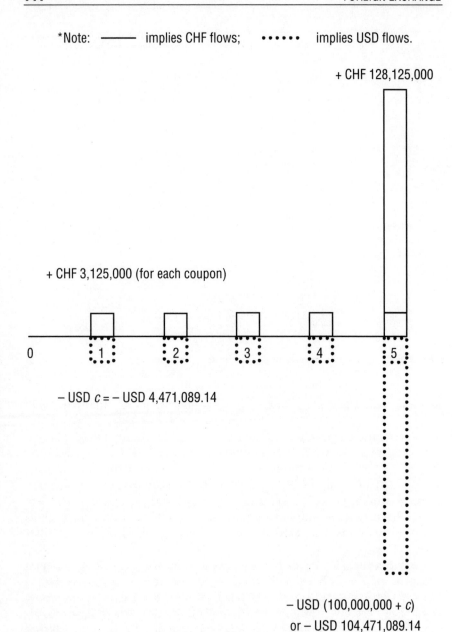

*Note: ——— implies CHF flows; • • • • • • implies USD flows.

+ CHF 128,125,000

+ CHF 3,125,000 (for each coupon)

0   1   2   3   4   5

− USD c = − USD 4,471,089.14

− USD (100,000,000 + c)
or − USD 104,471,089.14

FIGURE 8.3   Currency Flows Associated with the Cross Currency Swap

country valued this credit differently from the investors in their domicile. What are the "savings" from issuing in Switzerland and doing the cross-currency swap? Let's see.

There are two ways to approach this. First, we could have simply presented valued the Swiss Franc cash flows associated with the CHF side of the swap and added them up:[1]

$$(.9709)(CHF\ 3,125,000)$$
$$+ (.9426)(CHF\ 3,125,000)$$
$$+ (.9151)(CHF\ 3,125,000)$$
$$+ (.8885)(CHF\ 3,125,000)$$
$$+ (.8626)(CHF\ 125,000,000)$$
$$= CHF\ 122,136,562.50$$

Then again, the corporate receives CHF 125,000,000 for this CHF bond, netting a gain of CHF 2,863,437.50. In current USD, this is a cost savings of USD 2,290,750. Not bad!

To see where this savings is coming from, let's figure out the USD "coupon" that is fair. If the present value of all the cash flows associated with the Swiss Franc side of the swap equals CHF 122,136,562.50, then (with USD|CHF $S = 1.2500$) this equals USD 97,709,250. Solving for the coupon (c), which makes the present value of the swap on a notional face of USD 100,000,000 equal to this amount:[2]

$$(.9524)c + (.9070)c + (.8638)c + (.8227)c$$
$$+ (.7835)(USD\ 100,000,000 + c) = USD\ 97,709,750$$

implies that the USD coupon should be c = USD 4,471,089.14 or a little less than 4.50%. (See Figure 8.3 again.) Obviously, this is lower than the 5.00% USD funding that the corporation could have gotten at home!

Note that, looked at individually, all of the first four "coupon exchanges" are unfair, in the sense that the payer of USD is paying too much (even when interest rates are taken into account). The implicit exchange rate for the first currency exchange is .6989 (and that is, possibly disturbingly, Swiss Francs per Dollar). How is this possible? Although all of the coupon exchanges are unfair to the USD-payer = CHF-receiver, the final exchange of "coupon-plus-principal" is unfair to the USD-receiver = CHF payer (as can be seen after we calculate the forward USD|CHF exchange rates below).

The second way to analyze this is by using FX forward prices. Before doing the calculations, we should note that, due to the length of time associated with this borrowing horizon (five years), we should, indeed, calculate interest using a compounding convention, and as long as we are considering annual coupon payments, we will use annual compounding. What this means, for the calculation of the FX forwards is that, instead of equation (6.8), which uses simple interest

$$F = \frac{S(1 + r_{CH}t)}{(1 + r_{US}t)}$$

we will use equation (8.1)

$$F = \frac{S(1 + r_{CH})^t}{(1 + r_{US})^t} \tag{8.1}$$

which can also be written as

$$F = S\left[\frac{(1 + r_{CH})}{(1 + r_{US})}\right]^t = S\left(\frac{1 + r_{CH}}{1 + r_{US}}\right)^t \tag{8.2}$$

In this example, then (rounded to four decimal places), the one-year forward $F_1 = 1.2262$, the two-year forward $F_2 = 1.2028$, the three-year forward $F_3 = 1.1799$, the four-year forward $F_4 = 1.1574$, and the five-year forward $F_5 = 1.1354$.

If we then look at the respective currency flows for this swap at each point in time:

Year One	+CHF 3,125,000	−USD 4,471,089.14
Year Two	+CHF 3,125,000	−USD 4,471,089.14
Year Three	+CHF 3,125,000	−USD 4,471,089.14
Year Four	+CHF 3,125,000	−USD 4,471,089.14
Year Five	+CHF 128,125,000	−USD 104,471,089.14

and convert them to one currency (let's turn these into USD) using our forward FX rates

Year One	+USD 2,548,523.90	−USD 4,471,089.14
Year Two	+USD 2,598,104.42	−USD 4,471,089.14
Year Three	+USD 2,648,529.54	−USD 4,471,089.14
Year Four	+USD 2,700,017.28	−USD 4,471,089.14
Year Five	+USD 112,845,693.10	−USD 104,471,089.14

differencing and present valuing (using U.S. interest rates, as these are USD cash flows)

$$(.9524)(-\text{USD } 1,922,565.24)$$
$$+ (.9070)(-\text{USD } 1,872,984.72)$$
$$+ (.8638)(-\text{USD } 1,822,559.60)$$
$$+ (.8227)(-\text{USD } 1,771,071.86)$$
$$+ (.7835)(+\text{USD } 8,374,603.96) \approx \text{USD } 0.$$

This proves that the 4.47% USD coupon cash flow works. Going through this same exercise with U.S. interest rate at 5.00% (on a notional of USD 5,000,000 in the right-hand column of our numbers above) gives a net benefit of around USD 2,290,000, which is the number that we arrived at above—calling it the funding "savings."

If there were no arbitrage opportunity, the U.S.-based corporation would either be able to borrow at 5.00% in USD (fixed) at home, at USD LIBOR (floating) at home, at 3.00% (fixed) in CHF in Switzerland, or at CHF LIBOR (floating) in Switzerland, and these would all effectively be viewed, financially, as the same. Looked at today (in terms of the present value of the currency cash flows, given USD|CHF spot and the interest rates in the two countries), there is no reason to prefer one over the other. Having said that, if one's name/creditworthiness is perceived as being better abroad (meaning that one is able to borrow "cheaper" in another country and another currency), then it could pay to issue a bond abroad and do a cross-currency swap to eliminate or "hedge away" the exchange rate risk.

Some additional points about cross-currency swaps:

1. Because a cross-currency swap, as described above, often accompanies a bond issue in another country/currency, it is sometimes called a "bond swap"; the real reason, though, that a cross-currency swap is referred to as a bond swap is that it looks like the exchange of a par bond in one currency for a spot-equivalent-amount of another par bond in another currency.

2. If the U.S. corporation really wanted floating rate (i.e., LIBOR) USD debt, they could have simply layered a standard fixed-for-floating USD interest rate swap on top of the fixed-for-fixed cross-currency swap. This need not have even required another transaction (as the providers of cross-currency swaps generally also provide interest rate swaps). One can do fixed USD-for-fixed CHF cross-currency swaps, floating USD-for fixed CHF cross-currency swaps, fixed USD-for-floating CHF cross-currency swaps, and floating USD-for-floating CHF cross-currency swaps. This last swap might not seem fair as USD interest rates are higher than CHF interest rates, but, looked at today, as a snapshot, with the expected

appreciation of the Swiss Franc (as built into the forward rates), the net present value of the swap (when reduced to either currency today) is zero. In a floating-for-floating cross-currency swap, it's the case that (USD) LIBOR should "swap" for (CHF) LIBOR, regardless of the fact that these rates may be of different orders of magnitude.

3. When I first heard about these products, I asked whether the company doing the cross-currency swap usually made an up-front spot exchange or not. Hopefully it is obvious that such an exchange would not affect the valuation. Since the U.S. corporation in our example really just wanted cheap Dollars, but actually received CHF (upon issuing the fixed coupon CHF-denominated bond in Switzerland), they would want to do an up-front spot exchange. Using the numbers from our example, they would want to trade in the CHF 125,000,000 and receive USD 100,000,000. On the other hand, if the U.S. corporation wanted to open a new branch in Switzerland (and needed CHF to do so), they would likely not do the CHF-USD spot exchange.

4. While these are OTC contracts and are typically done at "fair value," that is, at the coupon rates that make any up-front cash payment by either counterparty unnecessary, once entered into, a cross-currency swap can and generally will take on a positive or negative value. As USD|CHF spot moves and Swiss and U.S. interest rates change, the mark-to-market value of this swap will change. In short, these swaps have market risk and credit risk.

5. We mentioned that there was counterparty risk associated with the cross-currency swap in our example because the USD-payer was overpaying on each of the periodic currency exchanges until the final swap. One way to mitigate this asymmetry and the associated cumulating counterparty exposure is to do a coupon-only FX swap (without the final exchange of "principal"); of course, the coupons would have to be adjusted to make this swap fair. Following up on this last point, the original FX spot-forward swap that we looked at appeared to involve an exchange of a zero-coupon bond in one currency for another zero-coupon bond in another currency. A typical cross-currency swap looks like the exchange of a par coupon bond in one currency for another par coupon bond of the same initial value but in another currency. A coupon-only swap is like an exchange of a strip of coupons in one currency for another strip of coupons in another currency.

6. In the more general case of non-horizontal yield curves, the coupon associated with both legs of a cross-currency swap would be the par coupon or swap rate [the same (fixed) swap rate embedded in a stan-

dard (plain vanilla) fixed-for-floating interest rate swap],[3] although the rates used for present valuing would be the respective zero rates.

CROSS-CURRENCY SWAPS EXERCISE

Using the numbers in our earlier example:

USD|CHF $S = 1.2500$, $r_{US} = 5.00\%$ and $r_{CH} = 3.00\%$ (for all maturities),

1. Show, in two different ways, that if the U.S. corporation issues a 3.00% annual coupon bond in CHF in Switzerland and does a cross-currency swap, then, effectively, it will be borrowing at 5.00% in USD.
2. Determine the fair USD coupon for a five-year coupon-only FX swap where one counterparty receives the 3.00% CHF on a notional of CHF 125,000,000.

EXAMPLE OF A (NONSTANDARD) CROSS-CURRENCY SWAP

Imagine the following five-year structured note that pays two large Australian Dollar (AUD) coupons followed by three small Australian Dollar coupons and then pays its principal in Japanese Yen (JPY). (See Figure 8.4 a.)

Who might have issued this product? Would you believe a Canadian utility company. Who was the investor? It was a Japanese investor who liked the Canadian corporation's name and credit. What is the biggest clue that it was a Japanese investor? The principal is repaid in JPY. What do issuers issue? What investors want! What drove this particular structure? Two things. First, the investor thought that the Australian Dollar (AUD) was going to outperform the Japanese Yen (JPY) over the next couple of years. Second, there was a change in the Japanese tax laws that gave beneficial tax treatment (between year 2 and year 3) if the investor could show that this investment traded under its face value, which, given the large up-front AUD coupon flows, was likely to be the case. For some reason, these became known as "vacation bonds."

What was a Canadian power company doing issuing a note with AUD and JPY FX risk? The Canadian capital markets are only so deep and, even though this company has a good name and good credit, the Canadian markets were not particularly inclined to want to lend them more money. In other words, the Canadian funding market was going to charge this firm for issuing (clearly) more paper (i.e., borrowing more money). By structuring this note to accommodate the interests of the investor and then immediately swapping out the FX components (see Figure 8.4 b), the Canadian corporation was able to effectively get five-year fixed-rate Canadian Dollar (CAD) funding at an interest rate well below what they could have gotten directly in the Canadian market!

(a) The Cash Flows for the Investor

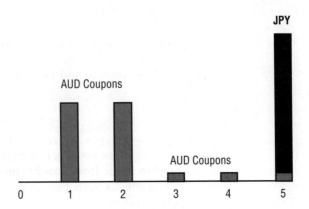

(b) The Cross-Currency Swap for the Issuer

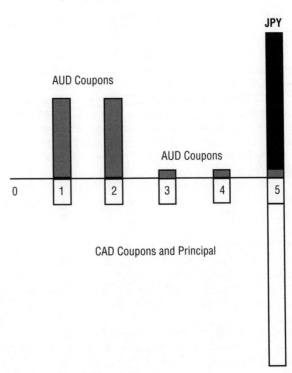

FIGURE 8.4 FX Structured Note

SUMMARY

There are many types of foreign exchange swaps. The most common is simply a standard FX forward trade with an offsetting FX spot transaction. The more interesting type of FX swap is the cross-currency swap or cross-currency interest rate swap or bond swap. These are often used in conjunction with international debt issuance and can result in lower borrowing costs both at home and abroad. Having said that, cross-currency swaps may be used to lock in the exchange rate for a series of firm commitment cash flows from operations; they may also be used for speculative purposes. Ultimately, though, cross-currency swaps are simply bundlings of FX forward contracts, and so introduce nothing new beyond our earlier spot-forward valuation relationship (aside from possibly interest rate compounding considerations); it is useful to keep this in mind for currency swap valuation and revaluation purposes.

CHAPTER 9

Foreign Exchange Options

"Foreign exchange:
It's not difficult;
It's just confusing."

"Foreign exchange options:
They're not really difficult;
They're just really confusing!"

OPTION BASICS

An option is an instrument that affords one the opportunity, if one wishes, to trade (either to purchase or to sell) a certain amount of a certain asset at a certain predetermined price on or before some date in the future.[1] Those who learn options from a textbook (or even in a business area other than foreign exchange) are usually told that there are two types of options: call options and put options. A **call option** is a contract that gives its owner the right (but not the obligation) **to buy** (or to "call" to oneself) a certain amount of a certain underlying asset at a fixed price (known as the strike price or the exercise price) on or before some set date in the future (known as the expiration date or expiry). Similarly, a **put option** is a contract that gives its owner the right (but not the obligation) **to sell** (or to "put" to someone else, namely, the seller of the option) a certain amount of a certain underlying asset at a fixed price (the strike or exercise price) on or before expiration.

Brief but careful consideration of these definitions indicate that an option is very much like a forward contract, although a forward contract does involve a bilateral obligation on the part of the two counterparties, whereas the acquirer of an option has just that, the choice to buy (in the case of a call) or to sell (in the case of a put), at his/her discretion.

The final part of the standard definition of an option ("on or before some date in the future") always sounds vague or unclear. This is because there are said to be two types of call options (and two types of put options): American and European [more formally, American-style-exercise calls (and puts) and European-style-exercise calls (and puts)]. It is well known that, in Switzerland (i.e., Europe), the trains, like the timepieces, are legend for being (exactly) on time, that is, they are precise, they are not particularly variable, whereas any rider on the commuter train lines around the United States (i.e., America) knows that their published schedules often seem more like a suggestion than a commitment; in the United States, we are far more flexible. If you can remember this, you can remember American- and European-style-exercise conventions (and how these relate to options):[2]

European options can be exercised only on their expiration date (they are not very accommodating in terms of the timing of their exercise), while *American options can be exercised at any time (up to and including expiration).* These designations have nothing to do with where they trade; European options are traded in America, American options are traded in Europe, and both types are traded everywhere else around the world.

For the record, if you do buy a three-month European call, you can always sell that option tomorrow; what you cannot do with a European call is utilize or "exercise" that call in order to buy the underlying asset for the exercise price prior to the expiration date.

In general, if two options are otherwise identical, but one is American and the other is European, then the American option should never trade for less, and may very well cost more, than the European option.

There are other types of exercise-style, such as Bermuda or Bermudan (so named because of Bermuda's location somewhere between America and Europe); this might refer, for example, to a six-month option that can be exercised on the first day of any month prior to expiration or on the expiration date itself; it would not be European, in that it *can* be exercised before expiration, but it is not American in that it *cannot* be exercised any time before expiration.

While it is not a hard and fast rule, exchange-traded options tend to be primarily American and over-the-counter (OTC) options tend to be mostly European. Both American and European currency options are listed on the Philadelphia Stock Exchange (PHLX).[3] Interestingly, when currencies began floating in the 1970s and currency options first started trading, the norm was to follow the convention used in the OTC equity options market, namely, they were American-style, but, in relatively short order, the entire OTC market flipped to almost exclusively European-style. FX options dealers can quote and trade American-style FX options, but American-style FX options make up only a very, very small fraction of FX OTC options volume.

And finally, just to be clear, American-style exercise and European-style exercise have nothing at all to do with American and European FX quotes.

To identify a particular option, you are required to specify a number of things. You would need to indicate whether you are interested in trading a call or a put. You further should know (though you don't always have to disclose) whether you want to buy that option or sell it. You have to be clear about what the underlying asset is. Furthermore, you must specify whether you want a European-style option or American-style option (though in the case of certain exchange-traded options, you may not have a choice of exercise style). Next, you need to select the expiration date. You may ask for a one-month option (with dating conventions similar to those used with OTC FX forwards), you could (though this is less common) ask for an option that expires on a particular day like December 15, or (in the case of an exchange-traded option) you can simply trade, say, the December option (aware that this contract has a designated, fixed expiration date associated with it). Then one must choose the exercise price or strike price. We use "X" to indicate the "eXercise" price or, if it is easier to remember, "X," which is used as the scoring mark for a strike in bowling (therefore, strike price). Some textbooks identify the strike price using "K," the symbol for a strike out in baseball. The method of settlement must also be agreed upon, depending on whether the option is to be physically settled or cash settled. Finally, one must indicate the size of the option (or the face amount or the notional). If a call option gives you the right to buy a certain amount of an asset, you must specify the amount of the underlying asset that the option represents or refers to or "covers."

Since a call option is like being long the underlying in the future (if the call owner wishes) or, stated differently, since a call is like being long a forward (without the downside), then, as the underlying price rises, any given call option (with a fixed strike price) should gain in value. In this sense, if you own (or are long) **a call**, it **is**, in some sense, **like being long the underlying** (in the future). If anything happens (as a result of owning or being long a call), you would buy the underlying (in the future). The owner of a call will, therefore, benefit as the underlying asset price rises.

Similarly, **a put** option **is like being short the underlying** in the future or like being short a forward (without the downside). If you own (or are long) a put, therefore, it is like being short the underlying asset, and a put owner will benefit from the underlying asset price falling.

These ideas are most easily seen with the use of graphs. For a (long) call with a fixed strike price (X), the **value** of the option (at expiration) will either be positive or zero depending on whether the option ends up "in-the-money" (with $S > X$) or "out-of-the-money" (with $S < X$). If you have a call option with a strike price of $X = 40$, then the graph of the value of that call at expiration will look like Figure 9.1a. If the spot price ends up at, say, $S = 36$, then the 40 call will be worthless (i.e., have a value of zero), whereas if the spot price ends up at $S = 55$, then this call option will have a value of 15 ($S - X = 55 - 40$) at expiration. After all, if you have an option to buy something at a price of $X = 40$ (the strike price) and the spot price in the market is 55, then, at expiration, that option will be worth exactly 15. We will denote this call with a strike price of $X = 40$ by writing 40C. The 40-strike price put (or 40P) has its value at expiration depicted in Figure 9.1b. Note that for both options, they "kink" (or start taking on a positive value) at the strike or exercise price and then go up in value point-for-point with the underlying asset price (for a call, as spot rises; for a put, as spot falls).

Note that we have not attempted to incorporate the cost of the option (the option premium) into this graph; if that is done, then it is typically referred to as a "P/L" (read "P n L" or "Profit/Loss") graph or a "breakeven" graph (because it highlights that spot price for which the investor "breaks even" (or exactly recovers their option premium).

To possibly make matters even more confusing, one can buy options or

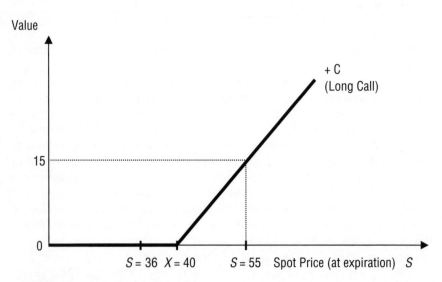

FIGURE 9.1a　　Value Graph of a Long Call at Expiration

Value

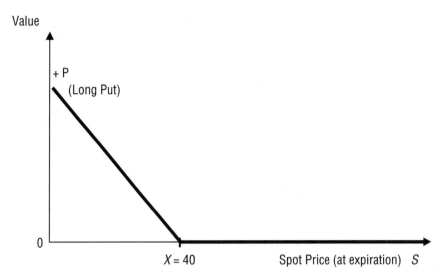

FIGURE 9.1b   Value Graph of a Long Put at Expiration

sell options. A long call is like being long the underlying (in that you want the underlying price to go up); if you sell a call option, you have given the "upside" to someone else (in exchange for the option payment or premium) and so you would like the underlying asset price to fall (or at least not rise), so the option ends up with little or no value. In this sense, being short (or having sold) a call is like being short the underlying. Similarly, having sold a put is like being long the underlying (because you have given the right to sell to someone else and if they choose to utilize that right, then you have to accommodate; if they want to sell, and it's their option, you have to buy). For graphical representations, see Figure 9.2.

If you own an option (regardless of whether it is a call or a put) and you wish to utilize or employ that option (whether to buy with your call or to sell with your put), then you are said to **"exercise"** your option. On the other hand, if you have sold an option and the owner of that option exercises the option, then you are said to be **"assigned"**; this language stems from the practice, with exchange-traded options, of identifying a counterparty who has sold an option and "matching" him/her with the owner of one of those options who is looking to exercise (and with exchange-traded options, it need not be the same individual with whom the original option transaction took place). In this sense, somebody who has sold an option is assigned to take the other side of the trade or exchange associated with the option exercise.

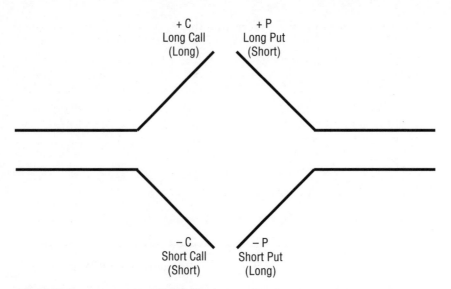

FIGURE 9.2 The Long and Short of Options
(The expression in parentheses refers to the comparable position in the underlying asset.) Note the relationship between the slope (positive, negative) and the corresponding position in the underlying (long, short).

At this stage, I'd like to say two things. First, most people who are exposed to options for the first time, which, nowadays, is often in an academic context, typically learn about equity options or options on stock/shares. For that reason alone, I'd like to briefly review the terminology and conventions used in the equity option world here, as many of those reading the book will already be familiar with equity options, and that may actually be a source of confusion. The reason we digress into equities (in an FX book), unlike the earlier instances in which we used equity examples (as we did in our chapter on forwards), is because equities and FX look at options differently, but often use the same language (to refer to different things); this potential source of confusion should become clearer as we proceed.

Second, someone, years ago, told me the following: "If you can trade equity options, you can trade anything, but if you understand foreign exchange options, then you understand options." I have come to understand this and believe it (now more than ever). Compared to the liquidity of, say, EUR|USD, many stocks are woefully illiquid. Some stocks pay large discrete dividends, which can change, a fact that has its own implications. There are events like mergers, acquisitions, bankruptcies, divestitures, and so on; stocks sometime split; there are other corporate actions; and there have been market regulations such as the up-tick or down-tick or short sale rule in effect. Trading stock options is difficult (then again, trading stock itself can be difficult). But the (classical) model of option valuation was first developed/derived for the case of nondividend-paying stock, and so enjoys a certain prominence/notoriety in academic circles. We deal with both equity option valuation and FX option valuation in the Appendix to this chapter.

EQUITY OPTIONS

The easiest place to start is with an example.

> Let's say you believe IBM stock will be going up significantly over the next three months. You might consider buying a call option on IBM common stock. If IBM stock is trading at, say, S = USD 99.50, your choice for the strike or exercise price might be X = 100. On the equity option exchanges, there are certain standardized "listed" strike prices. In this case, those might be X = 80, X = 85, X = 90, X = 95, X = 100, X = 105, X = 110, X = 115, and X = 120.[4]
>
> Now, if somebody asked for the three-month **at-the-money** call, then an equity option trader would understand that to be the call with a strike price equal to (or closest to) the current spot price (**X = S**). In this example, the at-the-money call and put would be the 100C and the 100P. With S = 99.50, the 80 call would be in-the-money (that is, it would have value relative to the current spot price, even if it could not be exercised right now because, for example, it is a European option). An equity option trader would say that this option, the 80C, has **intrinsic value** and that intrinsic would be 19.50 (S − X); the 100C, as well as the 125C, would have no intrinsic value.

In the OTC market for equity options, there is not a limited number and range of listed and traded strike prices. As these are individually negotiated option contracts, one can (in principle) trade any strike price for any expiration date. Some of the different things one will hear with OTC equity options (versus exchange-traded equity options) are quotations in percentages. If, say a stock is trading at S = 20, then you might hear someone talk about the 110 call, the 95 call, or the 95 put. These would be seriously out-of-the-money, slightly less out-of-the-money, and seriously in-the-money, respectively, if the strike price was being quoted in, say, Dollars, but the strike price here is being quoted as a percentage of the current stock price (and so these would refer to the USD 22 strike call, the USD 19 strike call, and the USD 19 strike put). Regardless of whether the option is listed on an exchange or traded OTC and regardless of whether it is American- or European-style-exercise, equity option references have traditionally been made relative to the spot price.

When talking about equity options, the convention usually involves quoting the premium on a per share basis. If the 100 call is quoted at 3.25 and that option is written on 100 shares, then it would actually cost USD 325.00. Of course this is just a scaling. In equity options, though, it is more common to talk about the premium in terms of USD per share (i.e., 3.25) as opposed to USD 325. We'll see that there are a large number of ways of quoting FX option premiums.

What are people using options for in the equity world? One of the most common uses of equity options is a "buy-write" or "covered call." This is a strategy in which one buys (or is long a particular stock) and sells (or "writes") a call against it. If you already own the stock, selling calls is sometimes referred to as an "over-write." If $S = 99.50$, you own the stock, and, over the course of the next three months, you do not think the stock will rise above 105, then you could consider selling the 105 call and "monetizing" the "upside" that you are effectively giving away. Buy-writes/over-writes are often referred to as "yield enhancement" or "income" strategies. Another investor may choose to buy a call option in lieu of buying the underlying stock. Unlike investing around USD 100 in the stock, the option may only cost about USD 3.25.

This investment brings up the notion of leverage and the idea of strike selection (i.e., some options may look more attractive than others, given your view). Still another tactical use of options may involve the purchase of a put against a long stock position; this is known as a "protective put" strategy. If the stock price drops, your equity position will lose value but your put option position can provide an opposite and offsetting financial impact for your portfolio. On the other hand, if the equity skyrockets, although you will have paid for that put option, you can participate in the entire upside associated with the stock. One final, and very popular, equity option example uses two different options. If you are long the stock and you would like to buy a put, but you are reluctant to pay the put premium, you may want to do a "collar." A collar involves buying a put and "financing it" by selling a call (usually with the exact same premium, so that it involves no up-front payment). This is really nothing more than a combined buy-write and protective put strategy rolled into one.

PUT-CALL PARITY WITH EQUITY OPTIONS

In 1969, Hans Stoll published a paper[5] identifying a fundamental arbitrage relationship between same-strike price, same-expiration European calls and puts. He recognized that if you buy, say, a three-month European call on IBM and simultaneously sell a three-month European put with the same strike price, then you are, in effect, going long IBM in the future. Specifically, you are entering into what an equity option marketmaker would refer to as a long IBM "synthetic forward" with a purchase price equal to the strike price of the two options. This is pictured in Figure 9.3. We said earlier that if you buy a call, it makes you kind of long the underlying asset ("kind of" because you may choose not to exercise your option). We also said that if you sell a put, it makes you "kind of" long the underlying asset

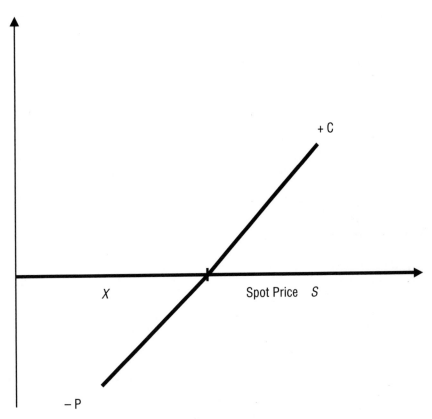

FIGURE 9.3 Long Synthetic Forward

("kind of," here, because you may not be assigned on the option you have sold). However, if you buy a European call and sell a same-strike European put, you are almost surely long the underlying (in the future).

With reference to Figure 9.3, if, at expiration, $S > X$, then your call will be in-the-money and you would exercise your call option (buying the stock at the strike price), while the put that you've sold will expire worthless. On the other hand, if $S < X$, then you will be assigned on your short put (requiring you to buy the stock for the strike price), while the call you bought will end up out-of-the-money. One way or the other, then, you will end up buying the underlying stock in three months for the strike price. Sound familiar? It should. It sounds like a forward, but you created or synthesized it yourself.

Presumably, if the actual forward was trading at a price different from the net price derived from the strike price and the option prices, there would be an arbitrage. At this point, those in equities usually start to fail to follow; they are not used to talking about forwards or futures on individual stocks (as opposed to stock indexes). The Securities and Exchange Commission (SEC) once turned down a request to list futures on individual stocks on exchanges in the United States; even worse, a law[6] was later passed making single stock futures illegal (for a time)! The point is that equity market participants historically did not trade futures and forwards on individual stocks (though there have been futures on U.S. equity indices listed since 1982) and so, equity option participants typically don't think in terms of forward pricing or "F."

Nevertheless, there is a relationship between options and forwards, and, as we know from Chapters 6 and 7, there is a relationship between forwards/futures and spot. What, then, does the relationship between options and the spot price look like?

Before we begin, we have to warn the reader to be careful when they see things like "+C." After all, what does that mean? Most people would say, it represents a long call, which, indeed, is certainly correct if one is thinking about **position** as in Figure 9.3, but if we want to talk about option values and option prices, then "+ C" would be used to refer to the fact that you receive the premium ("C") from selling a call, which means that "+ C" indicates a short or sold call, when you are discussing **cash flows**. A useful hint, if you are not sure what "+ C" represents, is to look around (e.g., at the surrounding terms) and see if there are any "r" (for the interest rate) or "t" (for time) terms, which would clinch the fact that you are looking at and talking about cash flows.

Unlike IBM stock, which currently pays a dividend, let's consider a nondividend paying stock, S; assume the stock is trading at $S = 30$. If you were to buy the stock, which makes you long, and sell a European 35-strike call and buy a European 35-strike put, which, together, make you short at the strike price, $X = 35$), then it looks as if you would have no net position at all. This is pictured in Figure 9.4. But on reflection, who wouldn't want to be long stock at $S = 30$ and short in three months at $X = 35$? Remember, one wants to buy low and sell high. Although we have no idea what either of the two options should trade for (at this point), we should be able to figure out what the difference in their prices must be.

If we were to consider the cash flows associated with this trade, (using S for the stock price, X for the strike price, C for the 35 call price and P for the 35 put price), we'd have

Cash Flow Today: $-S$ (buy stock) $+ C$ (take in call premium)
  $- P$ (pay put premium)

Cash Flow at Expiration: $+ X$

(Through the options, you will either exercise your put (if $S < X$) and sell stock for X or you will be assigned on your short call (if $S > X$) and sell stock for X.)

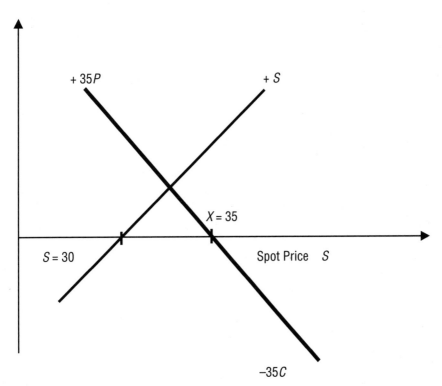

FIGURE 9.4 Put-Call Parity

Note, though, that these cash flows occur at different points in time. We can either look at these cash flows today, which would require present valuing the strike price cash flow):

$$+C - P - S + PV(X) \qquad (9.1)$$

or, employing an interest rate convention,

$$+C - P - S + X/(1 + rt) \qquad (9.2)$$

or using continuous interest,

$$+C - P - S + X_e^{-rt} \qquad (9.3)$$

or we could look at these cash flows at expiration (in which case, we would have to "carry" or "finance" or future value the options and stock cash flows into the future):

$$+C(1 + rt) - P(1 + rt) - S(1 + rt) + X \qquad (9.4)$$

There would be an arbitrage or free lunch if these expressions were not equal to zero [in which case, if it was positive, one could make a profit from doing these trades (buying stock, selling the call, and buying the put)—and, if it was negative, one could presumably profit by doing the opposite (selling stock, buying the call, and selling the put)].

Note: This nondividend-paying stock and same-strike European option relationship:

$$+C - P - S + [X/(1 + rt)] = 0 \qquad (9.5)$$

or

$$+C - P - S + Xe^{-rt} = 0 \qquad (9.6)$$

is sometimes referred to as a "no-arbitrage" relationship; it is also a version of what's known as "put-call parity," where the parity (or equivalence) can be seen by manipulating the formulas above:

Simple Interest	Continuous Interest
$C = P + S - [X/(1 + rt)]$	$C = P + S - Xe^{-rt}$ (9.7)
or	or
$C = P + [S(1 + rt)/(1 + rt)] - [X/(1 + rt)]$	$C = P + Se^{+rt}e^{-rt} - Xe^{-rt}$
or	or
$C = P + [S(1 + rt) - X]/(1 + rt)$	$C = P + [Se^{+rt} - X]e^{-rt}$

and recalling, for a nondividend-paying stock,

$$F = S(1 + rt) \qquad\qquad\qquad F = Se^{+rt}$$

then,

$$C = P + [F - X]/(1 + rt) \qquad\qquad C = P + [F - X]e^{-rt} \qquad (9.8)$$

Stated differently, put-call parity says that same-strike European calls and puts should differ by the present value of the difference between the forward price (F) and the strike or exercise price (X). Although it might not be clear, at this point, why this relationship is so important, it should be clear that it must hold for any European call and put values given by a theoretical option valuation model, and it will allow us to highlight, a little later on, another way in which foreign exchange options differ from equity options.

If we are thinking of a one-year time frame $(t = 1)$, interest rates are $r = 5.00\%$, the nondividend stock is trading at $S = 30$, and the 35 call is trading at 2.00, then at what price should the 35 put be trading?

One might think that the 35 put should trade for $35p = 7.00$ (since the trades in Figure 9.4 suggest that you will make 5.00 by buying stock at 30.00 and selling it in the future at 35.00) and so you should have to pay 5.00 for there not to be an arbitrage. One would pay 5.00 in this context by buying the put for 7.00 and selling the call for 2.00. We only forgot one thing, though; the question really is, "How much would you pay **to-day** for the chance to sell at (or take in) 35.00 in one year?" That is, we have to take the difference in the timing of the cash flows into account. To get 35.00 in a year, I'd pay the present value of 35.00 today; that would be (using simple discounting) 33.33. The stock costs 30.00 today, so the net option payment should be 3.33. If the 35 call is trading for 2.00, then the 35P should be trading at 5.33. If you then buy the stock (– 30.00), buy the 35 put (– 5.33), and sell the 35 call (+ 2.00), then your net investment today would be 33.33, and you'd (properly) receive 35.00 one year later. You can check that these numbers work using Equation (9.5).

EXAMPLE

If a nondividend-paying stock is trading at $S = 30$, (simple annualized) interest rates are $r = 6.00\%$, the three-month ($t = .25$) European 35 call is trading for 35C = 2.25 and the three-month European 35 put is trading at 35P = 6.50, what trades would you propose and how much would you make?

Answer:

$$C - P - S + X/(1 + rt) \text{ should} = 0$$

Here, $2.25 - 6.50 - 30 + 35/(1.015) = .27$ or so.

You are "being paid" to do this trade, so sell C, buy P, buy S.

Equity option marketmakers refer to that trade as a "conversion."

Understanding put-call parity once provided profitable arbitrage opportunities for option traders.

PUT-CALL PARITY EXERCISE #1

If a nondividend-paying stock is trading $S = 78.50$, the time frame is one year, interest rates are 4.00%, and the one-year 80 strike European call is trading at 80C = 3.75, where should the one-year 80 strike European put be trading (for there not to be any arbitrage)? If it's trading for .50 more than you think that it should, what trades would you do and how much profit will you make?

IN-THE-MONEY, AT-THE-MONEY, AND OUT-OF-THE-MONEY

In the world of foreign exchange, forwards are commonplace. They have been around for years, they are well understood, and they trade extremely liquidly. Also, an option is often viewed as an alternative to a forward. For these reasons, when FX market participants refer to "moneyness" or "intrinsic," they usually employ these concepts relative to the forward (as opposed to the spot).

In other words, if someone requested the one-year at-the-money USD call (= CHF put), the strike price on that option would be set equal to the one-year forward price ($X = F$). In an earlier USD|CHF example, we had Spot $S = 1.2500$ and the one-year forward at $F = 1.2262$. How would you label the CHF 1.2400 call on a Dollar and would it have intrinsic value? Contrary to the equity option vernacular, which would label this call in-the-money with an intrinsic value of CHF .0100, in FX (remember now, we're looking at the forward), we would label this "out-of-the-money" with zero intrinsic value. After all, who would want to buy a Dollar for CHF 1.2400 when the spot price is headed toward 1.2262—or so says the forward?

THEORETICAL OPTION VALUE AND OPTION RISK MEASURES ("THE GREEKS")

An option's theoretical value depends on the spot price (S), the strike or exercise price (X), time till expiration in years (t), the (annual) interest rate (r), the (annual percentage) volatility of the underlying (σ) and, of course, the type of option (e.g., American call, European put). This could be written succinctly (for a call) as

$$C = C(S, X, t, r, \sigma)$$

Theoretical option valuation models are presented in the appendix to this chapter.

This "black box" (or "Black–Scholes box") approach to theoretical option valuation is represented in Figure 9.5. The model gives the theoretical value of an option (below which an option marketmaker would want to buy and above which an option trader would want to sell). If any of the inputs into the option valuation model change, the value of the option will change; the model will also give numerical measures of these parameter or risk sensitivities. The Option Risk Measures or "Greeks" are known as: Delta (Δ), Gamma (Γ), Rho (ρ), Theta (θ), and Vega (v) [or Tau (τ)].

FIGURE 9.5 Theoretical Option Valuation

Delta (Δ)

Delta is a measure of spot price risk. We cannot use expressions like "Δy" to refer to a change in a variable y (since Δ is one of our fundamental option risk measures). We will, therefore, instead of a capital Greek "D" (that is, Δ), use a lower case "∂" to refer to "a change in." It is just notation; we aren't doing math or calculus. This allows us to write (for a call option):

$$\Delta = \frac{\partial C}{\partial S}$$

Delta is an option's primary risk. It indicates the sensitivity of an option's value to a change in the underlying asset's price. Option traders who hedge or offset this risk say they trade "delta neutral" or "flat" (as in, neither long nor short). Since this relates movements in the spot price to changes in the option value, it also tells the option trader how much of the underlying must be traded in order to hedge the option position. For this reason, delta is also known as the "hedge ratio." It tells you (effectively) how long or how short you are (as a result of having bought or sold the option). The deeper "in-the-money" a call option, the greater the delta, until eventually, in the simplest case of a nondividend paying stock, the option value and underlying asset price move one-for-one (100 delta). Delta is typically referenced in percentage terms. An option that is extremely "out-of-the-money" will have a delta close to zero. In the simplest case, a call's delta ranges between 0 and 1 ("100") and a put's delta (remember, a put is like being short the underlying) ranges from –1 ("– 100" or often just quoted as "100" without the "minus") to 0. For most (relatively short-dated) options, the "at-the-money" option will be around a 50 delta (.50). This means that, for a call, if the spot price moves 1.00, the call's value will change by .50; it also means that if one were to buy the call, one would hedge by selling around 50% of the underlying notional face that the call represents. Finally, some traders tend to think of delta as the probability that the option will be in-the-money at expiration. While this is not really 100% accurate, it's not a bad rule of thumb. For this reason, a trader might say that a deep in-the-money call with $\Delta = .90$ has a 90% chance of ending up being exercised.[7] A deep out-of-the-money Call might be a "5 (.05) delta." As mentioned, the at-the-money call tends to be around a 50 (.50) delta; the interpretation is that it is a "coin toss" (a 50-50 chance) as to whether the option will be exercised at expiration. If you buy calls or sell puts, you get long delta (or positive deltas); if you sell calls or buy puts, you're short delta (or you are effectively getting short the underlying via the options). Again, delta is a measure of how long or short you are (in terms of the underlying asset).

Gamma (Γ)

Gamma is a second-order risk measure. It reflects the fact that, as the underlying price changes, the delta changes.

$$\Gamma = \frac{\partial \Delta}{\partial S} = \frac{\partial^2 C}{\partial S^2}$$

In essence (remembering that delta is the hedge ratio), gamma indicates how quickly you become unhedged as the spot price changes. It is usually larger "around the money" and tends to get bigger (around the money) as you approach expiration. If you own options (calls or puts), you are said to be "long gamma," and you're "short gamma" if you've sold options.

Vega (Tau) (ν or τ)

Vega (or Tau as we call it in many areas of UBS) is a measure of option sensitivity to changes in volatility. Sometimes underlying assets fluctuate more (higher volatility) and sometimes they tend to oscillate less. As volatility changes (some would be more precise and replace this with, "As the market's perception of future volatility changes"), option values will change:

$$\nu \text{ or } \tau = \frac{\partial C}{\partial \sigma}$$

If you own options (calls or puts), higher volatility benefits your position and you are said to be long vega, long tau, long volatility, or simply, long "vol."

Rho (ρ)

Rho is the sensitivity of an option's value to changes in interest rates. Since an option is like a forward without the downside, and knowing that forward prices depend on interest rates, one would suppose changes in interest rates impact option values.

$$\rho = \frac{\partial C}{\partial r}$$

Interestingly, for a call, an interest rate increase will impact the forward (positively, which should make a call—with a fixed strike price—more valuable) but will secondarily impact a call value through a greater present valuing of any future payoff, which should make a call less valuable today). For the simplest case of a call on a nondividend-paying stock, rho is positive. For puts, rho is usually negative,

Theta (θ)

Finally, time impacts an option's value. Theta is a measure of how an option value will change as time goes by:

$$\theta = \frac{\partial C}{\partial t}$$

Usually, as time (that is, the time left in the option till expiration) approaches zero, the option will lose value. For that reason, theta has been referred to as "decay" or "erosion." Theta is usually negative (if you own options); if the only input to the option valuation model that changes is time, it is likely (with the exception of deep-in-the-money puts) that options will lose some of their value.

FOREIGN EXCHANGE OPTIONS

In the world of equity, it is obvious what the underlying asset is (e.g., IBM common stock) and no one even thinks about the other side of the trade (the USD—in terms of which the spot price is quoted, in terms of which the strike or exercise price is quoted, and in terms of which the option premium is quoted)—other than in the context of the option's payoff. In FX, money is the underlying and there must be another money involved on the other side of the option contract, as well as with the option premium. This is as disturbing as thinking about an option to trade four shares of Microsoft stock for one share of IBM. And how would the premium be quoted? In terms of Microsoft shares, IBM shares, USD? Confusing isn't it?

This is the one statement that should form the basis of one's understanding of FX options: **Every option is a contract to exchange one thing for another.**

Said slightly differently, every option gives the owner the opportunity (if they wish) to exchange one pile of "stuff" for another pile of "another stuff."

Let's go back to our IBM example (with $S = 99.50$), but this time let's consider the $X = 115$ call; this option would give the call option holder the right to buy IBM stock for USD 115 per share. Since the standard exchange-traded option contract (in the United States)[8] is written on 100 shares of stock, what this option, then, really represents is a contract in which the call option owner may (at their discretion) buy 100 shares of IBM stock in exchange for USD 11,500. Obviously, this is an IBM call, but do you see that it is also a USD put? After all, the owner of the IBM call option had the right to sell USD (in exchange for IBM). **An IBM Call is a USD Put.** Similarly, **an IBM Put is a USD Call.** Think about it.

In the world of foreign exchange, every option involves the potential exchange of one currency for another currency. For this reason, in FX, people know that **every call is a put and every put is a call.** Although the FX market has its way of talking about options, it is common to hear the following sort of statement on the dealing floor:

"I sell you a Swiss Franc call—Dollar put."

That refers to one option, not two.

Before moving on, everyone should understand that a CHF call is a USD put. (Of course, a CHF call could be a EUR put, a JPY put, or even a Nestle Stock put in Switzerland, but if the relevant currency pair is USD|CHF, a Swiss Franc call is a U.S. Dollar put.) See Figure 9.6.

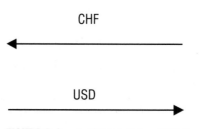

FIGURE 9.6 A CHF Call is a USD Put

PUT-CALL PARITY IN FOREIGN EXCHANGE

One of the fundamental relative value relationships with options is put-call parity. In the case of a nondividend-paying stock, we said it could be written as

$$+ C - P - S + [X/(1 + rt)] = 0 \qquad \text{or} \qquad + C - P - S + Xe^{-rt} = 0$$

(depending on your preference for interest rate conventions). These formulas are not correct for same-strike European-exercise-style options **on foreign exchange**. Why?

Returning to our earlier put-call parity thought experiment above, we started by asking what must be true if we bought a share of stock and then effectively sold that share through the simultaneous purchase of a European put and sale of a European call with the same strike price. More specifically, something has to be changed here with foreign exchange. With stock, we bought one share and traded two options each covering one share; in foreign exchange, this would be wrong. Why? Foreign exchange is money and money "grows." Consider USDICHF: If we buy a put on one Dollar and sell a call on one Dollar, our earlier inclination would lead us to want to buy one Dollar (to deliver against whichever of these two options ended up in the money at expiration), but if we did buy one Dollar, and we put that Dollar into an account that generated interest, we would have purchased more USD than we needed. Although it may sound odd, all we need to purchase today is "the present value of a Dollar" (some amount less than one Dollar, which will grow into one Dollar by expiration (for delivery versus the options).

Being more explicit, and staying with USDICHF, then the "no-arbitrage" condition would be based on

Cash Flow Today: Sell a call $+ C$ (a call on USD 1 quoted in CHF)
    Buy a put $- P$ (a put on USD 1 quoted in CHF)
    Buy the present Value of USD 1 (in CHF)

This involves buying not USD 1, but USD .9524, which is

$$1/(1 + r_{US}\, t) = 1/1.05 = .9524$$

Cash Flow at Expiration   Sell USD 1 for $+ X$ (which is quoted in CHF)

So, put-call parity in FX could be written (for our USDICHF example and in general):

Simple Interest	Continuous Interest

For USD|CHF:

$$+ C - P - S/(1 + r_{US}t) + X/(1 + r_{CH}t) = 0 \quad + C - P - Se^{-rUSt} + Xe^{-rCHt} = 0 \quad (9.9)$$

In general:

$$+ C - P - S/(1 + r_2t) + X/(1 + r_1t) = 0 \quad + C - P - Se^{-r2t} + Xe^{-r1t} = 0 \quad (9.10)$$

Rearranging into the form of put-call parity ($C = P +/- \dots$):

$$C = P + S/(1 + r_2t) - X/(1 + r_1t) \qquad + C = P + Se^{-r2t} - Xe^{-r1t} = 0 \quad (9.11)$$

And, if we substitute—converting our S into the corresponding F:

$$F = S\frac{(1 + r_1t)}{(1+r_2t)} \qquad \text{or} \qquad F = S\,e^{(r_1-r_2)t}$$

then,

$$C = P + [F - X]/(1 + r_1t) \qquad \text{or} \qquad C = P + [F - X]e^{-r1t} \quad (9.12)$$

where, in both forms, the discounting or present valuing is done using the interest rate associated with the currency units that are being quoted. For example, with USD|CHF, since S, X, C, and P are all quoted in terms of CHF, it is the CHF rate that is used to present value. There is an obvious similarity between equation (9.8) and equation (9.12). Furthermore, there are similarities between the continuous version of equation (9.11) and the Garman Kohlhagen Formula, which, of course, must generate European call and put option values that satisfy FX put-call parity.

USD|CHF EXAMPLE

If S = 1.2500, considering the one-year time frame (with r_{US} = 5.00% and r_{CH} = 3.00%), and looking at the one-year European 1.3000 call on USD 1 trading at CHF .0219 per USD 1, find the value of the one-year European 1.3000 put on USD 1.

$$C - P - S/(1 + (.05)(1)) + X/(1 + (.03)(1)) = 0$$
$$\text{CHF .0219} - P - \text{CHF } 1.2500/1.05 + \text{CHF } 1.3000/1.03 = 0$$
$$P = \text{CHF .0936}$$

Reality check: F = 1.2262, X = 1.3000 so the USD put is in-the-money. It has intrinsic value (relative to the forward) of CHF .0738, which, when present valued using Swiss rates, gives CHF .0717.

$$P \text{ (at CHF .0936)} - C \text{ (at CHF .0219)} = \text{CHF .0717!}$$

FX PUT-CALL PARITY EXERCISE #2

USD|JPY $S = 110.00$, $r_J = 1.00\%$, $r_{US} = 3.00\%$, $t = 3$ months ($t = \frac{1}{4} = .25$)

1. For the 107.50 strike ($X = 107.50$) three-month European options, by how much will the call and put differ and which will be more valuable?
2. If the 107.50 call is trading at JPY 2.62 per USD 1, where should the put be trading?

PERSPECTIVE MATTERS

If you accept the earlier assertion that a CHF call is a USD put, let's ask who would want a CHF call and who might want a USD put. By considering the perspective of the potential user, we will gain an additional insight into FX options.

Who would want the CHF call? If CHF is the underlying, then the interested party would be someone other than Swiss. For example, if a U.S. jeweler used Swiss works in his watches or a U.S. baker insisted on genuine Swiss chocolate for his pastries, they might be obliged to pay their suppliers in Swiss Francs; this is the American perspective. Recognizing that changes in exchange rates (in particular, if USD|CHF falls) can be painful for a U.S. purchaser of Swiss products (denominated in CHF), the U.S. jeweler and the U.S. baker could protect themselves (from FX risk) by acquiring a call option on Swiss Francs. In this way, worst case, they would be able to obtain CHF at the strike price. From the U.S. perspective (again, with CHF as the underlying asset), one might consider the spot price in terms of USD per CHF, the strike price in USD, and these American market participants would probably like to have the premium quoted in USD.

Now consider a Swiss company that sells its products (like Swiss army knives or Swiss cheese) in the United States. Further suppose that their receivables (that is the cash flow from their business in the United States) are in Dollars. They might like to know that, if the Dollar weakens against the Swiss Franc, they can get back at least a certain amount of Swiss Francs for each Dollar they take in. In other words, they might want to ensure the economic viability of these off-shore businesses. They would like a USD put (= CHF call). Since the underlying, from their perspective, is USD, they would look at the spot price in terms of Swiss Francs, they would set the strike price in CHF, and they would like the premium in terms of CHF.

In some way, we should be able to go back and forth between the CHF call and the USD put. Let's look at an example. Starting with USD|CHF $S = 1.2500$, $t = 1$ (year), $r_{US} = 5.00\%$ and $r_{CH} = 3.00\%$ (and we'll assume these are continuous rates), $X = 1.2195$, and USD|CHF volatility $\sigma = 10.00\%$.

Which option will we look at first? The natural option here has the USD as the underlying (so it is the Swiss or European perspective). More precisely, this is a Dollar put that would allow a Swiss market participant the opportunity to sell ("unload") their Dollars in exchange for CHF 1.2195 each. Using the Garman–Kohlhagen Model (the FX version of the Black–Scholes Model), we arrive at a USD put option value of CHF .0445 (per USD 1). Is it in-the-money or out-of-the-money?

To see the other (American) perspective, we should turn everything upside-down. To be more explicit, the U.S. perspective looks at Swiss Francs as the underlying "asset" and so this should involve CHF|USD quotes. Keeping everything aligned, now $S = .8000$, $X = .8200$, the interest rates don't change (but they have to be "flipped" when used in the Garman–Kohlhagen formula), and volatility is volatility.[9] Not forgetting that we are valuing a Swiss Franc call (as opposed to the earlier Dollar put), we get .0292. What went wrong? I thought a Swiss Franc call was a Dollar put? Oh, yeah, I forgot; this option value (the value of the CHF call) is in USD whereas the option value of the USD put is in CHF. No problem. If we convert these to the same currency (say, CHF), then these should be equal, right?

Let's try: The USD put value = CHF .0445. The CHF call value = USD .0292. We know USD|CHF spot is $S = 1.2500$, so let's turn the CHF call value (currently in USD) into CHF (by multiplying by spot):

$$USD\ .0292 \times \frac{CHF\ 1.2500}{USD\ 1} = CHF\ .0365$$

It didn't work! CHF .0365 (the value of the CHF call translated at the spot exchange rate) isn't equal to CHF .0445 (the value of the USD put). What's going on here? Think about this for a moment. Although it is true that a CHF call is a USD put, it is not true that a call on one Swiss Franc is exactly the same as a put on one U.S. Dollar. See Figure 9.7.

How do we get this to work? We must have an additional conversion. Any thoughts? What would make these two contracts the same size? Remember, every option is an option to exchange one pile of stuff for another pile of stuff?

The final adjustment is to ensure that the contracts are identical. The price that determines the relative size of the piles to be exchanged is the strike or exercise price. Since Swiss Francs are smaller than Dollars, we have to scale up the Swiss Franc call (by the strike price of 1.2195):

$$USD\ .0292 \times \frac{CHF\ 1.2500}{USD\ 1} \times 1.2195 = CHF\ .0445$$

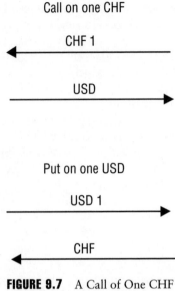

FIGURE 9.7 A Call of One CHF
Is NOT a Put on One USD
These two option contracts are
not the same size. Need to scale
(by the strike price) to make them
identical.

Now it works!

Summarizing, one can go back and forth between the values of FX options from the two perspectives (call and put); that relationship will look like this:[10]

$$C \times S \times X = P \qquad (9.13)$$

This is not put-call parity; I have heard this referred to as international put-call equivalence, put-call duality, and put-call symmetry (although there are many symmetries between puts and calls).

FX OPTION PREMIUM

When it comes to quoting option premiums, there are a variety of ways in FX. If we are considering a put on USD = call on CHF, we could quote the premium in terms of a total amount of USD or a total amount of CHF, or CHF per Dollar or USD per Swiss Franc, or percent of the USD notional or percent of the CHF notional, or in volatility terms.

Let's return to our example from the last section. If one was interested in the option to sell USD and buy CHF on a notional of USD 10,000,000, how might the premium be quoted? First, note that if this is a put option on USD 10,000,000, then it represents a call option on CHF 12,195,000, which follows directly from the strike price. This option involves the opportunity to receive CHF 12,195,000 in exchange for USD 10,000,000. The USD put value, which is easier to think about because it uses the USD|CHF convention that we have become accustomed to, was CHF .0445 (that is, CHF .0445 per USD 1). This is analogous to the way equity option market participants usually think of option premium: It is in CHF per share, where here, a share refers to one U.S. Dollar. To get the total CHF premium, just scale by the number of Dollars that the option represents: CHF 445,000. And, for the record, just to add to the confusion, it would be common to hear this USD put premium quoted as "445," that is, 445 CHF pips per USD 1.

To quote in USD, we simply convert at spot: USD 356,000. There's no need to adjust for strike as the "notional amounts" take care of that for us. If we knew that the value of the CHF call was USD .0292 (or quoted in USD pips: USD 292 per CHF 1), we could have scaled this amount by our Swiss Franc notional and would have gotten to USD 356,000 this way as well; this reinforces the idea that we're doing things correctly.

One of the nice reasons for quoting pips per unit of currency is that the counterparty can simply scale up the premium for the notional option size they are contemplating. Another common approach in FX is to quote the option premium as a percentage of the face amount of either/both of the currencies. In the previous example, we believe the total USD premium is USD 356,000 on a USD face or notional of USD 10,000,000. It would be quoted as 3.56% of the USD face. Sometimes it disturbs people to hear that the percentage face in the other currency is more or less, but, especially when the option is in- or out-of-the-money, there's no reason why the two "piles" (to be exchanged through the option) have to have anywhere close to the same value. In our example, the CHF premium was CHF

445,000 on a notional of CHF 12,195,000; this translates to an option premium of 3.65%.

One last point (though we will not belabor it by going through the numbers): It is common in the interbank FX option market to hedge the option with the counterparty (especially if both sides of the trade are banks or broker/dealers). What this really involves is an option trade and an exchange of currency (in the spot market) analogous to doing a spot trade in conjunction with a forward trade. With options, traders will often talk about trading the "deltas" or the spot equivalent in order to be "hedged." That said, in FX, we sometimes go one step further. It is not uncommon to hedge the option premium, which may be perceived as involving an additional currency risk in conjunction with the underlying exposure that the FX option represents.

Finally, there is one additional way in which option premium is quoted in foreign exchange: volatility. There is a unique correspondence between volatility and option value/option premium. If you quote a volatility, it implies an option price. It is also true that if you see an option price in the market, this "implies" a volatility.

Our previous example did not incorporate a bid–ask spread as one would experience in the real marketplace. One can easily imagine a spread being placed around any of the preceding quotes. That said, one of the more common ways of quoting an option bid–ask is through a volatility market or "'vol' quote." Our example was based on an annualized volatility of σ = 10%. Since option values go up when vol goes up, and option values go down when vol goes down, one could quote volatility, which would then translate into our other quotes. The important point to note is that we can quote volatility (and understand each other) only if everyone else agrees on all of the other inputs to the model *and agrees on the model.* That is, everyone must be using the same model, which, in FX, even if you believe the Garman–Kohlhagen model is wrong, provides a useful tool for communication and remains the market standard.

A typical vol quote might be 9.90–10.10 (indicating that the dealer would buy the option in question on a σ = 9.90% volatility, putting that number into their option valuation model and deriving the price or premium bid, and the dealer would sell that option on a 10.10% volatility. This vol bid–ask would result in a bid–offer for the option in our earlier premium example of CHF 441,000 at CHF 450,400.[11] This specific vol quote would be given for a particular currency pair for a particular expiration and for a particular strike price.

Let's summarize these methods of FX option premium quotation in Figure 9.8.

FIGURE 9.8 Methods of Quoting Option Premium

For a USD|CHF option, the option premium could be quoted in terms of

Total CHF amount

Total USD amount

(or could even be quoted in terms of EUR or JPY for premium payment, though this would be relatively unusual).

CHF pips per USD 1.

USD pips per CHF 1.

% of the USD face amount.

% of the CHF face amount.

Volatility (in terms of % per year).

FX OPTION PREMIUM EXERCISE #3

You telephone an FX option dealer/bank and ask for a three-month ($t = .25$) at-the-money European option on EUR|JPY on a notional of EUR 40,000,000. Spot is currently trading at $S = 140.00$, Japanese interest rates are 1.00%, and Euro rates are 5.00%.
The dealer/bank quotes the premium in Yen pips: 263.

1. What is the strike price, X?
2. What is this option (i.e., call or put, on what currency)?
3. Calculate the option premium in terms of total EUR, total JPY, percent of Euro face, percent of Yen face, and in terms of Euro pips per Yen.

VOLATILITY

If you ask option traders what they do, many will say, "We trade 'vol.'" They really trade options (calls and puts), but they think about the volatility value embedded in those options.

One of the stranger notions associated with volatility is that there are several types of volatility. There is **historical volatility**, which one would think would be cut and dried, but this is open to interpretation. For starters, although historical volatility is calculated giving equal weight to all of the observations in the sample, the volatility will be determined by the data that you examine; one person may look at three years of data, another may look at three months of data. Further, even if two people looked at the same time horizon (e.g., one year), one might examine high frequency or "tick" data while the other may look at daily (e.g., "closing") prices. Most FX option traders will tell you that past volatility doesn't matter; that it is really future volatility that they care about. Equity option traders are generally more interested in historical volatility than their FX counterparts because equity volatility is said to exhibit a property known as "mean reversion," which is simply a fancy expression to indicate that, while volatility may jump or drop relative to its typical historical level (that is, there is volatility to volatility), it tends to drift back to its long-term average over time.

Since options (like many financial market instruments) are forward looking, perhaps one would like to try to **forecast** future **volatility**. Time-series models have been developed that use past data in an to attempt to arrive at a best guess of a future variable. In this sense, estimated or forecast volatility sounds like historical, but a time-series model will typically not give equal weight to the observations in your sample, typically placing greater weight on the more recent observations. One class of these models, Generalized Auto-Regressive Conditional Heteroskedasticity (GARCH) models, has received a great deal of attention in the financial community.

Actual future **volatility**, which is what an option trader would really like to know, is potentially different from historical and forecast volatility, but, unfortunately, you cannot know it in advance, until it happens—in which case it will be historical volatility and some traders would go on to say that then it doesn't matter.

The most talked about volatility among option market participants is **implied volatility**. This is most easily explained with reference to a diagram; see Figure 9.9. Instead of inputting a volatility into the option valuation model and generating a theoretical value, one can input the option's market price or premium (backwards) into the model and solve for the volatility that, in conjunction with the other inputs (spot price, strike price,

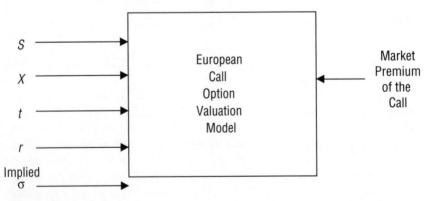

FIGURE 9.9 Implied Volatility

interest rate, and time), arrives at an option value that is equal to the option's market premium. Compare this graph to Figure 9.5.

In some sense, at any point in time, if three-month USD|CHF implied volatility is 10.00%, then this must be the market's opinion about how this currency pair will fluctuate or oscillate over the next 90 days or so. This leads to what at first appears to be a possible contradiction. If you look at a low-strike three-month European (out-of-the-money put) option, an at-the-money three-month European (call or put) option, and a high-strike three-month European (out-of-the-money call) option, one would think that these should all trade on the same implied volatility. But no! How can the market have more than one opinion on how USD|CHF will fluctuate over the next three months? Good question.

What one actually observes is known as the "volatility smile." If one were to plot the implied volatilities of these three different three-month USD|CHF options, they might very well all be different. See Figure 9.10. Traders tend to "explain" this by appealing to "demand and supply"; financial engineers are more likely to indicate that the model (and in particular,

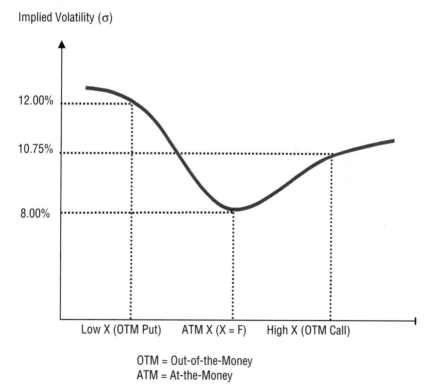

FIGURE 9.10 Volatility Smile

the probability distribution reflecting where the spot price might be in the future) is wrong, that is to say, the real world (or at least the market's perception of the real world) does not align with the model. The volatility smile is the market's reflection that the model does not conform to reality. Usually the "wings" (that is to say, the out-of-the-money or low-delta options) are "bid" or priced higher (in volatility terms) over the at-the-money options. Furthermore, the lower strike (put) options may have a higher implied volatility than the same (but different sign) delta higher strike (call) options; FX option traders refer to this asymmetry as "skew." There is a third explanation for the volatility smile. If you believe, as the spot price moves, that the volatility on which any given option will change, then this, too, could generate a vol smile. Usually, the longer-dated the option (that is, the further off the option's expiration), the less prominent the vol smile (i.e., the vol smile tends to flatten out). Regardless of its justification or rationalization, vol smiles are a real phenomenon in the FX options market.

Finally, just as different strike options with the same maturity have different implied volatilities, it is also the case that different maturity options (typically looked at in reference to those at-the-money forward), will also have different implied volatilities. The graphical representation of this "term structure of volatility" is most commonly referred to as a "volatility

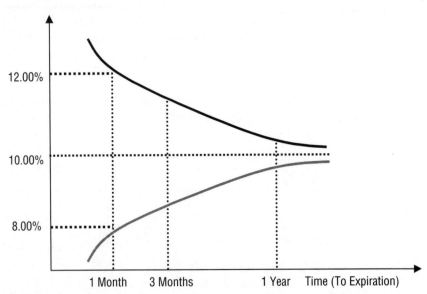

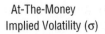

FIGURE 9.11   Volatility Cones

cone." Vol cones (as pictured in Figure 9.11) often look like either the upper curve or the lower curve (depending on whether near-term events are more or less volatile relative to the long-term historical volatility).

Exchange-traded FX option marketmakers want to know two things every morning before going to work on the floor: What are the at-the-money volatilities (for the different expirations) and what do the volatility smiles look like? They are able to "back out" implied volatility by looking at the at-the-money (forward) options; the norm is to see where the at-the-money **straddle** (a long straddle is made up of a long call and a long put with the same strike price) is quoted/trading. They then look at the 25 delta **risk reversal**, another spread that compares the out-of-the-money 25Δ call (say, long) versus the out-of-the-money −25Δ put (say, short) to see if the market was "leaning" more toward the "upside" (higher spot prices in the future) or toward the "downside," (which would then be labeled "puts over calls").

There are actually other types of volatility as well: seasonal volatility, historical implied volatility, stochastic (or variable) volatility, and so on, but further exposition would take us beyond the scope of this book.

How do foreign exchange volatilities compare with volatilities in other financial product areas? A typical U.S. equity volatility (including NAS-DAQ stocks) might be between 25% and 40%. Equity indices (like the S&P 500 and Russell 2000) tend to have volatilities lower than the average volatility of their constituent securities, because on any given day some stocks will be up and some stocks will be down; common equity index volatilities range from 15% to 25%. What about FX? Today, many FX options on the major currencies trade on implied volatilities between 8% and 12% (with the majority of FX implied volatilities ranging from 5% to 16%), which many find interesting given that there is nothing concrete behind the U.S. Dollar (so one might think it would be more protean or variable or "volatile" than, say, IBM stock).

Given that volatility is one way the FX markets talk about options (through the mechanism of quoting option premium in volatility terms), some familiarity with this idea is essential for FX market participants.

USES AND STRATEGIES

How do market participants use FX options? Options are used to hedge risks that one does not want and to implement one's view on the market.

Though hedging activity may be more common, let's start with a purely speculative use of FX options. Global macro hedge funds usually enjoy the flexibility to position their portfolio opportunistically based on current economic conditions. Let's be explicit and walk through a (mildly realistic) scenario.

Assume that we are in the midst of the Asian crisis several years ago. USD|JPY spot is at $S = 125.00$. The belief is that this situation will get worse before it gets better (in the sense that Asia is in for relatively difficult times). Your personal view is that, in one year, USD|JPY spot will be trading around 142.00. Also, for the record, the one-year forward is quoted and trading at $F = 120.24$. What can you do? Your first thought should be to buy USD spot = Sell JPY spot. This, though, may limit the size of your exposure (based on your available financial capital). You can generally take on a larger (or more levered or leveraged) position using forwards (specifically, buying USD forward = selling JPY forward), but, although you think spot in one year will be around 142, you do not **know** that it will be around 142; a large forward position would be risky. This, then, brings us to options. It says in most textbooks that if you buy options, the worst that you can do is to lose your option premium. Options provide leverage and generally trade at a fraction of the price of the underlying asset. But which option? Under these circumstances, you would want a USD call (= JPY put). Since we quote USD|JPY in terms of Yen per Dollar, let's think of this in terms of the USD call. But which one?

Let's limit your choices to the following one-year European options (quoted in JPY pips per USD 1): the 100 call, the 120 call, the 125 call, the 130 call, the 135 call, the 140 call, and the 141.50 call. The premiums and returns (if held till expiration and S in one year actually does end up at $S = 142.00$) are found in Table 9.1.

TABLE 9.1 Speculative Example

These are all one-year European calls (USD call = JPY put)

	Premium	Return (in JPY per USD 1 if $S = 142$ in 1 year)
Buy S	125.0000	13.60%
100 Call	20.1774	108.15%
120 Call	4.8622	352.47%
125 Call	2.8448	497.58%
130 Call	1.5388	679.83%
135 Call	.7704	808.26%
140 Call	.3580	458.66%
141.50 Call	.2806	78.19%

Sample Calculations

Spot: Buy USD 1 for 125; in one year, sell for 142; 142/125 = 1.1360 or 13.60% return.

125 C: Buy 125C for 2.8448; in one year, worth 17.00; 17/2.8448 = 5.9758 or 497.58% return.

Had you simply bought USD 1 spot for JPY 125.00, then your return (in JPY) would have been 13.6% (not a bad return at all), but you see the magnification effect you get with options. That said, if you buy the 141.50 call and spot goes to 141.50 (so you were almost exactly right), you don't get zero; what you get is a −100% rate of return on your investment. The point of this example is to show that, given your view (and this is as true for a hedging situation as a speculative play), one option may look more attractive than the others. This general idea, which is referred to colloquially as "strike selection," recognizes that, with options, one needs to consider which strike price, as well as what expiration date best fits one's views and needs.

One can consider scenario analysis (if S in one year, for example, were to equal 138 or 155) and also sketch out the breakeven graphs. The "breakeven" graph for the 125 call is pictured in Figure 9.12; the "breakeven spot price" is $S^* = 127.84$. Most textbooks identify the breakeven price as that spot price at expiration that gives you your money (your premium) back, but this is misleading. If you *knew* (for certain) that the spot price in one year was going to be $S = 127.84$, then

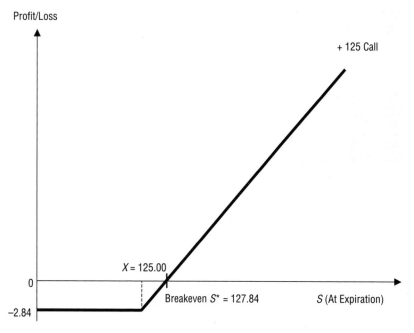

FIGURE 9.12   FX Option Breakeven (The 125.00 Call on USD 1 with an Option Premium of JPY 2.84)

you would rather sell this option, put the money into the bank (even if all you got on your premium was the Japanese interest rate of 1%), and buy the option back at expiration for 2.84 in a year. My point is that breakeven analysis must be taken lightly; it confuses money today (the option premium) and money in the future (the option payoff or option value at expiration). That said, many traders will talk "breakevens" for shorter dated trades, where the difference in the timing of the cash flows is less of an issue.

FX OPTION BREAKEVEN GRAPH EXERCISE #4

1. Sketch the P/L (profit/loss) or breakeven graph of a long three-month 125.00 put with a premium of 6.58. Identify the breakeven spot price, S^*. Does it matter whether this is a three-month option or a one-year option? Briefly explain.

Now let's consider a more realistic, hedging example. If a U.S. corporation sells its product in Europe and has Euro receivables, then, like many U.S. corporations, it may simply sell their EUR (= buy USD) forward. But if this corporate Treasury had reason to believe that the EUR was going to strengthen against the USD (especially if the forward points are negative), they might be inclined not to lock in the rate at which they repatriate their profits. Further, they might be concerned that their global competitors will not hedge, enjoy the expected EUR appreciation, and outperform their financials for this year. At any rate, not hedging may be an option, but there would be risk if the EUR weakened (= USD strengthened); this would mean that the EUR receivables would translate into fewer USD in the future. For this reason, a corporation might think about buying a EUR put (= USD call). Of course, which call depends on a number of considerations.

To be explicit, assume EUR|USD $S = 1.2500$, let's say there are three months left in the year, and the three-month forward is quoted at $F = 1.2380$. As corporate treasurer, the forward sale of your Euro is unappealing at 1.2380; then again, the risk of not hedging is not comforting. So you consider a EUR put (= USD call). Which one? You can buy the 1.2500 put, the 1.2250 put, and the 1.2000 put. Their respective premiums are (quoted in USD per EUR 1): .0300, .0150, and .0100. You may decide that the slightly out-of-the-money option (the 1.2250 put) is the most attractive at USD .0150 (1½ U.S. pennies per Euro). How much can you lose? That actually depends on how you account for both the currency and the option. Nevertheless, if EUR|USD spikes to 1.3600, you'll receive a windfall gain on your long Euro, which you didn't sell out at 1.2380. If EUR|USD falls to 1.0000, you'll feel like Rocky for having bought this option ("saving" the company around 22.5 cents per Euro, though independent of the cost of the option). What is the worst case scenario? Most would say that it occurs if EUR|USD ends up exactly at 1.2250. In this case, you get nothing back from your hedge and you've lost your option premium (USD .0150). Well, at least the textbooks say that the worst thing you can do is lose your option premium. Wrong! In this case, you would lose USD .0250 (relative to the original spot) or at least USD .0130 (relative to the forward) per Euro 1 as well as the option premium of USD .0150. This is similar to a statement about automobile insurance: "All it can cost you is the insurance premium." If you have a USD 1,000 deductible built into your insurance policy (which is like using out-of-the-money options to hedge), you are obliged to incur some of the cost before your insurance kicks in. When you use options as part of a portfolio, you have to be careful about any statement that starts with, "All you can lose. . . ."

There was an interesting exchange (in print) a number of years ago between Ian Giddy and Christopher Bourdain in the magazine *Derivative Strategy* regarding the corporate use of FX options;[12] the interested reader is strongly encouraged to obtain, review, and evaluate their arguments.

Some FX option market participants will identify a specific option (like the 1.2250 Euro put in our last example), but, on the FX options desk, one is just as likely to hear a request for a 20Δ call, an option that costs USD 4,000, or an option that is 10% out-of-the-money.

As a final wrap-up, we include, in Figures 9.13 and 9.14, two screen shots of typical foreign exchange option trading tools. The option in question is a one-month European at-the-money (ATMF standing for "at-the-money-forward") EUR|USD call (call on Euro = put on Dollars) written on a notional of EUR 1,000,000. The premium is quoted (with a bid–ask spread) as a percent of the Euro face amount. The commentary box on the first screen identifies this as a 50 delta call (requiring an exchange of EUR 500,000 [50% of the Euro notional] as a hedge). The second screen shows a tool known as FENICS FX (pronounced "Fee-niks" as in "phoenix" and, tongue-in-cheek, standing for "Foreign Exchange Nuclear Interplanetary Computing System"); FENICS has been the industry standard FX option trading tool since the 1980s. Created by Peter Cyrus (recognized by *Risk*

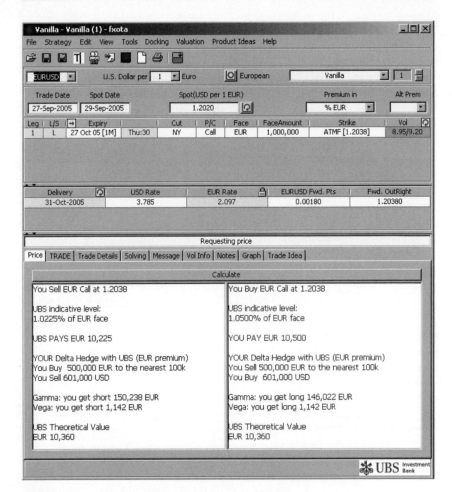

FIGURE 9.13   Typical FX Option Trading Tool (UBS)
Source: © 2006 UBS Investment Bank. Reprinted by permission.

magazine as one of the 50 most important individuals in derivatives and risk management (see *Risk*: December 2002) and now owned by GFI Group Inc., it values the same option with the same parameters in a slightly different format.

Finally, the only aspect that is not explained is the "cut." Most FX options are either New York-cut or Tokyo-cut; this indicates the precise time

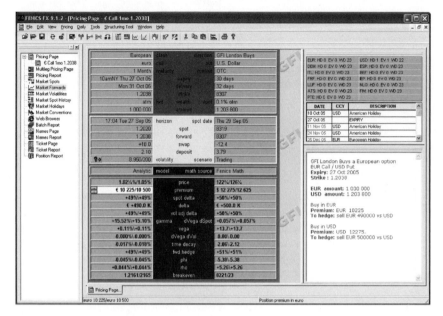

FIGURE 9.14 FENICS Option Screen Shot
Source: FENICS, GFI Group Inc.

of expiration. A New York-cut FX option will expire at 10:00 A.M. New York (U.S. East Coast) time, whereas a Tokyo-cut FX option will expire at 3:00 P.M. local time in Japan.

One Last Thing

Foreign exchange options are very powerful tools for the management of financial risk, but, like any power tools, they should be well understood and used appropriately. It is our hope that this chapter has been a useful review of the most important elements in support of this objective.

APPENDIX: Theoretical Option Valuation

". . . traders now use the formula and its variants extensively. They use it so much that market prices are usually close to formula values even in situations where there should be a large difference."[1]

—Response by Fischer Black to an assertion that the Black–Scholes Model is one of the most successful theories in all finance and economics

THE BINOMIAL MODEL

Although the binomial model first appeared six years after the Black–Scholes model was published,[2] it is usually taught to students first (as the requisite mathematics are more elementary); it can, in the limit, reproduce Black–Scholes option values, and it is much more generally applicable (that is, it can value a much broader range of options) than Black–Scholes.

Like with all models, the standard binomial model makes a number of simplifying assumptions. Typically, it is assumed that there are no transaction costs, no commissions, no bid–ask spreads, no taxes, perfect markets [in the sense that one can trade as much (underlying) as one wishes and there will not be any impact on the market price], no issues associated with selling an asset you do not have, full use of short stock proceeds, one constant interest rate, and a constant volatility (associated with the returns) of the underlying asset. Of course, many of these assumptions can be relaxed, but we stick to the most elementary case.

As Louis Bachelier understood in his now famous dissertation, "Theorie de la Speculation" (1900), you have to "model" spot price movements before you "model" option values. The assumption in the classical binomial and Black–Scholes cases is that there is multiplicative uncertainty (also known as Geometric Brownian Motion). What this means is that the (unknown) spot price in the future is a scaled version of the current spot price (scaled up or scaled down); that's the "bi" in "binomial." The spot price is assumed to take on one of only two possible spot prices in the future. In an example of the generic binomial case, the spot price "process" is as pictured in Figure 9A.1.

Interestingly, this process is, in general, not symmetric. The asymmetry is more pronounced (although usually not graphed to scale in the textbooks) when there are more time "steps" than one. In Figure 9A.1, the time frame (that is, the time till expiration) is one year ($t = 1$) and the time step, sometimes represented by dt, is one year ($dt = 1$), but the time step

Spot Price

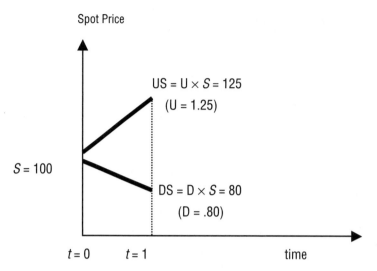

FIGURE 9A.1 One-Step Binomial Spot Price Process

can be a year ($dt = 1$), a quarter of a year ($dt = \frac{1}{4}$), a month, a day, an hour, a minute, or a second.

The Classical Nondividend-Paying Stock Binomial Model Example

Assume the spot price is currently at $S = 100$ and that in one year (here, we assume that $t = dt = 1$), S can either go to 125 or 80. The upper spot price will be denoted by US (really $U \times S$) and here $US = 125$, so $U = 1.25$. Similarly, the lower spot price will be denoted by $DS = 80$, and so $D = .80$. U and D reflect the multiplicative uncertainty.

Let's consider the one-year European 115 call. Although we don't know what the option is worth today (yet), we know exactly what this option is worth at expiration. If you own the 115 call and spot at expiration is $US = 125$, this call option is worth 10. If $DS = 80$ at expiration, the 115 call is worthless (i.e., worth 0).

In general, a call will be worth the following: $\text{Max}[(S_{\text{EXPIRATION}} - X), 0]$ where this simply means the maximum of either the difference between "the spot price at expiration and the strike price" or "zero," whichever is larger. In our specific example, if spot were to go up, the 115 call option value at expiration will be denoted C_U (where, here, the "U" is simply a subscript indicating that spot went "up") and we can write $C_U = \text{Max}[(US - X), 0] = \text{Max}[(125 - 115), 0] = 10$. Similarly, if spot were to drop to $DS = 80$, we would write $C_D = \text{Max}[(DS - X) 0] = \text{Max}[(80 - 115), 0] = 0$.

Now what is the option worth today? We need a little more information. We know $S = 100$, $X = 115$, $t = 1$, and, given our spot process, we actually know something about volatility (though not as an annualized percentage number). What we still need to know is the interest rate, r. Remember, there is assumed to be one constant volatility associated with the underlying and one constant interest rate. Assume the interest rate $r = 6.00\%$.

Now, stepping back for a moment, we know that buying a call makes you "long the underlying," so one could, in principle, "hedge" or offset the spot price risk by trading (more specifically, selling) the correct amount (Δ) of the underlying.

$$+C - \Delta S \qquad (9A.1)$$

An old floor trader once told me that "to hedge" meant to do a trade in order to try to Hold (or capture) the **EDGE** (or theoretical profit) in your trade. One would be successfully hedged if the outcome is the same whether the spot price goes up or down. What amount (Δ) of spot should you trade today in order to be hedged?

Let's start at the end and work backward. If you're trying to create a hedged portfolio (long call and short delta spot or "$+ C - \Delta S$") and you want to achieve the same outcome regardless of whether S goes up or down (or, said another way, if you wish to be indifferent to the spot price rising or falling), then this would imply that, at expiration,

$$C_U - \Delta US = C_D - \Delta DS \qquad (9A.2)$$

Rearranging this expression results in the following

$$\Delta = \frac{C_U - C_D}{US - DS} \qquad (9A.3)$$

which is strangely similar to our definition of delta. In our example, $\Delta = (10-0)/(125-80) = .2222$.

The Black–Scholes insight was based on the fact that, in this model, the only risk comes from the spot price (the sole source of uncertainty). The strike price, volatility, and the interest rate are all assumed constant, and, although time will pass, it is not a risk per se. Thus, if one is able to construct a "hedged" or "riskless" or **"risk-free" portfolio** ($+C - \Delta S$), Black and Scholes noted that it ought to return the risk free rate of interest; in other words, it's like a default-free bond. To keep it simple, if a bond today is worth B, then the value of the bond in the future, using simple interest, should be worth $B(1 + rt)$.

Manipulating the following,

$$+C - \Delta S = B$$
$$C_U - \Delta US = C_D - \Delta DS = B(1 + rt) \qquad (9A.4)$$

Using either the first or second terms, we can get an expression for B. The final step simply involves a rearrangement of the first equation of (9A.4).

Solving for C, we get

$$C = \Delta S + B \qquad (9A.5)$$

(and the expression for B, for the record, will be a negative number).

This is known as the **"replicating portfolio."**

What is a call option? It is an instrument that makes you (effectively) long the underlying asset (here the stock) and short the money to purchase it (a stock call is a Dollar put). How long the stock are you? Delta long. How short the cash? B short. Now, substituting the expressions of Δ and B into equation (9A.5) and rearranging a bit, we get

$$C = \frac{1}{(1+rt)}\left[\left(\frac{(1+rt)-D}{U-D}\right)C_U + \left(\frac{U-(1+rt)}{U-D}\right)C_D\right] \qquad (9A.6)$$

though it is usually written in a manner similar to the following

$$C = \frac{1}{(1+rt)}[pC_U + (1-p)C_D] \qquad (9A.7)$$

where

$$p = \left[\frac{(1+rt)-D}{U-D}\right] \qquad (9A.8)$$

but sometimes is written using continuous (as opposed to simple) interest. In our example, $p = .5778$ (rounded to the fourth decimal place) and $C = 5.45$.

Equation (9A.7) seems to indicate that an option's value can be viewed as the present value of some future payoff, where p looks like the probability (and, indeed, it will behave like a probability) that the spot price goes up (and, therefore, results in the payoff C_U).

Interestingly, if we ask what the expected future spot price will be with this "pseudo" or "risk neutral" probability, p, we find that

$$pUS + (1-p)DS = (1+rt)S = F \qquad (9A.9)$$

The term "p" acts like that probability that makes the expected future spot price equal to the forward price.

In general, we can derive the call option value process from the spot process. Graphically, this is pictured in Figure 9A.2.

There is a similar looking relationship for a European put:

$$P = \frac{1}{(1+rt)}[pP_U + (1-p)P_D] \qquad (9A.10)$$

Call Option Value

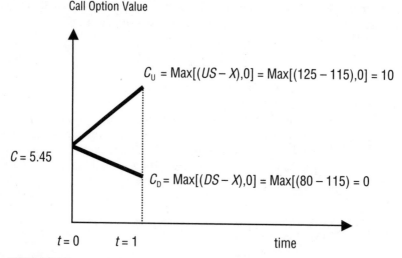

$C_U = \text{Max}[(US - X),0] = \text{Max}[(125 - 115),0] = 10$

$C = 5.45$

$C_D = \text{Max}[(DS - X),0] = \text{Max}[(80 - 115) = 0$

$t = 0$ $t = 1$ time

FIGURE 9A.2 One-Step Binomial Call Option Value Process

where

$$P_U = \text{Max}[(X - US),0]$$
$$P_D = \text{Max}[(X - DS),0]$$

p is the same as before, as in equation (9A.8). Just to be sure we're on the same page, which is likely larger, P_U or P_D?

If we attempt to extend this approach to value a two-year option ($t = 2$), but we continue to let each time step be one year ($dt = 1$), the spot process would look like that pictured in Figure 9A.3. Note that the second year spot price process is simply the first year spot prices scaled by the same multipliers, U and D; note also the asymmetry in future spot prices that is implied by the assumption of constant volatility. The analogy (not using numbers from our example) is that if spot starts at 100 and goes up 20%, it goes to 120, and if it goes up another 20%, it will end up at 144, whereas if spot starts at 100 and goes down 20%, it goes to 80, and if it goes down another 20%, it will end up at 64. Spot could go up 44, but down only 36.

To see the impact of extending the expiration date, let's value the two-year European 115 call option (in other words, let's leave the strike price the same). What would you guess would happen to this call option's value?

The call valuation approach is the same as for a one-step process, again starting at expiration. Indeed, the relationship we derived earlier is

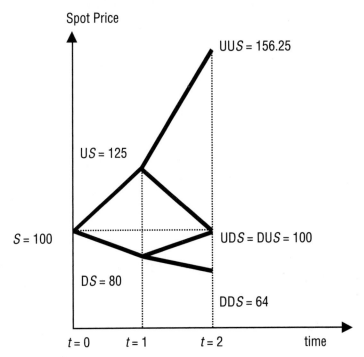

FIGURE 9A.3 Two-Step Binomial Spot Price Process

still applicable on a "node by node" basis, but we have to be careful about the notation and the subscripts:

$$C_{UU} = \text{Max}[(UUS - X),0] = \text{Max}[(156.25-115),0] = 41.25$$
$$C_{UD} = C_{DU} = \text{Max}[(UDS - X),0] = \text{Max}[(100-115),0] = 0$$
$$C_{DD} = \text{Max}[(DDS - X),0] = \text{Max}[(94-115),0] = 0$$

Interestingly, *p* is exactly the same as before, but each point on our "binomial tree" will have its own delta (Δ):

$$\Delta_U = \frac{C_{UU} - C_{UD}}{UUS - UDS}$$

$$\Delta_D = \frac{C_{DU} - C_{DD}}{DUS - DDS}$$

The implication is that one would have to dynamically hedge (i.e., rehedge) at each step.

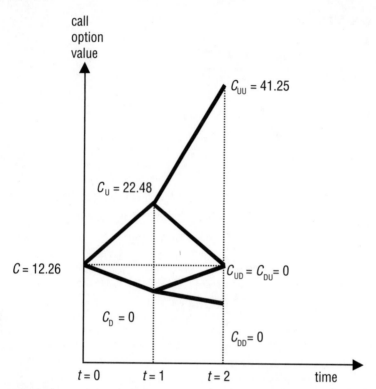

FIGURE 9A.4 Two-Step Binomial Call Option Value Process

The fundamental option valuation relationship is "recursive" (i.e., is applied over and over). Here we find that $C_U = 22.48$ ($\Delta_U = .7333$), $C_D = 0$ ($\Delta_D = 0$), and so the two-year European 115 call value is $C = 12.26$ with an initial delta of $\Delta = .4996$ (as first defined). See Figure 9A.4.

If instead of our relationship equation (9A.7), which must hold at each and every step (otherwise, there is an arbitrage), we wanted a formula for a two-year, two-step European call, it would look like this:

$$C = \left(\frac{1}{(1+rt)}\right)^2 \left[p^2 C_{UU} + 2p(1-p)C_{UD} + (1-p)^2 C_{DD}\right] \quad (9A.11)$$

The reason we spell this out is because we would like to draw an analogy to the Black-Scholes equation (which refers to a process) and the Black-Scholes formula.

The FX Binomial Model

The earlier arguments for the classic binomial model on a nondividend-paying stock all continue to hold, but we need to make one adjustment and one clarification. First, when one calculates delta (the hedge ratio) with FX as the underlying, you should "present value your deltas." That is, the asset that is being used to hedge "grows," so the correct spot delta for FX options will look like this:

$$\Delta = \left(\frac{1}{(1+r_2 t)}\right)\left[\frac{C_U - C_D}{US - DS}\right] \tag{9A.12}$$

where r_2 is the interest rate associated with the asset (currency) that is being used as a hedge. Ultimately, this derives from our original hedging relationship:

$$C_U - \Delta US = C_D - \Delta DS$$

but recognizing that, in the case of foreign exchange (which receives interest), this would really look like this:

$$C_U - \Delta(1+r_2 t)US = C_D - \Delta(1 + r_2 t)DS$$

One share of stock, in a year, is still one share of stock, whereas one Dollar today will not be one Dollar in a year. This was the "adjustment."

The clarification involves our p. Rewriting the earlier equation (9A.8):

$$p = \left[\frac{(1+rt) - D}{U - D}\right]$$

we need to know which rate goes into this relationship. I think the easiest way to see what r goes in here is to return to equation (9A.9):

$$p\, US + (1-p)\, DS = F$$

but, in FX, we know that

$$F = S\left[\frac{(1+r_1 t)}{(1+r_2 t)}\right]$$

so, we should really rewrite p as

$$p = \left[\frac{\left[\frac{(1+r_1 t)}{(1+r_2 t)}\right] - D}{U - D}\right] \tag{9A.13}$$

This works more elegantly with continuous interest, where we could write

$$p = \left[\frac{e^{rt} - D}{U - D} \right]$$

and

$$p\text{US} + (1 - p)\text{DS} = Se^{rt} = F = Se^{(r_1 - r_2)t}$$

so

$$p = \left[\frac{e^{(r_1 - r_2)t} - D}{U - D} \right] \tag{9A.14}$$

and so the r in the p relationship is actually $(r_1 - r_2)$ from the spot-forward scaling factor.

A practical modeling consideration: You should use many small time steps (dt "small"). In the limit (and the math necessary to prove this is beyond the scope of this book), the binomial model values will approach the Black–Scholes values.

THE BLACK–SCHOLES/GARMAN–KOHLHAGEN MODEL

The only difference between the binomial model and the Black–Scholes Model is the way in which time is handled. In the binomial approach, time is treated as a discrete variable (e.g., an integer such as $t = 0, 1, 2, \ldots$ or as taking predetermined time "steps" as in the following sequence where $dt = \frac{1}{4}$: $t = 0, \frac{1}{4}, \frac{1}{2}, \frac{3}{4}, 1, \ldots$) and as such time moves in distinct increments, whereas the Black–Scholes approach assumes that time is a continuous variable and that time flows. As a matter of fact, the usual assumption is that returns (properly defined) are normally (in a formal statistical sense) distributed. If returns are assumed to be normally distributed, then prices are assumed to be what is referred to as "lognormally" distributed.

By essentially following the same arguments as we did in the binomial case, we arrive at criteria that must hold at each and every point in time (else an arbitrage exists). This is (a second-order differential equation) known as the Black–Scholes Equation:

$$\frac{\partial C}{\partial t} + rC = rS \frac{\partial C}{\partial S} + \frac{1}{2}\sigma^2 S^2 \frac{\partial^2 C}{\partial S^2} \tag{9A.15}$$

While this may look daunting, it has a nice economic interpretation. In economics, everyone knows that optimal behavior (maximizing utility, maximizing profits, minimizing costs) involves doing things to that point where the marginal cost equals the marginal benefit. The left-hand side is the marginal cost associated with holding a call for a very small period of time (the decay, theta, or θ and the financing cost of the option = interest on the premium), while the right-hand side reflects the marginal benefit stemming from the fact that, through the call option, you are effectively long and (since the spot price is presumed to be headed up to the forward price) the price is going up (your delta) and your long exposure (or delta) will rise as spot goes up (the second-order exposure referred to as gamma).

This Black-Scholes Equation can be written using three of our option risk measures:

$$\theta + rC = rS\Delta + \frac{1}{2}\sigma^2 S^2 \Gamma \tag{9A.16}$$

Equations (9A.15) and (9A.16) are the analog to equation (9A.7); these indicate a relationship that has to hold at each and every point in time.

Solving this, in the simple Black–Scholes case which isn't that simple unless you've studied differential equations, results in the following Black-Scholes Formula (for a European call option):

$$C = S\,N(d_1) - X\,e^{-rt}\,N(d_2) \tag{9A.17}$$

where

$$d_1 = \frac{\ln\left(\dfrac{S}{X}\right) + \left(r + \dfrac{\sigma^2}{2}\right)t}{\sigma\sqrt{t}} \tag{9A.18}$$

$$d_2 = \frac{\ln\left(\dfrac{S}{X}\right) + \left(r + \dfrac{\sigma^2}{2}\right)t}{\sigma\sqrt{t}} = d_1 - \sigma\sqrt{t} \tag{9A.19}$$

and N(.) refers to the standard normal distribution (a statistical construct with nice mathematical properties).

Equation (9A.17) is analogous to equation (9A.11).

To be precise, a call makes you long spot. How long? Look at equation (9A.17). Here, $N(d_1)$ is your spot delta. A call option also makes you short cash (USD)? How short? In the extreme case of a deep, deep in-the-money call option, you might think it makes you short the strike price, X, but, in reality, you're not effectively short that entire amount today. As a matter of fact, even if you knew that you were going to have to hand over the strike price in the future, today you would effectively only be short the present value of that cash (i.e., you'd only have to set aside the present value of X: $X e^{-rt}$). And this assumes that the option *will* be exercised; the equivalent short cash position is contingent on the likelihood that the option will be exercised at expiration. It can be shown that $N(d_2)$ can be interpreted as "the probability that this option will end up in-the-money" or "the probability that this option will be exercised at expiration" (given our assumptions and in the risk neutral world where the expected future spot price is the forward price).

Maybe one last insight. Mildly adapting equation (9A.17), we could write

$$C = Se^{+rt} - r + N(d_1) - Xe^{-rt} N(d_2) = e^{-rt} [Se^{+rt} N(d_1) - X N(d_2)]$$
$$= e^{-rt}[F N(d_1) - X N(d_2)]$$

Recognizing that $N(d_1)$ and $N(d_2)$ are "probability-like" terms, the Black–Scholes Formula seems to say that an option's value is the present value of some expected future payoff where that payoff is based on the difference between the forward and the strike price. This should ring a bell with another relationship we saw earlier, namely put-call parity (equations (9.7) and (9.8)).

One of the nice things about a formula is that you can analyze it, graph it, and often derive some additional information from it. Some of the things that we might like to derive are our option risk measures or "Greeks" [and here, unlike when we defined the terms delta, gamma, theta, and so on, we would have to do the math (i.e., differentiation)].

Let's hold off and give the formulas for the FX option risk measures after introducing the Black–Scholes Formula for foreign exchange. Even though Robert Merton (1973) spelled out this case in print almost immediately after the original Black-Scholes Formula was published, the foreign exchange version of Black–Scholes has come to be known as the Garman–Kohlhagen Formula (presumably based on their publication in 1983). Several publications appeared that year dealing with European foreign exchange option valuation.

It should not be surprising to see that the FX version looks very similar to the original Black–Scholes Formula, but, just as we had to be careful with interest rates in the binomial case, we have to be careful here, too.

The Formula derives from the partial differential equation:

$$\frac{\partial C}{\partial t} + r_1 C = (r_1 - r_2)S\frac{\partial C}{\partial S} + \frac{1}{2}\sigma^2 S^2 \frac{\partial C^2}{\partial S^2}$$

For the case of European-style FX options, the Garman–Kohlhagen Formula looks like this:

$$C = S\, e^{-r_2 t}\, N(d_1) - X\, e^{-r_1 t}\, N(d_2) \tag{9A.20}$$

This should both make sense (based on our discussion of present valuing the hedge, which explains the extra discounting term in the first part of the Formula) and recall the FX put-call parity formula Equation (9.11).

What about the rest of the Formula (in particular, d_1 and d_2)? Since

$$d_1 = \frac{\ln\left(\dfrac{S}{X}\right) + \left(r + \dfrac{\sigma^2}{2}\right)t}{\sigma\sqrt{t}}$$

we need to know which r to use. As mentioned earlier, this r is the one that takes the spot price from S to F (and so, using continuous interest, for the Garman–Kohlhagen Formula),

$$d_1 = \frac{\ln\left(\dfrac{S}{X}\right) + \left((r_1 - r_2) + \dfrac{\sigma^2}{2}\right)t}{\sigma\sqrt{t}} \tag{9A.21}$$

which can be rearranged to give

$$d_1 = \frac{\ln\left(\dfrac{S e^{(r_1 - r_2)t}}{X}\right) + \left(\dfrac{\sigma^2}{2}\right)t}{\sigma\sqrt{t}} = \frac{\ln\left(\dfrac{F}{X}\right) + \left(\dfrac{\sigma^2}{2}\right)t}{\sigma\sqrt{t}}$$

and similarly for d_2:

$$d_2 = \frac{\ln\left(\dfrac{S}{X}\right) + \left((r_1 - r_2) - \dfrac{\sigma^2}{2}\right)t}{\sigma\sqrt{t}}$$

The Garman–Kohlhagen Formula for a European put value is

$$P = X\,e^{-r_1 t}\,N(-d_2) - S\,e^{-r_2 t}\,N(-d_1)$$

One last manipulation of the Garman–Kohlhagen call option value formula (9A.20):

$$
\begin{aligned}
C &= Se^{-r_2 t}N(d_1) - Xe^{-r_1 t}N(d_2) \\
&= Se^{-r_1 t}e^{+r_1 t}e^{-r_2 t}N(d_1) - Xe^{-r_1 t}N(d_2) \\
&= e^{-r_1 t}[Se^{(r_1-r_2)t}N(d_1) - XN(d_2)]
\end{aligned}
$$

or

$$C = e^{-r_1 t}[FN(d_1) - XN(d_2)] \qquad (9A.22)$$

Kind of reassuring, isn't it?

THE GARMAN–KOHLHAGEN OPTION RISK MEASURES OR "GREEKS"

We simply enumerate the following Garman–Kohlhagen risk measures associated with a European FX call option (without showing the derivations):

$$\text{Delta } (\Delta) = \frac{\partial C}{\partial S} = e^{-r_2 t}N(d_1)$$

$$\text{Gamma } (\Gamma) = \frac{\partial \Delta}{\partial S} = \frac{\partial^2 C}{\partial S^2} = \frac{e^{-r_2 t}\frac{\partial N(d_1)}{\partial d_1}}{\sigma S\sqrt{t}} = \frac{e^{-r_2 t}\frac{1}{\sqrt{2\pi}}e^{-\frac{(d_1)^2}{2}}}{\sigma S\sqrt{t}}$$

$$\text{Vega (or Tau) } (\nu \text{ or } \tau) = \frac{\partial C}{\partial \sigma} = e^{-r_1 t}S\sqrt{t}\frac{\partial N(d_2)}{\partial d_2} = e^{-r_2 t}\frac{S\sqrt{t}}{\sqrt{2\pi}}e^{-\frac{(d_1)^2}{2}}$$

For the record, Vega, which is not a Greek letter, has also been known as tau (τ)—at O'Connor and UBS, kappa (κ), lambda (λ), and zeta (ζ)

$$\text{Theta } (\theta) = \frac{\partial C}{\partial t} = -r_2 e^{-r_2 t}SN(d_1) + r_1 e^{-r_1 t}XN(d_2) + \frac{e^{-r_2 t}\sigma\frac{S1}{\sqrt{2\pi}}e^{-\frac{(d_1)^2}{2}}}{2\sqrt{t}}$$

Since there are two interest rates in the Garman–Kohlhagen Formula, we distinguish between

$$\text{Rho } (\rho) = \frac{\partial C}{\partial r_1} = te^{-r_1 t} XN(d_2)$$

and

$$\text{Phi } (\phi) = \frac{\partial C}{\partial r_2} = -te^{-r_2 t} SN(d_1)$$

There is sometimes talk of other higher-order risk measures, many recognized as having been popularized (or at least "labeled") by Mark Garman (of Garman–Kohlhagen fame) which have been called "charm" (the change in delta given a change in time), "speed" (the change in gamma given a change in the underlying spot price), and "color" or "colour" (the change in Gamma given a change in time). An industry-standard FX option tool/platform called FENICs also lists "vanna" (the change in delta given a change in volatility) and "vomma" (the change in vega given a change in volatility) which at least sounds like "vol gamma."

There is also "Omega" (ω or, more commonly, Ω), which measures the elasticity of an option's value to changes in the underlying spot price (more precisely, the percentage change in the option's value divided by the percentage change in the spot price). This is often considered to be a measure of an option's "leverage."

Anyone interested in pursuing the formal mathematical modelling of these options is directed to any of a number of excellent references that are available today, one of which is *Options, Futures, and Exotic Derivatives: Theory, Application and Practice* by Eric Brys et al.

CHAPTER 10

Exotic Options and Structured Products

Creations proceeding from our own heat-oppress'd brains.
—Mark Rubinstein

While the options proposed by the academics were cute and exemplified some interesting theoretical problems in option valuation, surely they were not to be taken seriously by men and women of practical affairs.
—Mark Rubinstein

the economic equivalent of crack cocaine
—George Soros

WHAT IS AN EXOTIC OPTION?

Perhaps the best definition of an "exotic option" that I have heard comes from Robert Jarrow, a professor at Cornell University. Jarrow defines an exotic option as "anything but vanilla." By this he means any option that has any associated feature that differs from a standard European (and some would extend this to include a standard American) option.

If you were to characterize the two primary reasons why people use options, they would be "to hedge" and "to implement a view on the market." Why would someone use an exotic option? In short, to either get more tailored financial "insurance" or to position a more precise "view" (or some would substitute "bet") on the market. Having said that, the majority of salespeople whose clients use these products would say that they use exotic options because they are "cheaper." This assertion has always troubled a financial engineer that I know, who tends to respond to that statement, "You get what you pay for." Nevertheless, an exotic option often involves a lower option premium than the otherwise identical vanilla option, but there are good reasons why. We return to valuation later.

Derivatives over the years have received a great deal of negative press—for a variety of reasons. The majority of the disasters date back to the early 1990s. Some of the higher profile names involved in these include Metalgessellschaft, Gibson Greeting, Bankers Trust, Procter and Gamble, Barings Bank, Orange County, and Long Term Capital Management (LTCM). Some banks even stopped using the appellation "derivative," replacing it with the less emotionally-charged expression "risk management product." It is my opinion, to paraphrase the long-standing opinion put forth by the National Rifle Association, that derivatives don't kill people, people kill people. Many of the derivative incidents, which resulted from a variety of mistakes, ultimately were not caused by the derivative products themselves (the forwards, futures, swaps, calls, puts, and structured notes), but from some aspect of human error: a bad trade, a mismatch between cash flows, selling and/or buying an inappropriate product, excessive leverage, and downright fraud. Many of these regrettable incidents still could have happened even in the absence of derivatives. Gary Gastineau, under the "derivative instrument or product" entry in his *Dictionary of Financial Risk Management*, gives, among other more precise formal characterizations, the tongue-in-cheek definition:

> "in the financial press, any product that loses money."[1]

Many of us in the financial community today, given the opportunity, would probably choose to characterize "exotic options" with a different label. The most natural would be the identification of those options that have some sort of "other than vanilla" feature or features as "nonstandard options." Exotic vacation destinations, exotic drinks, exotic dancers, exotic options. Who wouldn't want to buy an exotic option? Some have tried to rename these instruments "second-generation" options, "path-dependent" options (though not all exotic options are path dependent), and so on, but, unfortunately, the expression "exotic option" is probably too deeply ingrained at this point (at least in FX) to attempt to change it.

Exotic Currencies

As always, in FX, there may be confusion with the expression "exotic." For some, trading exotic currency might involve trading less liquid or downright uncommon currency pairs, such as Namibian Dollars against the Russian Ruble.

NONSTANDARD OPTIONS

What can be nonstandard about an option? Just about everything! The type of option may be nonstandard. With a typical European call or put, the payoff is a linear function of the underlying (spot) price (at expiration), but there are options (for example digital or binary options) which have a constant (nonlinear) payoff. Also, there are power options in which the payoff is nonlinear. An option's underlying is typically a traded asset, but an exotic option may have a payoff based on some nontraded underlying (such as the weather or volatility). Also, a standard call option typically has a payoff based on the level of the underlying asset price at expiration in relation to the strike or exercise price; for a standard European call, we can write

$$C = \text{Max}[(S_{\text{EXPIRATION}} - X), 0]$$

Imagine the following scenario (for which a three-month call was purchased as a hedge against rising spot prices): ABC Corporation uses oil in the manufacture of their product and are disadvantaged when oil prices rise. Crude oil is currently trading at $S = $ USD 58 per bbl and the concern is that oil prices may jump. To "hedge" this oil price risk, ABC might choose to purchase a three-month out-of-the-money call on oil, struck at $X = 60$. As feared, oil prices spike and remain around 75 for almost the entire three months, but drop down and dip below 60 on expiration. You receive nothing back from your hedge. See Figure 10.1.

Obviously if the hedger only buys oil every three months (i.e., only has risk at these intervals), then ABC will avoid those high prices over the next three months, but if they buy oil every day, their exposure and their hedge won't match very well. This would be analogous to buying automobile insurance that only pays out if you get into an accident on a day that starts with an "S"; then again, if you drive only on weekends, you would find this acceptable.

If, on the other hand, ABC purchases oil every day, this would be an ineffective hedge. Maybe a better option would be one in which the payoff is determined, not by the level of the spot price at expiration, but by the average daily spot price (calculated with an averaging procedure that is presumably somewhat objective). This sort of option would be referred to as an average-price option, an average-rate option, or an Asian option.[2] An average-price or Asian call's value at expiration, then, would be

$$C_{\text{AVERAGE PRICE}} = \text{Max}[(S_{\text{AVERAGE}} - X), 0]$$

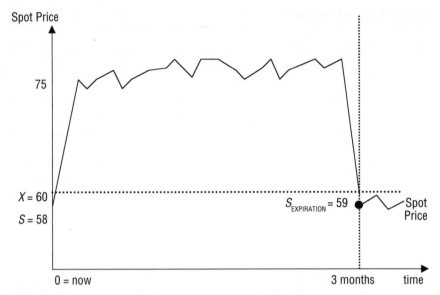

FIGURE 10.1 Standard European Call Option—Expiration Risk

Another way to make an option exotic is to make the strike price contingent on where the spot price has traded. For example, one could define a call's payoff in the usual way, but instead of a fixed strike price, the strike on this call could be defined as the lowest spot price realized over the life of the option. Because you want to "buy low," and this option identifies as the strike price as the lowest realized spot price, this is one version of what is known as a "lookback option."

$$C_{\text{LOOKBACK}} = \text{Max}[(S_{\text{EXPIRATION}} - S_{\text{MINIMUM}}), 0]$$

Another version of the lookback option would have a fixed strike but a payoff replacing the spot price at expiration with the highest spot price realized over the life of the option.

$$C_{\text{LOOKBACK}} = \text{Max}[(S_{\text{MAXIMUM}} - X), 0]$$

It is usually the case that these types of options are European-style exercise. Moreover, one could attempt to come up with the valuation formula for, as an example, a put option that has no expiration date. A perpetual put is certainly an interesting and exotic-sounding option.

There is also an entire class of exotic options that have a payoff contingent upon some event "happening" or "not happening." The most common of these are barrier options and their contingency is typically made dependent upon where the spot price trades (or does not trade).

With reference to Mark Rubinstein's second quote at the start of this chapter, some of the challenges associated with the valuation of nonstandard options (for the academics as well as those in the derivatives business) stemmed from either the problems posed by the mathematics or the computational limitations on computing power at that time.

Even if some of the early exotic options were scholarly exercises, many of them have come to hold prominent places in the financial community and especially in the FX markets.

DIGITAL OR BINARY OPTIONS

An option that pays you, say, USD 1,000,000 if GBP|USD is less than $S = 2.0000$ in one year and zero otherwise is known as a digital option (digital as in "on" or "off"), a binary option (binary as in "0" or "1"), an all-or-nothing option, a cash-or-nothing option, or even an asset-or-nothing option (depending on what is paid out). Over the years, these have also been referred to as lottery options and bet options.

A digital or binary option is one in which there is a fixed payout if the underlying asset price is above or below a certain level. Since calls pay out when the spot price rises, we identify a binary or digital call as one that pays off when the spot price is above a certain level. Similarly, a binary or digital put is defined as having a payoff when the spot price falls below a certain level. That unique point where the option crosses from having zero value to the constant payout value is sometimes referred to as the strike (in deference to the point where standard options start taking on value). These are pictured in Figure 10.2.

Again, these are typically European-style. If one can exercise a digital option at any time, that is, if it is an American digital option (unlike a regular American option, which, even though it is in-the-money relative to the spot price, may not be designated as an "early exercise"), there would be no point waiting to exercise. Since the payoff is a constant, you might as well capture that payoff as soon as you can. These are sometimes known as one-touch options. The only thing that needs to be specified, then, is whether you get that payoff immediately or on the expiration date (but this simply involves accounting for the discounting).

While we do not go into exotic option valuation in any great detail in this chapter, we can ask what a digital call might be worth. Imagine EUR|USD $S = 1.2500$. We could ask what you would pay for an option

A Digital Call

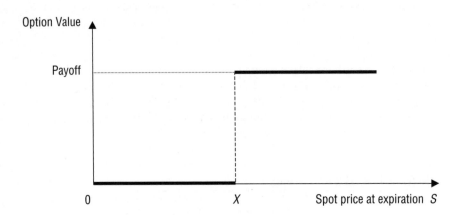

A Digital Put

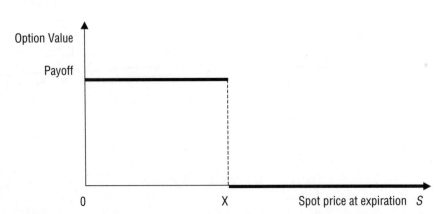

FIGURE 10.2   Digital Options

that will pay out USD 1,000,000 if, in three months, EUR|USD spot is above
1.3500. Would you pay USD 1? Probably. Would you pay USD 995,000?
Probably not. What does it depend on? What would you really like to
know? I'd like to know the probability that $S > 1.3500$ in three months'
time. Although we don't really know what this is, the Black–Scholes model
gives us some insight into that figure. At least in the "risk-neutral" world

(where the best forecast of the future spot price is the forward price), we said that $N(d_2)$ is the probability that a call option will be in-the-money (i.e., $S > X$) at expiration. If you believe this, then the value of a digital call would be

$$\text{Digital Call} = \text{the Present Value of } [\text{Payoff} \times N(d_2)]$$

If you trade technicals and you think a currency is "range bound," you could put on a digital call spread. For example, if you thought that EUR|USD was going to be trading between 1.3500 and 1.4000 in three months, you could buy the 1.3500 digital call and sell the 1.4000 digital call.

Another type of option that seems designed for technical trading is a lock-out option. Lock-outs have a constant payoff at expiration unless spot has traded beyond some level (at any time during the life of the option). In this sense, it anticipates our discussion of barrier options. If one is very confident that spot will stay within a trading range, for example, if you thought USD|JPY was going to remain between 115.00 and 120.00 for the next three months, you could trade a double lock-out. This is pictured in Figure 10.3. As long as spot stays below 120 and above 115, you will

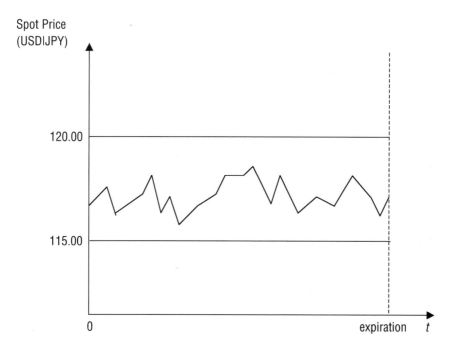

FIGURE 10.3   A Double Lock-Out (Receive a Constant Payoff if neither Upper nor Lower Barrier is touched/crossed)

get a constant payoff (say, USD 1,000,000 at expiration), whereas if spot crosses either 120 or 115, you get zero. While this might make sense for a variety of reasons (not the least of which is the fact that, as a trader, it is difficult to make money in markets where there is no volatility), it would be regrettable if, on the last day, spot crossed one of the significant levels. This is the analogue to Figure 10.1. For that reason, a more "forgiving" derivative has been designed. It might pay out a fraction of the total payoff depending on the percentage of days that USD|JPY stays within that "band." These are known as range-accrual options.

BARRIER OPTIONS

The most common type of exotic FX option is a barrier option. Barrier options have the same specifications as standard options [call or put (they are primarily European), a strike or exercise price, an expiration date, settlement features] with the added feature of a "barrier" and the understanding that if the spot price either hits or crosses the barrier, then the option either goes away (as in "terminates its existence"—an "out" option) or comes into existence (as in "initiates its existence"—an "in" option). Just to be clear, "terminates its existence" does not mean that the option expires; what it means is that the option goes away, ceases to remain, disappears.

One of the most confusing things about barrier options is the terminology, which is, even now, in the process of becoming more "standardized" between market participants. As an example, consider a three-month European put with a strike price of $X = 110$, with spot at $S = 100$ and an out barrier at $B = 90$. See Figure 10.4. How would you refer to this option?

Some would name this a "knock-out put" (because it is a put that may "go out"); others might call it a "reverse knock-out put" (reflecting the more common practice of putting the barrier in the out-of-the-money direction, which in this example would imply a barrier above the 110 strike price); some identify this as a "down and out put" (incorporating the spot price direction on which the option's termination is contingent); still others refer to this as an "up and out put" (reflecting the fact that intrinsic value goes up as the option goes out); it is also known as a "parity out" (because this option "disappears while it has some value relative to the spot price); and some, like UBS, refer to this as a "kick-out put" (using the word "knock" for an option that has a barrier in the out-of-the-money direction and "kick" for an option that has a barrier in the in-the-money direction. If there is a lesson to take from these different naming conventions, it is a warning that there is no standardized language yet for the entire range of FX exotic options.

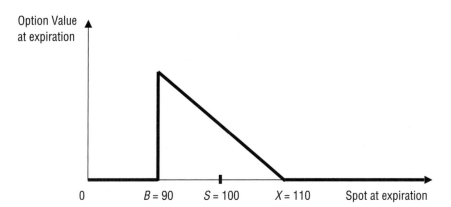

FIGURE 10.4   A Put Option with an Out Barrier (assuming the barrier has not been touched)

For the record, we have labeled the barrier with a "B," but one will also see that level referred to as an out-strike, which may be represented by "OX" or "KO".

EXOTIC OPTION EXERCISE

What would you label a put option with spot at $S = 22.50$, strike price at $X = 20.00$, and an out barrier at 21.00? What if, instead, it was a call?

Obviously the knock-out option will trade at a discount to the otherwise identical vanilla option. In some cases, especially if the barrier or out-strike is placed very close to the current spot price, these barrier options can involve significantly cheaper premiums. As a matter of fact, you can have a double-barrier option (with one barrier in the out-of-the-money direction and another in the in-the-money direction). This will reduce the premium further still. Some barrier option users appreciate a rebate (a return of cash) when their option goes out; although effectively this is simply long a one-touch (and would be priced in accordingly), it may serve some clients' needs.

We will examine two uses of barrier options: a speculative use and later a corporate hedging application. Returning to our example of a hedge fund during the Asian crisis, your view on USD|JPY is that it is headed from the current spot of $S = 125.00$ monotonically (as in, straight up) to 142.00 in one year. You could buy USD = sell JPY spot; you could buy USD = sell

JPY forward; you could buy a call on USD (= put on JPY) for 3.75% of the USD notional; or you could inquire about a barrier option.

The at-the-money call on USD with a barrier at 120.00 will still be over 3.00% of the USD notional, but if you move the barrier to 123.50, the premium might drop to .75% of the notional. George Soros admitted to using these instruments during the Asian crisis. Apparently, the spot price, which eventually went to around 142.70, dipped below the equivalent of our 123.50 barrier, and Soros lost around USD 200,000,000. Two weeks later, he appeared before Congress recommending that these dangerous derivatives be banned. Soros has written, "Knock-out options relate to ordinary options the way crack relates to cocaine." Further, he has implicated barrier options as a proximate cause of the implosion in currency markets in Asia in the 1990s.

Whether sore loser or concerned citizen of the world, Soros does suggest that barrier options could induce an unscrupulous FX market participant to attempt to push spot around in order to eliminate their option obligations. Aware, for example, that EUR|USD is one of the largest, deepest, most liquid markets in the world could impose an awesome cost on a dealer attempting to knock out their own short barrier option position.

In the early days of barrier options, the bank/dealer (simply and conveniently) informed the owner of a knock-out or kick-out that spot had hit or crossed the out-strike and that their option had gone away. The market has become more sophisticated, with the requirement for example that at least 10,000,000 of the underlying spot must trade (without the option dealing bank as one of the counterparties), observable in the broker/dealer market, and so on. That said, it is often the case that, in order to hedge these barrier options (especially the kick-outs), the option dealing bank must trade—sometimes in large volume—as the out-strike is approached. Most FX derivative dealers include a disclaimer to that effect right in the trade confirmation for a barrier option.

Nevertheless, a rumor has circulated among the financial markets approximately once every year (for the past several years) that Alan Greenspan is dead. The most recent was on Wednesday, March 31, 2004 (one day before April Fools' Day). One would think that repeated telling would mitigate the effectiveness of the tale, but perhaps not. What impact did it have? "The dollar weakened broadly . . . after rumors that Federal Reserve Chairman Alan Greenspan had suffered a heart attack roiled the markets, traders said. The Fed declined to comment on the rumors. The euro rose to a session high just above $1.23, a gain of more than 1%, according to Reuters data. The dollar fell over 1% against the Swiss franc to 1.2671 francs. 'The dollar is selling off across the board on fears that Greenspan may no longer be at the helm,' said Jeremy

Fand, senior proprietary trader with WestLB in New York."[3] A year earlier, Paula Lace, in a web article, "Greenspan Isn't Dead" (August 26, 2003) noted: "The dollar reached its lowest level against the euro in four months, dropping to \$1.0874 per euro after hitting \$1.08 earlier in the day." On at least one of these occasions, the source of the rumor was said to be an off-shore bank with a large outstanding short position in barrier options.

Just as there exist relationships between vanilla options, there are some interesting relationships as well between barrier options. Imagine that you buy a three-month European knock-out call with spot at $S = 100$, a strike price of $X = 105$, and an out barrier at $B = 95$. The only thing that we can say about its value is that it will be worth less than the vanilla three-month European 105 call. Now consider an in option. This is an option that does not exist until spot crosses a barrier, but, if it does, this option will come alive (regardless of where spot might subsequently trade). To be specific, let's consider the three-month European 105 knock-in call with an in barrier at $B = 95$. Obviously, this too should be worth less than the vanilla three-month European 105 call. These options are pictured in Figure 10.5.

Either the barrier is not hit (in which case, you get the payoff from the 105 knock-out call, which has not knocked out and the knock-in never existed) or the barrier is hit (and the knock-out disappears, but the knock-in comes alive and you get the payoff from this 105 call). One way or the other, you will receive the payoff from a 105 call. In short, a three-month European 105 knock-out call with an out barrier at $B = 95$ and a three-month European 105 knock-in call with an in barrier at $B = 95$ will

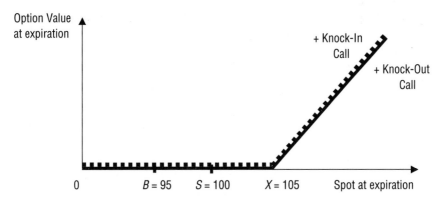

FIGURE 10.5 Knock-Out—Knock-In Parity ("Knock-out 105 call with barrier at $B = 95$ + knock-in 105 call with barrier at 95" is equal to the vanilla 105 call.)

together be worth the same as three-month European 105 call. Interestingly, an option trader doesn't need both a knock-out model and knock-in model over and above their standard (vanilla) option valuation model; that would be redundant.

On to our second exotic option application.

Perhaps the most conservative FX market participants are corporations. Would a corporation ever use a knock-out option? Perhaps. Let me describe a scenario in which it might make sense (though I am, in no way, advocating the general corporate use of these options).

Assume a U.S. company has six-month GBP receivables of GBP 40,000,000. Let GBP|USD spot be trading at $S = 1.8500$. The six-month forward may be trading at $F = 1.8200$, which makes a forward sale of the GBP look unattractive. Furthermore, if the company believes GBP|USD will be around 1.9200 in six-months, they do not want to lock in the lower exchange rate today. The rub? There is risk that GBP|USD could go to $S = 1.7000$ in six months (though this is viewed as remote). The company could leave their GBP receivables unhedged, but they might prefer the comfort of knowing they can sell their GBP at an economically-viable rate. The six-month at-the-money European GBP put (= USD call) is quoted at 2.00% of the notional, which seems way too expensive. Is there any other option? Consider an at-the-money GBP put with an out-barrier at $B = 1.9200$. This will reduce the GBP put premium. Is there a disaster scenario? Yes (as we saw with our hedge fund earlier); spot could run up to 1.9200 or 1.9201 and then whipsaw back to 1.7000 (in which case, the company's hedge would have disappeared). But what if, in conjunction with this knock-out Sterling put you placed a limit order to sell GBP 40,000,000 forward (to your receipt date) if spot ever hits 1.9200? Sounds reasonable, doesn't it? About the only risk is that you cannot be exactly sure of the forward points you'd lock in under the (positive) contingency that GBP|USD goes to 1.9200. Maybe not so exotic after all.

Just as we showed a standard FX option trading template for standard FX options, we include a screen shot of a barrier option in Figure 10.6.

OTHER EXOTIC OPTIONS

There is a wealth of other nonstandard options. We can value an option on an option (or a compound option), an option where you only have to pay for it when it ends up in-the-money at expiration (known as a premium-contingent option), a forward-starting option (where the strike price is set in the future—usually based on where S or F are trading—though the

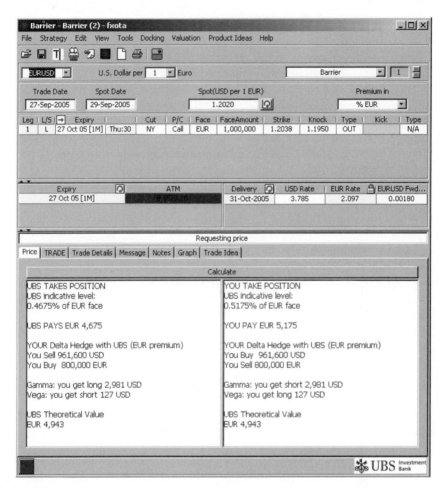

FIGURE 10.6 FX Exotic Barrier Option Trading Tool Screen Shot
Source: © 2006 UBS Investment Bank. Reprinted by permission.

volatility is locked in today), a quanto-option, which pays you the return from, say, a German stock, in U.S. Dollars, and a host of others.

FX-LINKED NOTES

There has been increasing interest from smaller investors in foreign exchange products. As is the case with many equity-linked notes, clients may not be able to trade options directly, but many of these structured products have relatively straightforward embedded FX options that, given one's views, can provide attractive returns. Many of these are created to provide at least a degree of capital protection.

One of our FX salespersons once asked the Financial Engineering team (the "Quants") if they could structure an FX-linked note with an embedded barrier option that didn't go out when spot crossed the out-strike once and that didn't go out when the spot crossed the out-strike a second time, but only went out when it crossed the out-strike for the third time. Three (out-) strikes and you're out; the salesperson really wanted to name it The Baseball Option Note.

Based on standard (or vanilla) options, digital or binary options, and barrier options, one can structure almost any payoff profile you'd like. Fischer Black once said, "You tell me the payoff structure you'd like, and I'll tell you how much it costs."

Barrier options, even if one does not use them, are an integral part of the FX market. The dynamic hedging by the banks/dealers, the impact on spot price movements, and the knowledge of a big position in a barrier out-strike are all factors that have an impact on where the FX spot markets are going.

Exotic options may be exotic, but they are not at all uncommon in the world of FX.

CHAPTER 11

The Economics of Exchange Rates and International Trade

*From the time Bretton Woods became effective, it was inevitable it
would break down. . . . It tried to achieve incompatible objectives:
freedom of countries to pursue independent internal monetary
policy; fixed exchange rates; and relatively free international
movement of goods and capital.*

— Milton Friedman (1975)

MONEY VERSUS CURRENCY

Currency is money, but money need not be currency. In the earlier chapters,
we seemed to identify money and currency, but they are not the same. To
an economist, money can be defined either narrowly or broadly. The U.S.
central bank, which once closely tracked and even targeted the money supply as a policy instrument, draws these three distinctions in the definition of
money (among others). (1) M-1 consists of currency in the hands of the
public (but not the banks), checking accounts, which are also referred to as
"demand deposits", travelers checks, and automatic transfer service account balances. (2) M-2 consists of M-1 plus savings accounts, also referred to as "time deposits," up to USD 100,000 (the maximum federally
insured amount per account in the United States), money market mutual
funds, and some overnight repo and EuroDollar accounts. (3) M-3 consists
of M-2 plus time deposits exceeding USD 100,000, institutional money
market funds, and longer-term repos and EuroDollar accounts. M-1 defines
money rather narrowly; M-3 includes less liquid monetary instruments.
Other central banks define money similarly.

As banks have created money substitutes over the years (such as charge cards, credit cards, debit cards), the Fed has given up trying to target the money supply in the United States. This is not true of other central banks around the world. Bill Gross contends, "Modern-day governments perform many functions, but two of the most important are establishing budgets and controlling the supply of money."[1] While the U.S. Fed may have chosen not to pursue the proximate goal of targeting the money supply, the European Central Bank continues to monitor several monetary aggregates and reserves the right to attempt to control the money supply of the Euro-Zone—with the primary goal of price stability or, put differently, curbing inflation.

Economists understand that you can intervene in any market and fix the price (in the case of the money market, this price is the interest rate) or you can fix the quantity (in this case, the supply of money), but you cannot fix both simultaneously. Although the government may claim to be the sole legitimate producer of currency, banks are often acknowledged as institutions that can create money. Let's explain this briefly. If someone drops off their weekly paycheck in cash at the bank (for, say, USD 1,000), that bank can then lend out the money. Most banking systems involve fractional reserve requirements; what this means is that they have to "retain" or "place on reserve" (often with the central bank) a fraction of their holdings/obligations. If the reserve requirement is 10%, they are subsequently only able to lend out USD 900 (of the original USD 1,000) which, once spent, will constitute a deposit in some other bank. And this process will continue until the initial deposit of USD 1,000 plays out to an increase in available funds for the banking system of USD 10,000. [In this example, the increase in the money supply is determined by calculating [USD 1,000/(fractional reserve requirement)] or [1,000/(.10)]. And the central banks, while they generally do not actively tinker with reserve requirements on a daily basis, can and occasionally do change them (sometimes in an attempt to either stimulate or slow economic activity by altering the nation's money supply, which, in turn, will influence interest rates and credit conditions in the economy).

Economists (whether academic, Fed central bank, or governmental) engage in a general attempt to gain an understanding of the economy: how it works, how to steer it, and what policies would most effectively bring about desired consequences. Part of these inquiries include getting a handle on the empirical impact of changes in controls such as reserve requirements, the various money supplies, and/or interest rates. In the United States, the Federal Reserve Bank sets the "discount rate," the rate charged to member banks in the event of a cash liquidity shortfall, but, more importantly, the Fed targets the Fed funds rate, the market rate that member banks charge each other to cover their reserve requirements. On some days, a bank may have excess reserves (to be lent out) and on other days, they may need to borrow to meet their reserve requirement.

Although in the financial press it sounds as if the Fed sets the Fed funds rate, in reality it is a market rate and sometimes needs assistance to move to the level that the Fed has targeted. The primary activity in which the Fed engages to influence interest rates is known as an "open market operation." If the Fed wished to raise interest rates—called a "tightening" (for example, in an effort to slow an overly exuberant economy)—they would enter the market and sell Treasury securities that would, in turn, remove money from the hands of the public, and therefore the banking system. Less money in the system would cause competition for funds to raise the cost of money (i.e., interest rates). Similarly, if the Fed wished to stimulate a sluggish economy, they might want to lower interest rates—called an "easing" (in an effort to stimulate business investment and induce consumer spending and credit card debt). The Fed would then buy in Treasury securities, putting money into the hands of the public and, therefore, the banking system. The increased cash in the system would seek (the unfortunately less productive) investment uses, and, short term, rates would fall.

Since most central banks can have a direct impact on the level of interest rates in their country, they are able to influence foreign exchange rates (the global price of their money) by changing the return on that asset known as their currency. But should they? More on policy later.

TYPES OF FX EXPOSURES

As we mentioned back in Chapter 4, there are many types of parties involved in the markets for foreign exchange. At this stage, with a better understanding of many of the FX instruments that are actually traded, let's look more closely at the FX market participants and try to gain some insights into the nature of their FX exposures.

UBS has arranged its client coverage into five groups: (1) the Corporate coverage team, whose clients are multinational companies doing business all around the world; (2) the Real Money (or Unleveraged Institutional) Investors team dealing with the foreign exchange requirements of major global investment, pension, and mutual funds; (3) the Hedge Fund coverage team, which interacts with perhaps the most sophisticated and most actively trading investor base; (4) the High Net Worth (or Wealth Management or Private Client or Private Banking) team, which also serves as a distribution point for many of the FX-based retail structured products; and finally (5) the B4B (or Bank-for-Banks) group, which acts as a wholesaler of FX products and services for a cadre of regional banks, commercial banks, and even some investment banks who have decided to keep to a minimum their direct exposure to FX market risk. Central banks and supranationals are categorized as clients based on the nature of their FX market needs and activities.

While this client breakdown may be somewhat idiosyncratic to UBS, it does recognize that the various types of foreign exchange market participants view their need for FX coverage and FX products differently.

Corporates

Every company that does international business has to deal with foreign exchange. Interestingly, multinational corporations have multiple types of FX exposures. The first, and easiest to understand, is **transactional exposure**. A global provider of fine Scottish cuisine, headquartered in the Midwestern United States, may generate cash inflows in a multitude of different currencies. As an example, let's say that, among other places, they sell their product in London, England (in GBP, obviously); this business may generate a quarterly cash flow of GBP 40,000,000. If today GBP|USD $S = 1.8000$, but the money will not arrive for three months, there is a FX price risk. If in three months, GBP|USD $S = 2.0000$, the company will receive even more USD per GBP than they may have anticipated. On the other hand, if $S = 1.5000$ in three months, the economic profitability of the overseas business may be called into question. This is FX transaction risk and arises every time a firm enters into a business arrangement in which movements in exchange rates influence their bottom line (in their reporting currency). One of the most common ways corporates hedge this transactional risk is to sell their expected foreign currency revenues forward (especially if these cash magnitudes are a firm commitment—meaning that they know exactly how large the currency flows will be) and purchase their foreign exchange payables forward—presumably at an acceptable level.

If a USD-based corporate treasurer with GBP receivables is told that he/she can lock in a three-month forward exchange rate of $F = 1.8400$ (with spot today at 1.8000, the Pound is then said to be trading at a premium in the forward market), this usually sounds good; it looks like they are making an extra four U.S. cents on every Pound that is sold forward. On the other hand, if the forward is quoted at a discount, say $F = 1.7600$, this looks unattractive—almost as if they are giving away four U.S. cents per Pound.[2] Nevertheless, if the company specializes in food products and does not have an opinion (or "ax") on FX rates, perhaps this is the prudent approach to transactional FX risk management.

Corporates are also sensitive to the hedging activities of their industry rivals, which could, therefore, impact their relative competitiveness. For this reason, they sometimes "layer" in their hedges as their business activities develop throughout the year, that is, as their foreign exchange needs become more certain. Also, corporates often budget for a certain FX rate (a "hurdle" rate) which they may attempt, more or less actively, to better.

An entirely different type of foreign exchange risk for a multinational firm is **translational exposure**. What this highlights is the fact that large international businesses may own subsidiaries, factories, plants, and inventories outside their home country. Since most publicly-traded companies must file quarterly and annual reports, and since these firms must convert all assets into their reporting currency, movements in exchange rates will affect the value of their institution—if only through their corporate financial statements; it is our understanding that most firms do not actively hedge this exposure.

There is a third, different type of FX risk that businesses have: **economic exposure**. This is most easily explained by an example.

> *Imagine that you are the CEO of RunCo, a U.S. company that produces a new portable CD player—the Runaround. Further, assume that you only make these in the United States, that you only use parts manufactured in the United States, that you employ only U.S. workers, that you pay for the inputs and wages exclusively in USD, and that you refuse to sell your product outside the United States. Finally, assume you sell each Runaround for USD 150.00. Do you have FX risk? It may seem as if you do not (as there does not appear to be any need for, or exposure to, foreign exchange), but you do have economic risk. If RunCo competes in a global marketplace, you must recognize that your product competes (in the United States) with other products manufactured outside the United States—like the TrotMan, which is made in Japan. This competitor, the TrotMan, is priced in JPY (say, at JPY 16,000), which at a USD|JPY exchange rate of S = 110.00 means that it sells in the United States for USD 145.45. Now the U.S.-manufactured Runaround may still do well (even though it is a bit pricier than its Japanese rival), but it will probably lose market share if USD|JPY rises to 146.00. Under that scenario, the Japanese TrotMan will trade below USD 110 and is likely to capture at least a portion of the market segment that does not possess strong brand loyalty.*

Because there has been a trend in the accounting rules (such as FAS 133) that effectively require corporations to mark-to-market their derivatives positions for the purpose of financial reporting, many companies do not even think about hedging their economic exposures, because doing so would add volatility to the accounting statements. Having said that, a private company, which isn't obliged to justify their hedging or balance sheet volatility to shareholders, may be more inclined to address this risk.

When asked to identify three chocolate companies, many people name Hershey, Nestlé, and M&M/Mars. When asked which one is different, most people single out Nestlé (as it is headquartered in Switzerland; Hershey and M&M/Mars are both U.S. companies), but, in this context, the standout is M&M/Mars, which is a private company while Hershey and Nestlé are both publicly traded). Presuming M&M/Mars loses market share and sales to Nestlé when USD|CHF spot rises (Dollar strengthens = Swiss Franc weakens), M&M/Mars may consider trading foreign exchange products that compensate them as USD|CHF goes up.

For the record (literally), one can review quarterly (10-Q) and annual (10-K) corporate financial statements and obtain some sense of a company's foreign exposure and what, if anything, they might do to manage FX risk. In the case of McDonald's, we see (from their 2004 Annual Report):

> *Impact of Foreign Currencies on Reported Results*
> *While changing foreign currencies affect reported results, McDonald's lessens exposures, where practical, by financing in local currencies, hedging certain foreign-denominated cash flows, and purchasing goods and services in local currencies.*
>
> *In 2004 and 2003, foreign currency translation had a positive impact on consolidated revenues, operating income and earnings per share due to the strengthening of several major currencies, primarily the Euro and British Pound.*
>
> *The Company uses foreign currency debt and derivatives to hedge the foreign currency risk associated with certain royalties, intercompany financings and long-term investments in foreign subsidiaries and affiliates. This reduces the impact of fluctuating foreign currencies on cash flows and shareholders equity.*[3]

Institutional Investors

When it comes to international investing, Bill Gross, the chief investment officer of PIMCO, the Pacific Investment Management Company, one of the largest bond funds in the world and a real money investor, has identified the following as attractive criteria for successful international investing:

> *. . . you want to have as high a return and as little risk as possible. That combination is best achieved by investing in countries with*

the following characteristics: (1) economic policies that promote high real GDP growth; (2) a stable political environment; (3) a sound and disciplined central bank; (4) a competitive currency without potential sinkholes; (5) low amounts of debt; and (6) a legal system emphasizing protection of individual property rights.
—William H. Gross, *Everything You've Heard About Investing Is Wrong!* p. 41 (1997)

Institutional investors are often referred to as the buy side [based on their requirement, spelled out in their respective prospectuses, to be, say 75% or more, invested in (i.e., long) the securities identified in their universe of targeted assets]. As such they buy stocks and bonds. Sometimes, a U.S. fund is allowed to buy, say, European stocks. What Gross seems to be advocating in the preceding quote is the purchase of foreign securities whose prices are denominated in currencies that are likely to gain (or at least not lose) in value relative to their reporting currency and investor population.

As an example of what can go wrong, say a U.S. fund were to purchase BASF shares (as was remarked in the movie *The Graduate*, "plastics!") in Euro at the start of 2005. As of November 2005, the price of BASF (in Euro) was up 12.70% year-to-date. An excellent addition to one's portfolio, one would think—especially in a year where equity markets have been less than spectacular. Nice stock-picking! Oh, one thing, though: Your investors lost money. Huh? That's right. EUR|USD fell 12.96% year-to-date, so, as a fund manager, if you had not hedged your U.S. investors' exposure to foreign exchange, overall they experienced a loss.

Understanding the motivation of traditional investment funds is an important prerequisite to understanding their FX needs. Funds have historically been compensated based on a percentage fee of their assets under management. One of their goals, therefore, has been, among other objectives, to be "big." One way to grow is to outperform one's competitors—even in weak markets. It is for this reason that the traditional investment funds industry is sometimes referred to as the "relative returns" industry. Your objective is to do better than the next fund (higher returns) with smaller risk (lower volatility).

These two elements figure into Morningstar's criteria for rewarding investment funds (where five stars is the ultimate distinction). If every other fund in your category (e.g., large-cap, value stocks) is down 20%, but your fund is down only 15%, it's a great year (even though you have lost a great deal of your investors' money). It is this sort of perspective that may explain how these funds operate. More specifically, it is worth knowing that each fund is trying to outperform its peers.

The real question is, "What is your benchmark?" A common international equity index is the Morgan Stanley Capital International—Europe, Australasia, and Far East Equity Index (MSCI—EAFE). If your goal is to outperform this benchmark, it may be worth knowing that there's more than one of these. One measures returns in local currency (independent of any repatriation of those returns—in other words, without any consideration of foreign exchange appreciation or depreciation); one measures returns in USD (without having hedged any of the foreign exchange risk—in other words, returns on the equity as well as the associated foreign exchange); and another looks at USD returns with a one-month rolling foreign exchange forward hedge. The first of these methodologies would record the BASF return as 12.70%; the second of these would calculate the USD return as –.26%.

Suffice it to say that equity returns can be swamped by foreign exchange movements. The inclination of any given fund to hedge their foreign exchange risk may depend on what they view as their benchmark and their view (and the associated degree of conviction) on the respective currencies to which they are exposed.

At any given point in time, one can look at the year-to-date performance of currencies against one another using Bloomberg; the WCRS function displays the best and worst performing currencies versus your choice of base currency. See Figure 11.1.

Hedge Funds

Hedge funds are distinguished from traditional investment funds (mutual funds, retirement funds, pension funds, and so on) in a few different ways. In the United States, hedge funds are not allowed to advertise and solicit investment money from the general public. They fall outside the control of the Investment Company Act of 1940 (although most are now being required to register with the SEC). They can go short (that is, sell securities they do not own—something traditional funds are not allowed to do); they can employ leverage in their investment strategy or investment process; and they often use derivatives (forwards, futures, swaps, and options) to obtain that leverage.

George Soros, sometimes referred to as "the Man who broke the Bank of England" for his successful speculative shorting of GBP in 1992, is known for (but not unique in) his willingness to magnify his position through the use of leverage. John Train has written, "A typical Soros maneuver, such as going long yen and shorting sterling on margin both ways, while immensely profitable when it works, can also have disastrous results if it doesn't."[4]

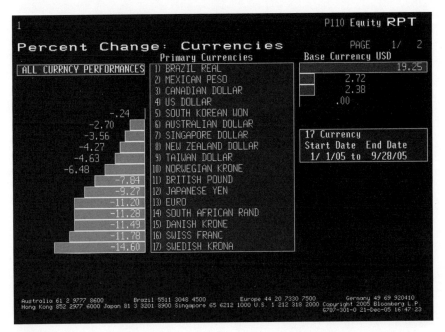

FIGURE 11.1   Bloomberg World Currency Returns Screen (WCRS)
Source: © 2006 Bloomberg LLP. All rights reserved. Reprinted with permission.

Global Macro Hedge Funds are viewed as singularly opportunistic alternative investment vehicles. For starters, they hold out the possibility of positive returns even if the usual securities and asset markets are floundering, but this is true for all hedge funds. For this reason, hedge funds are sometimes referred to as "absolute returns" funds.[5] To date, they have not been "benchmarked," though there seems to be pressure to develop and implement hedge fund indices. Many hedge fund strategies, as the name suggests, "hedge" or focus their trading on a very specific opportunity in the market. As an example, an equity long-short fund may buy one auto manufacturer's stock and sell another's, concentrating on the relative performance of these two firms—independent of the level of the market and independent of the performance of the automobile sector. Convertible bond arbitrage has typically involved buying convertible corporate debt (corporate bonds that can be "turned in" for a fixed number of shares of common stock), selling that same company's stock against the "convert," and dynamically managing that position. Risk or merger arbitrage involves buying the stock of a firm being targeted for a takeover and selling the stock of the potential acquirer. Fixed income arbitrage involves trading one bond against another.

The scope of trading by Global Macro Hedge Funds ranges from conservative "carry trades" (e.g., borrowing money in Japan where interest rates are close to zero and investing in relatively safe securities in Brazil where interest rates are around 14%) to outright directional bets on currency movements (like Soros and the Pound), and everything in between. There are convergence trades (as countries join the EuroZone), trades based on international trade flows (with record trade deficits, many think the U.S. Dollar eventually has to weaken, so some hedge funds have positioned their portfolio to benefit from the anticipated decline of the Dollar), event trading (as China bends to political pressure that would require the Renminbi to strengthen), and even opportunistic interday trading based on market flows, economic data, news, technicals, and even rumors.

Most equity long-short hedge funds do not employ leverage beyond, perhaps, 2 to 1 (meaning, that if they have USD 1,000,000 to invest, they would not put on a position worth more than USD 2,000,000). The way in which they can do this is by borrowing and/or using derivatives. Fixed income arbitrage hedge funds have been known to lever their positions 25 to 1 (in an effort to generate "absolute returns" from relatively small arbitrage opportunities). Global Macro Hedge Funds have shown the propensity to lever their positions tactically as market conditions present opportunities for profitable foreign exchange trades.

High Net Worth Clients

As the notion of foreign exchange as an asset class gains acceptance, individuals have taken an interest in exploring this realm of the financial markets. Banks have offered investments and deposits that have a currency component, ranging from structured notes that pay out based on the performance (and possible trading range) of an exchange rate to money market products that may offer the possibility of above-average returns, but with the additional provision, for example, that you may receive those returns in either one of two currencies (as selected/determined by the broker/dealer).

Many of these products are structurally a combination of a money market instrument or account with an embedded or associated derivative component. These are known by a number of fancy names and acronyms such as Speeders, Quantos, PIPs, GROIs, Bulls, ARNs, DOCUs, CUDOs, and so on.

Other Banks

Banks, whether commercial, investment, central, or supranational, are intimately involved in the markets for foreign exchange. Commercial banks are sometimes asked to assist their local clients with their foreign exchange risk. Investment banks tend to be more active, but this depends on the reason for their FX trading (facilitating client transactions, hedging their business exposures, cross-border issuance, international mergers and acquisitions, and even proprietary trading). Central bank activity ranges from the management of their foreign reserves through active FX market intervention.

Of course, if exchange rates never moved (i.e., if they were fixed), then much of the trading activity (whether hedging or implementing views on the market) would cease. Having spelled out the economic rationale for many of the trades undertaken by the FX market participants, we now consider the possible implications of fixed exchange rates.

FIXED VERSUS FLOATING EXCHANGE RATES

Economists have long debated the advantages, disadvantages, virtues, shortcomings, merits, costs, and benefits of a fixed exchange rate system versus a floating exchange rate system. "Does the choice of exchange rate regime matter? Few questions in international economics have sparked as much debate and yielded as little consensus."[6]

Fixed Exchange Rates

The attraction of fixed exchange rates is the presumed stability they provide for those engaging in international transactions. If USD|JPY is fixed at 120.00, then a U.S. software firm can enter into trade agreements in which their product will sell for JPY 6,000 in Japan—comfortable that they will receive USD 50 as a result of that sale. Similarly, a Japanese automobile manufacturer might sleep better knowing that their cars, selling in the United States for USD 20,000, will appear on the bottom line as JPY 2,400,000.

Sounds good.

The real problem, though, with fixed exchange rates is that someone must keep them fixed. If the institutions charged with maintaining the exchange rate (which, if it indeed requires active support, is obviously not set at the market clearing rate) are either unable or unwilling to maintain the peg, then there are potentially large impacts associated with formal devaluation (reduction in a currency's value) or revaluation (appreciation of a currency's value). As with agricultural price supports, the minimum wage and rent control, any interference with market prices creates inefficiencies, distortions, and influences behavior in a way that may not be desirable.

What are the ultimate negative implications of fixing an exchange rate (or maintaining the price of foreign exchange within a band)? There are two primary issues. First, as experienced by Norman Lamont, Chancellor of the Exchequer, and the Bank of England in 1992, while attempting to maintain the GBP exchange rate within its tight ERM range, and in the face of mounting speculation (or a "speculative attack" as the media seems to like to call it), the central banking authorities could run out of the foreign exchange reserves necessary to preserve the value of their currency in the market. When that occurs (especially without the collaborative support of other central banks), the fixed rate of exchange will presumably collapse (as it did for the Pound on Black Wednesday). Second, by formally linking one country's currency to another country's currency at a fixed rate of exchange, disparities in monetary policy will invariably tend to cause imbalances that will ultimately culminate in a breakdown of that peg. For example, a country with a monetary policy that induces a relatively rapid growth in their money supply (relative to a neighboring country), under a fixed exchange rate regime, can "export" their inflation to their neighbor. The transmission mechanism is through increased spending on the part of the country with the expanding money supply (some of which will be directed to imports). As these growing funds find their way into the other country, there will be a natural pressure for the "inflated" currency to depreciate, but the central banks and monetary authorities will have to maintain the fixed exchange rate (by buying up the expanding currency).

The result will be ever mounting reserves of the relatively faster growing currency in the coffers of the monetary authorities, and the "forced" purchase of that currency on the part of the less expansionist country. In effect, their money supply must be "grown" to maintain the FX peg and will have the impact of inducing inflation in a country that would otherwise have had less.

This leads to the notions of "open economies" (as opposed to "closed economies") and "openness," which are intended to indicate the relative importance of the international trade sector for an economy and the exposure for such an economy to policy impacts or other "shocks" (monetary or real) abroad.

A current, real world example of a "pegged" exchange rate and the imbalances that result can be seen in the case of international trade between the United States and China. The United States has been running record trade imbalances (to be more precise, "trade deficits," which implies that the United States is importing more goods and services than they are exporting; this is sometimes called a "current account" deficit). What this really means is that the United States is exporting Dollars in exchange for products from around the world (and increasingly from China). In September 2005, the monthly trade deficit was an unprecedented USD 66.1 billion; for the first nine months of 2005, the cumulative trade deficit was USD 503 billion. The natural implication of all this is that the USD should weaken, but China has maintained a (somewhat) pegged exchange rate, meaning that they have had to "absorb" those Dollars. If China were to sell these Dollars on the world market, the value of the Dollar would fall, Chinese products would look more expensive to American consumers, U.S. products would look cheaper to the rest of the world, and there would be an automatic force at work (Adam Smith's "invisible hand" operating on a global scale) to reverse those imbalances. As it is, China has actively kept the Renminbi weak (thereby encouraging Chinese exports and real economic growth in China). The way in which the Central Bank of China has kept the Renminbi weak has been through their willingness to absorb the U.S. Dollars they have received via international trade. What has China done with the Dollars they have accumulated?

What did the U.S. government do with the milk they purchased as a part of their dairy product price support program (initially enacted in 1949)? They turned the milk into cheese; they warehoused and guarded the cheese; and then, in an act that vilified President Ronald Reagan in the dairy states, in December 1981, they gave the cheese away ("released 30 million pounds of federal cheese surpluses").

What has China done with the Dollars? China (in 2005) has foreign exchange reserves exceeding USD 750 billion, with around USD 500 billion in U.S. Dollar-denominated securities. China has taken its Dollars and turned around and bought mostly U.S. Treasury securities (over USD 250 billion) as well as U.S. agency securities and mortgage-backed securities. There has been talk of a bubble (that is, the disaster scenario if China were to dump their U.S. Treasury holdings), but it has also been pointed out that China, in so doing, would shoot themselves in the foot, negatively impacting the value of their own portfolio holdings. The trend of China recycling trade-generated Dollars into U.S. Treasury securities shows no sign of slowing, but, at some point, many recognize that something will have to give.

"Beggar Thy Neighbor"

Fixed (or otherwise manipulated) exchange rates allow for what older British economists referred to as a "beggar thy neighbor" policy. Under this strategy, a country actively tries to keep their currency weak in order to encourage exports (their exports will look "cheap" to external consumers), to discourage imports (products abroad will look "expensive"), to build up foreign exchange reserves, and, most importantly, to benefit from the real economic growth in their local economy that derives from taking production away from their neighboring countries.

It may sound counterintuitive to implement a policy that keeps one's currency weak ("Shouldn't our country want our currency to be strong?"), but it is the stimulus to real economic growth that drives this objective. This sort of "weak money" policy was alleged to have been periodically carried out (intentionally or unintentionally) by the countries of continental Europe. The phrase "beggar thy neighbor" implies that, by "stealing" industry from another country (since it is less expensive for foreigners to import products from you), a country can impoverish a neighboring nation (as their jobs are lost to foreign producers).

Floating Exchange Rates

Under a floating exchange rate regime, a sustained trade imbalance (e.g., USD out) will eventually result in a depreciating currency (USD weakens), the perception that imports are increasingly expensive, the view from abroad that your products are "cheap" (stimulating your exports), and a natural reversal of the trade flows. Much of the rationale for a floating exchange rate regime hinges on the belief that an unregulated global economy will serve to advance the interests of all countries collectively (even if it is not the case that every single individual benefits from that flexibility).

Milton Friedman tells us that if foreign exchange rates are determined in a free market, they will settle at whatever level will clear that market. His classic treatise, "The Case for Flexible Exchange Rates," produced in the early 1950s, in the middle of the Bretton Woods fixed exchange rate regime, was a spectacularly unorthodox defense of the power of competitive world markets.[7] "What about the argument that we must defend the dollar, that we must keep it from falling in value in terms of other currencies—the Japanese yen, the German mark, or the Swiss franc? . . . The price of the dollar, if determined freely, serves the same function as all other prices. It transmits information and provides an incentive to act on that information because it affects the incomes that participants in the market receive."[8]

If, to a U.S. consumer, Japanese automobiles are attractive relative to the alternatives, then why should the U.S. government either induce (possibly via tariffs) that consumer to buy the more expensive U.S. product or spend the consumer's tax Dollars to artificially maintain a strong Yen = weak Dollar? It may sound somewhat less dramatic today, but the Friedmans report that the U.S. government lost around USD 2,000,000,000 between 1973 and early 1979 defending the U.S. Dollar.

IMPLICATIONS OF MONETARY POLICY

Economists have investigated, developed theories, and modelled the effects of monetary and fiscal policy under different exchange rate regimes. These studies have resulted in a number of theories involving the transference of monetary phenomena, the overshooting of inflation with changes in monetary policy (which can, obviously, have foreign exchange market implications) and an entire field known as open-economy macroeconomics.

To the extent that monetary policy affects money markets, interest rates, and, therefore foreign exchange markets, its theoretical foundations should not rest on factors such as inelastic (unresponsive) consumer demand for imports, behavior that shows myopia or inconsistent expectations, or ignore the import of the trade sector for a country's economic objectives. To the extent that volatile foreign exchange prices have repercussions for real economic variables, there is an FX chicken-and-egg problem. Recognizing that more extensive treatment is beyond the scope of this book, we end by quoting Paul Krugman, a noted, prolific, and popular author, a distinguished economist, and an occasional contributor to policy discussions and debates: "The policy implications of unstable exchange rates remain a subject of great dispute."[9]

TRADE DEFICITS: A CURSE OR A BLESSING

Few economic issues have received more attention recently than the twin deficits (the budget deficit and the trade deficit). Although the budget deficit (and the cumulative national debt) has caused some concern, economists recognize a few things worth noting. First, unlike an individual's charge card or credit card debt, the national debt need not be retired (by any particular date—or, indeed, at all). Second, given the role government plays in steering the nation's economy, most economists view a balanced federal budget as absurd. When times are good, a nation's treasury should enjoy a surplus; when times are tough, government should spend more than it's taking in. Third, although people have been troubled by the astronomical, whirling numbers on the National Debt Clock on a billboard near Times Square in New York City for years, economists recognize that it is not the size of the debt that matters, so much as the percentage of GDP that the debt represents. Far from its being a chronic impediment, burden, or disease, Alexander Hamilton thought that a national debt could, indeed, be a national blessing.

The same general issues are relevant for trade deficits. In terms of financing, a net import flow of goods and services for the United States must be paid for, but this can come from an export of Dollars, an exchange of capital assets (Treasury securities, stock, bonds, etc.), or a sale of real assets (such as the sale of much of Rockefeller Plaza to Japanese investors in 1989). This last phenomenon is sometimes called foreign direct investment (such as a South Korean automobile company buying, opening, and owning a production facility in the United States). What can go wrong? If the value of the Dollar were to collapse, this could cause short-term difficulties with the trade deficit (as the United States has allowed, if not encouraged, low-tech manufacturing to go abroad). Then again, the Japanese sold Rockefeller Plaza back to us at a discount to its original purchase price and, unlike London Bridge, much of this cannot be appropriated (i.e., "They can't take it with them"). A large trade imbalance, in and of itself, does not necessarily mean any impending disaster. Of course, there are certainly short-term negative implications associated with offshoring and U.S. jobs going overseas.

But the ratio of net imports-to-GDP has been growing at a very rapid pace, and this worries some economists. In 2004, this ratio was around 6%. The prevalence of language such as "unsustainable trade deficits and current account deficits" is growing. The upshot is that we (in the United States) will increasingly owe foreigners for our cheap import consumption today (through non-U.S. ownership of Treasury securities and the future tax liabilities that they represent), we will sell our country to non-Americans, and/or we will hurt the international value of the Dollar. Then again, if we can get Japanese cars, Swiss watches, German beer, and South Korean electronics for pieces of green paper, really, what's the problem?

POLITICS AND ECONOMICS

Although there may be compelling **political** arguments for fixed exchange rates, that does not alter the compelling economic argument that free trade and, by definition, freely determined prices tend to allow resources to gravitate to their most highly valued and productive uses. It's been noted that the American Economic Association has, without fail, for over 30 years, included at least one session (and often organized several sessions) on the optimal or appropriate exchange rate regime. The reason, I believe, is that what one means by "optimal" depends on your objective (or "objective function," to use a more mathematical expression). Those who would protect U.S. jobs, restrict capital flow into the media and communications sector in many Southeast Asia countries, limit immigration, preserve or implement tariffs, taxes, embargos, duties, and so on would all do so at an economic cost. Politically, though, this cost may seem small relative to the larger benefits whether they are security, protection, defense, immunization, and so on.

Jagdish Bhagwati, in his excellent book *Protectionism* (MIT Press, 1988), attempts to document the sources of, and justifications for, trade interferences, embargoes, and other forms of protection. *The Economist* summarized it best in the review of Bhagwati's book: "Trade protection is probably the biggest avoidable cause of economic harm in the world. There are plenty of excuses for it, but none of them is any good."

In the end, I am still a University of Chicago-trained economist, and as such, maintain a healthy skepticism about the efficacy of fixing prices (i.e., a fixed exchange rate regime) and the effectiveness of government intervention in international markets in general and in the foreign exchange markets in particular. I also continue to believe, as a rule, in the efficiency of free markets.

The nature of economics, though, is all about analyzing trade-offs. Although a given policy may bring about some desired consequence or consequences, there is typically an associated inefficiency or set of costs that arises from the government's intervention in the marketplace. Robert Heller, in a statement that most professional economists would agree with unequivocally, told us that, "It can be shown that unrestricted international trade increases welfare for the world as a whole."[10]

And yet, the policies and interventions promulgated by the governments and central banks around the world often are contrary to the ideal of free, unencumbered international trade. Milton and Rose Friedman implicate this activist inclination by central banks for many of the problems that arise on an international scale. "Why the repeated foreign exchange crises? The proximate reason is because foreign exchange rates have not been determined in a free market. Government central banks have intervened on a grand scale in order to influence the price of their currencies."[11] Further, they have written that the Federal Reserve System in the United States "blames all problems on external influences beyond its control and takes credit for any and all favorable occurrences. It thereby continues to promote the myth that the private economy is unstable, while its behavior continues to document the reality that government is today the major source of economic instability."[12]

This statement leads nicely into the topic of our next chapter, where many would say that clearly something had gone wrong in the cases documented there: Currency Crises.

CHAPTER 12

Currency Crises

When the Bretton Woods system of fixed exchange rates broke up in the early 1970s, most international economists were not dismayed. Not only did they believe that greater flexibility of exchange rates was a good thing; they also believed that they understood reasonably well how the new system would work. They were wrong. The last 20 years of the international monetary system have involved one surprise after another, most of them unpleasant, all of them forcing economists to scramble to keep up with new issues and unexpected turns in old ones.
—Paul R. Krugman in *Currencies and Crises* (1998)

Since money has been used, there have been occasional crises. After all, money is a matter of faith, and faith has been known to waver.

When most of us think of a crisis or crash, we tend to think of a spectacularly dramatic fall in the stock market (i.e., a large and general drop in stock prices across the board). Less intuitive, though no less painful, are the similarly high profile spikes or upward jumps in commodity prices (oil, gold, orange juice). It has been said that equities tend to crash down; commodities tend to crash up. Where is foreign exchange in all this? Interestingly, if one currency crashes down, its counterpart must be skyrocketing (in relative terms). Unlike the case of equities where a substantial decline is painful to everybody (after all, "the world is long stock"), significant movements in foreign exchange rates serve to benefit some and inflict pain on others.

Charles P. Kindleberger tells us, "A crash is a collapse of the prices of assets, or perhaps the failure of an important firm or bank. A panic, 'a sudden fright without cause,' from the god Pan, may occur in asset markets or involve a rush from less to more liquid assets. Financial crises may involve one or both, and in any order."[1]

More to our topic at hand: foreign exchange, Chiodo and Owyang tell us, "A currency crisis can be defined as a speculative attack on a country's currency that can result in a forced devaluation and possible debt default."[2]

In this chapter, we selectively examine some of the more prominent modern FX crises with an eye to their cause and possible similar future recurrences.

THE END OF BRETTON WOODS

The Bretton Woods Conference (1944) established a fixed exchange rate regime for many of the world's major currencies. There were occasional adjustments to the par exchange rates established at Bretton Woods; these periodic changes were known as "creeping pegs." In 1967, Sterling was attacked. In November of that year, the Bank of England (assisted by other central banks) was unable to protect the British Pound and it was devalued; this was the first post-Bretton Woods failure on the part of the central banks to intervene in the market to maintain the fixed rate of exchange. In 1968, the U.S. Dollar was under pressure. Germany was obliged to absorb (i.e., buy) Dollars to keep the Deutsche Mark from getting stronger; the Deutsche Mark eventually appreciated in 1969. Two years later, U.S. President Richard Nixon suspended the Dollar's convertibility into precious metal and imposed wage and price controls in the face of a weakening Dollar. Something had to be done.

In December of 1971, Bretton Woods was superseded by a new arrangement that allowed for a wider range of fluctuation (2.25%) around the central or par rates and that increased the Dollar-gold peg to USD 38 per ounce. Signed at the Smithsonian Institution in Washington, D.C., this accord was innovatively known as the Smithsonian Agreement. In 1972, the European Economic Community (EEC) decided to halve the width of these bands for their respective currencies in order to reduce intra-European currency risk. This allowed for some FX movement (not a "fixed peg," but not the wider band instituted by the Smithsonian Agreement). Membership, though, in this cooperative was voluntary, and many countries came and went as they pleased. In 1973, in the words of one market commentator, "the snake died" and the U.S. Dollar devalued by 10%. This metamorphosis effectively marked the change from the old fixed exchange rate regime to the new floating exchange rate regime; this is a major landmark in FX history.

In 1985, another international conference composed of G-7 representatives met at the Plaza Hotel in New York and agreed to engage in a concerted effort to lower the value of the U.S. Dollar; this was known as the Plaza Accord. By the next year, the Dollar had fallen approximately 25%. By 1987, the negative repercussions of the Dollar's free fall were apparent and many central banks intervened to reverse (or, at the very least, to halt) this directional move. We might ask, how far does a currency have to move before it is labeled "a crisis"?

There have been foreign exchange crises that did not necessarily involve dramatic exchange rate moves.

BANKHAUS HERSTATT

One of the issues with global foreign exchange settlement was that the currency deliveries often took place at different times during the day (and, indeed, may have taken place before or after local business hours for the counterparties to an FX transaction); in other words, the currency you paid may have left while you were sleeping, while the currency you were expecting to receive may not have arrived until the middle of your work day. Although one might think that this should not have been particularly problematic (and, if one were used to U.S. banking hours, this may not have even seemed particularly surprising), settlement risk has been a real issue in FX. Perhaps one of the most prominent examples involved Bank Herstatt.[3]

On June 26, 1974, Bankhaus Herstatt (a smaller financial institution in Cologne) had their banking license revoked by the German regulators and were, literally, shut down at the close of the local business day and ordered into liquidation. An active FX market participant, Bank Herstatt had received payments (in Deutsche Marks) while open, but were unable to reciprocate the offsetting payments associated with those receipts in subsequent (e.g., U.S. Dollar) time zones. Herstatt's correspondent bank in the United States suspended any outgoing payments pending the regulatory investigation. This event did not involve marginal revaluation risk; the full notional or face value of the settlement was lost. "The failure of Bank Herstatt caused three days of disruption in the settlement of foreign exchange transactions in New York."[4] This event has been characterized as having contained elements of settlement risk, regulatory risk, credit risk, liquidity risk, market risk, replacement risk, legal risk, price risk, time-zone risk, and so on. This particular sort of risk is currently being mitigated by continuous linked settlements (CLS™), a process facilitated by CLS Bank International,[5] which ensures the bilateral exchanges of currencies, but, although this covers "the majority of cross-currency transactions across the globe," it only allows for settlement in 15 currencies—so settlement risk still remains an issue in FX.

THE ERM CRISIS OF 1992

In 1979, most of the countries making up the European Union (EU) entered into an arrangement known as the European Monetary System (EMS). One of the unique aspects of this system was the creation of a novel currency unit called the ECU or "ecu" (effectively a basket of currencies, neither legal tender nor a means of payment, but an accounting unit); by linking the individual currencies to the ECU at a central or par rate, exchange rates between member currency pairs were similarly tied. Central bank intervention was required when the exchange rate reached 75% of its maximum-allowable divergence. While there were occasional adjustments to the ERM rates, this system held up until 1992.

In September and October 1992, amid political turmoil surrounding the ratification of the Maastricht Treaty in France, the lack of coordinated efforts of the EU central banks, and a certain lack of credibility about the ability on the part of the Bank of England to keep GBP within its band, George Soros and others attacked the Pound. In attempting to defend their currency, on Wednesday, September 16 alone—a day that became known as Black Wednesday—the Bank of England squandered around USD 15 billion worth of foreign exchange reserves buying Pounds; eventually they ran out of reserves and GBP was forced out of the Exchange Rate Mechanism (ERM) along with Italian Lira. On September 16, Soros made a profit of approximately USD 2 billion based on his short Pound and short Italian Lira positions as well as additional bets on Swedish Krona, and other currency and equity markets around the world. This day earned George Soros the title "The Man Who Broke the Bank of England."[6]

The inability of central banks to maintain an artificially supported price in the foreign exchange markets is a common theme of FX crises. At the time, George Soros himself said of speculation:

> *Measures to stop it, such as exchange controls, usually do even more harm. Fixed exchange rate systems are also flawed, because they eventually fall apart. In fact, any exchange rate system is flawed and the longer it exists the greater the flaws become. The only escape is to have no exchange rate system at all, but a single currency in Europe, as in the U.S. It would put speculators like me out of business, but I would be delighted to make the sacrifice.[7]*

Perhaps Soros should also be credited with the nickname, "The Godfather of the Euro"!

Interestingly, while this quote at first seemed to advocate free markets and floating exchange rates, Soros also believes that, "freely floating exchange rates are cumulatively destabilizing."[8] The logical extension of the Soros worldview and the doctrine of what he calls "reflexivity" (referring to the feedback by which market participants' beliefs, decisions, and actions influence what actually happens in the future) manifest themselves in his opinion that "financial markets are inherently unstable." This assertion is not new with Soros; it has been articulated in a variety of ways from an incredibly wide range of sources (from Keynes to Grossman and Stiglitz) for very different reasons. Perhaps FX crises are unavoidable?

THE ASIAN CRISIS OF 1997

The Asian Crisis was actually more of an equity bubble that had foreign exchange implications than an FX bubble that resulted in a flight from Asian stock markets. The proximate cause of this crisis, which actually began in the summer of 1996, was a herd-mentality exodus from the equity market in Thailand. The Thai Baht was also the target of concerted speculative attacks, but the floodgates really opened when Western investors started to flee from Baht-denominated assets—with the associated selling of Thai Baht. One of the interesting aspects of the Asian Crisis was the transmission of this frenzy into other nearby countries—from Thailand, to Malaysia, to Indonesia, to the Philippines, and to South Korea. Presumably the deterioration of the Thai Baht had negative implications for its neighbors and trade partners.

In one of the more interesting exchanges (verbal, not financial) at the time on September 20, 1997, Malaysian Prime Minister Mahathir, during an address at an IMF/World Bank conference in Hong Kong, stated that "currency trading is immoral and should be stopped." The next day, George Soros responded, "Dr. Mahathir is a menace to his own country."

Stanley Fischer, in a 1998 address "The Asian Crisis: A View from the IMF," expressed his belief that "They (Thailand, Indonesia, and Korea) have all suffered a loss of confidence, and their currencies are deeply depreciated. Moreover, in each country, weak financial systems, excessive unhedged foreign borrowing by the domestic private sector, and a lack of transparency about the ties between government, business, and banks have both contributed to the crisis and complicated efforts to diffuse it."[9]

THE RUSSIAN CRISIS OF 1998

This crisis, usually identified as the Russian Debt Crisis, was triggered by a formal devaluation of the Russian Ruble on August 17, 1998 and the default on Ruble-denominated debt by the Russian central bank. There followed a panic security sell-off in Russia, which only exacerbated the Ruble's fall; the Ruble floated on September 2. Within a relatively short period of time, the Ruble lost 80% of its value (peaking at around 21 Rubles per Dollar, compared to a predevaluation exchange rate of 6.29). Perhaps in a display of aggressor–victim turnabout, this time, as opposed to the hedge fund being the slayer of the government and/or central bank, the tables were turned: Russia's unilateral decision to simply renege on its outstanding bonds was one of the material factors that took down Long Term Capital Management (LTCM), probably the largest, best known, and most celebrated hedge fund at that time. Not long ago, someone on the trading floor said, "Long Term Capital Management," and someone else swung around in their chair and said, "They were neither. They didn't last long and they didn't manage their capital very well, did they?"[10]

THE TURKISH LIRA CRISIS OF 2001

This crisis was a bit different in that the currency collapse stemmed from political controversy and a lack of confidence in the banking system as opposed to market pressure. On February 19, 2001, President Ahmet Necdet Sezer and Prime Minister Bulent Ecevit clashed in a National Security Council meeting at which Turkey's prospects for EU membership was discussed. There followed personal attacks, allegations of political corruption, and investigations into the "graft ridden" "corruption-plagued" state-owned banking system. Compounding these problems, Turkey had experienced particularly high inflation, massive government debt, negative real economic growth, and serious unemployment. Before the political fallout, one U.S. Dollar traded for 650,000 Turkish Lira; by October 21, 2001, one U.S. Dollar traded for 1,678,822 Turkish Lira. The Turkish Lira was notable, at that time, for being the least valued currency unit in the world. Headlines around the world read "Europe Holds its Breath as Turkish Lira Dives," "Turkish Lira takes Pounding," and "New Financial Crisis Causes Currency Value to Plunge 40%." A local Turkish pensioner was quoted as saying, "I am in shock, I cannot even comment." The International Monetary Fund sent in a "swat team" to sort things out. On January 1, 2005, the Republic of Turkey replaced the old Turkish Lira (TRL) with a new currency—the new Turkish Lira—which has an ISO code that perhaps reflects at least a modicum of hope (TRY): 1,000,000 TRL = 1 TRY.

THE ARGENTINEAN PESO CRISIS OF 2002

After years of economic instability, excessive inflation, and political uncertainty, Argentina decided to support their currency, the Argentinean Peso, with the introduction of a U.S. Dollar-based Currency Board on April 1, 1991 (under which the Central Bank of Argentina would hold one Dollar for every outstanding Argentinean Peso). The benefits of backing the Peso with the Dollar include providing some confidence in the currency, which had been lacking in the past, curtailing inflation (unless imported from the United States), and instilling some fiscal discipline that may have previously been difficult to implement.

Through the 1990s, Argentina had been one of the most prosperous economies in Latin America. One of the contributing factors leading up to the crisis in Argentina was the fact that Brazil (an important economic trade partner) had devalued by over 30% in 1999—making Argentina's economy significantly less competitive in international markets. Further, the U.S. Dollar, to which the Argentinean Peso was pegged one-for-one, strengthened between 1999 and 2001—dragging the Argentinean Peso along with it. Obviously this had a negative impact on those sectors of the Argentinean economy that were more "open" (or vulnerable to changes in exchange rates).

In late 2001, Argentina threatened to stop servicing its USD 155,000,000,000 in debt. International investor confidence in Argentina evaporated and there was a subsequent accelerating flight of financial capital from the country—driven by the fears of external investors. Moreover, there was a simultaneous deterioration in the confidence associated with the banking system within Argentina. Individuals in Argentina began withdrawing large amounts of Pesos from their bank accounts and sought to convert them into Dollars; the government responded by effectively freezing those bank accounts, which only added to the panic. In January 6, 2002, the Currency Board was abandoned and the Peso was allowed to float against the U.S. Dollar. Within a month, the Argentinean Peso had lost more than half its value (versus the USD).

The abandonment of the currency peg led to a massive Argentinean Peso devaluation, a return to large double-digit inflation, widespread unemployment, and other economic ills. To add to these problems, on November 14, 2002, Argentina actually failed to repay a debt obligation to the World Bank (though they did pay the interest on that debt). This constituted a "credit event" (e.g., default, missed payment on borrowed money, bankruptcy, moratorium, restructuring under duress), which triggered credit default swaps—an increasingly common credit derivative instrument. These allowed the buyers of credit default protection, many of whom were investors in Argentinian debt (and who had paid a "premium" similar to an insurance premium for their protection) to deliver their defaulted securities for their face value (to the sellers of credit default protection).[11] It is significant that settlement of these credit default swaps occurred in an ordinary orderly capital markets (e.g., two-day settlement) fashion—as opposed to requiring a legal workout, as is the case with many bond defaults, which can take months to resolve.

Since that time, Argentina has not only rebounded, but the government has had to actively manage the appreciation of the Peso (so as not to reverse the beneficial trade flows that have resulted from their weak currency). Although inflation is currently around 12%, real economic growth is over 10%. This combination, for the majority of Argentinians, appears to be very welcome—a far cry from an urban population recognizable for their practice of banging pots and pans in the street and, literally, attacking banks and foreign businesses.

SUMMARY

A "crisis," according to most dictionaries, is a critical moment, an uncertain and worrisome time, an unstable situation, or a prelude to a breakdown or disaster. It is the Chinese term for "crisis"—"wei ji"—that I find interesting; it is a composite of two words meaning "danger" and "opportunity."

Without attempting to be too overarching, some of the common themes that are evident in examining many of the modern foreign exchange crises involve attempting to support the local currency at an unreasonable level without sufficient international foreign exchange reserves, lack of confidence in a currency brought on by a lack of confidence in the government and/or banking system, weak underlying macroeconomic conditions, debt considerations (especially when liabilities are not denominated in local currency), the absence of an overseeing international body with the authority to intervene in the foreign exchange markets, and the presence of market participants (often hedge funds) who are willing to act (i.e., risk financial capital) in an effort to profit from the significant foreign exchange moves that often accompany these circumstances.[12]

How important are these "speculators/arbitrageurs" in precipitating FX crises?

As long as there are free markets, there will be situations when prices will move—and occasionally move radically. Bill Gross, a high-profile fixed income investment professional, has identified what he refers to as "capital market vigilantes"—hedge fund managers, international mutual fund managers, and stock, bond, and currency traders; these aggressively seek returns and occasionally "attack on the 'wires' by selling and depreciating currencies."[13] He cites the example of Mexico in 1994 when, with an exploding trade balance, the "vigilantes" identified the Peso as "significantly overvalued" and, over the course of just a few days, withdrew "billions of Dollars in international investments." This meant a massive selling of the Peso; Mexico had to devalue its currency by 50%. Gross continues, "Well-publicized financial confrontations around the globe, such as those in Argentina, France, Italy, and Spain in recent years, all serve as reminders of the power of the vigilantes."[14] Is there anything that can be done to stop the FX "vigilantes"? Over the years, central banks have occasionally engaged in certain practices to discourage speculation in their currency. In 1993, for example, Ireland's central bank pushed overnight interest rates to 100% to penalize those with short Irish punt positions. Nevertheless, the resources necessary and the costs involved in challenging the weight of the financial markets can be quite daunting. Dick Nanto, in a CRS report to Congress in 1998, wrote, "The mammoth size of the world exchange markets makes them virtually impossible for governments to control."[15]

When Milton Friedman and Anna Schwartz first postulated this idea in 1971 in their landmark treatise *A Monetary History of the United States, 1867–1960*, it was a radical notion:

> *Then we get to the conclusion, . . . there is likely not enough reserves anywhere in the world, particularly in a central bank, to defend the wrong exchange rate. But who wants to have the wrong exchange rate? We always want the right exchange rate. The fact of the matter is, if you look at the history of all speculative attacks against countries, if there is such a thing, they are always happening to governments that are attempting to defend a price that is different than what has been determined in the marketplace.*[16]

CHAPTER 13

Technical Analysis

I always laugh at people who say they've never met a rich technician.

—Martin Schwartz

I've never met a rich technician.

—Jim Rogers

Disclaimer: This chapter is not meant to provide a tutorial in technical analysis. There are a number of classic references on this subject: John Murphy's *Technical Analysis of the Financial Markets*, Martin Pring's *Technical Analysis Explained*, and Jack Schwager's *Getting Started in Technical Analysis*. What we hope to do here is to ensure that the reader knows the names of some of the more popular approaches, to try to explain why it may be worthwhile gaining some familiarity with one or more of these techniques, especially in the FX markets, and to identify how this "art" is evolving into a "science."

INTRODUCTION

As we mentioned briefly in our discussion of marketmaking, there are two primary avenues of analysis that attempt to gain an insight into whether a market is going up or going down: fundamental analysis and technical analysis. Fundamental analysis (also known colloquially as "demand and supply") purports to provide an understanding of the underlying economic factors that are influencing buyers and sellers, and, thereby, to gain some insights or advantages in predicting future price movements. Technical analysis is an entirely different paradigm. Utterly eschewing the underlying economic drivers, technical analysts focus solely on past price movements, trends, and patterns in an effort to gain an understanding of where markets are headed next.

When I was studying economics and finance at the University of Chicago, most of my professors (most of whom had Nobel Prizes in Economic Science) told us that technical analysis was (using singularly stronger language than what I report here) "nonsense"; their justification usually turned on an argument set forth by Milton Friedman, who reasoned that it would take only a very small number of entrepreneurial individuals to exploit any market inefficiency and, in doing so, to make the markets efficient (in the sense that consistent arbitrage would not be possible). Or, at the very least, if the data were conscientiously obtained and analyzed properly, this would reinforce the notion that there is "no free lunch" available in the financial markets.

Because past price data is now generally and widely available and because there are presumably a large number of smart market participants looking at it, examining it, modeling it, searching for patterns, opportunities, signals, recurring themes, the thought that there might be value for any one individual in analyzing that same information is, at best, tenuous. The notion behind efficient markets—that the market's best guess of where the price is going next is where it is right now—suggests that technical analysis cannot "work." Friedman might even add that, if someone did stumble across a process that purported to identify a profitable trading strategy based on reviewing some past price history, then the act of trading on that information would tend to eliminate the profitability of that strategy and the informational content of the data.

What was I to think, then, when I left the academic community (still brandishing my University of Chicago "efficient markets" tattoo) and entered the rank and file of market practitioners, who every morning, often before the sun came up, pulled out their charts, examined their resistance and support levels, analyzed their Elliott waves, reviewed their Japanese candlesticks ("Oh my, it's a shooting star!"), consulted their Fibonacci numbers, and looked at their flags, pennants, relative strength indices, momentum figures, and so on?

My professors, for the most part (independent of their million dollar Nobel prizes), were living in unimpressive homes and apartments on the south side of Chicago and drove old Chevy Impalas; these traders drove brand new Jaguars and Ferraris and lived in multi-million dollar estates in the suburbs. Is there something to technical analysis? I believe that there is probably some value to this discipline, but we have to ask, "What and why?"

Bill Gross, CIO of PIMCO, has written, "Technical analysts are the witch doctors of our business," but, in the same breath, Gross confesses, "Well, there's something to it, I'll admit . . ."[1]

WHAT IS TECHNICAL ANALYSIS?

Technical analysis is that umbrella-like characterization associated with the various methods of examination of past price data (in one representative form or another) with a view to gleaning from that information some insight into where that market price is headed. Most of those who practice this art will describe it as such (that is, "an art"), but increasingly "(i)n recent years . . . more open minded academics and practitioners have joined forces and created the nascent field . . . (s)upported by advanced risk management techniques, mathematical theories, and the power of modern computers".[2] There are sometimes more efficient ways of looking at data and, increasingly, market participants have employed the following modern tools as they have become more widely accessible: artificial intelligence, neural networks, and genetic algorithms.

Traditionally, technical analysis was synonymous with charting. If one traded, say, soybeans, then one could attempt to discern the direction of their market price based on the past price history of soybeans (and usually one **only** looked at the past price history of soybeans). There are some aphorisms that tend to circulate around the financial markets. One of the most common is, "The trend is your friend." If the price of soybeans has been rising, buy them, because the trend is positive or upward; if the trend were southerly, sell them. Prior to the availability of modern computers and access to historical price databases, many market participants kept track of (i.e., recorded) these prices themselves. The most common form of representation for this data was a chart—a picture of the numbers transmitted to graph paper. Many of the approaches employed by technicians (those engaged in the practice of technical analysis) involve attempting to identify the trend (and patterns within the trend, and deviations from that trend, and reversals of the trend, and so on).

METHODS OF TECHNICAL ANALYSIS

There are many ways to summarize past price information. The simplest approach is simply to connect the dots (i.e., to look at a continuous graph of past prices). See Figure 13.1.

Whenever you analyze data, though, one must make a number of decisions (i.e., "judgement calls"). Will you look at continuous data or high

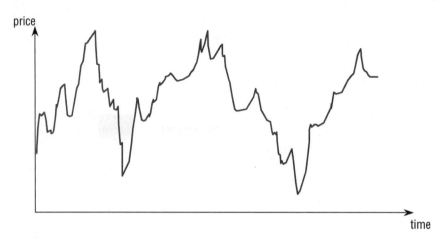

FIGURE 13.1   A Chart of Past Price History

frequency data (sometimes called "tick data") or periodic data (e.g., prices at 10-minute intervals) or daily closing prices or weekly price moves? Will the prices you examine be trade prices or the bid–ask spread or midmarket prices? If looking at periodic trade data, what will you do if there was no trade? Can you look at prices and traded volume simultaneously? If you decide to summarize or compress daily data, what might you like to be able to see? You might like to know where the asset price opened that day, the highest price realized that day, the lowest price realized that day (and, obviously, knowing the high and the low, you would know the daily range in which that price moved), where the asset price closed on the day. How to summarize all these facts? One approach that is very popular is known as **Japanese candlesticks**. This method summarizes a time interval's price action in a simple picture. The body of the candlestick is white if the end (closing) price is higher than the start (opening) price; it is black when the close is lower than the open. The range is identified by the height of the candlestick—including the wick(s) or shadow(s) that extend from the top and bottom of the candle. See Figure 13.2.

In condensing the day's trading data from a time series of prices into a vertical pictogram, you lose detail (as is always the case when you summarize information). In other words, the precise path that the prices followed is unknown. To see this, observe the very different looking price paths in Figure 13.3, which generate the same candlestick.

Moreover, looking at the shape and "color" of one Japanese candlestick is said not to be, in any way, sufficient to indicate market direction. A

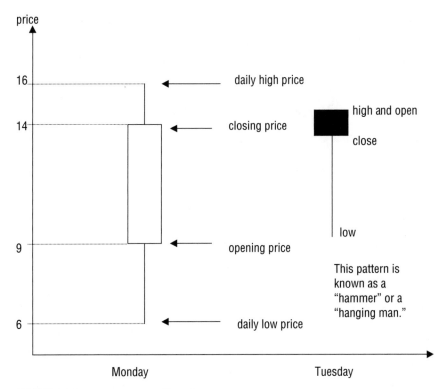

FIGURE 13.2　Japanese Candlesticks

candlestick history (a collective pattern of shapes and trends) is presumably needed to really tell the whole story.

Bar charts, summarizing similar information (open, high, low, and close) are also used by technicians, but the ease of reading Japanese candlesticks presumably makes them an attractive (and often preferred) graphing or charting instrument. The difference between a Japanese candlestick and a bar chart can be seen in Figure 13.4.

Other Approaches

Data can be represented in many forms. If one believes that trade or market data is "noisy" (in the sense that there are a great deal of fluctuations about the true underlying trend), then the technician may be inclined to try to "smooth" the time series. This can be done with the assistance of **moving averages**. A moving average simply summarizes the running "statistical

Both of the following price histories would result in the same Japanese candlestick.

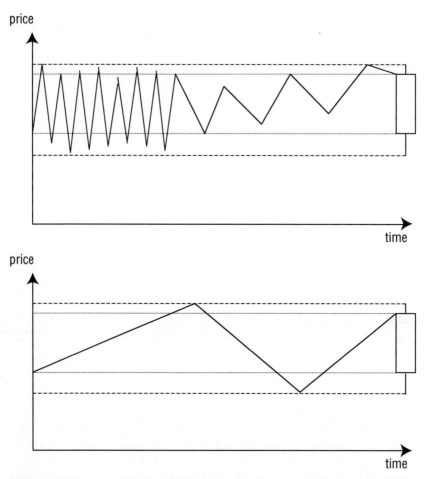

FIGURE 13.3   Different Data—Same Candlestick (Some Pictures Summarizing Data Lose Detail)

mean," which, if a set of consecutive data points are used to generate each average "point," will tend to smooth the numbers and presumably help identify a trend. Significance (market, not statistical) is often attributed to that point in time when a moving average of a certain length (say, the 30-day moving average) "crosses" a moving average of another length (say, the 90-day moving average). Just as identifying a trend is one of the goals

Japanese Candlestick   Bar Chart

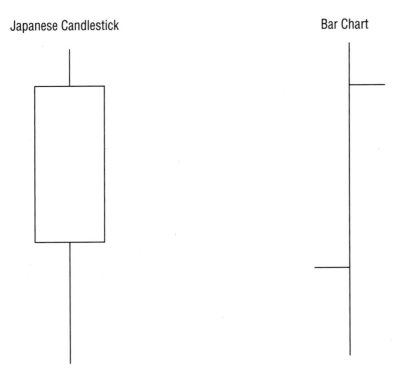

FIGURE 13.4   Japanese Candlestick versus Bar Chart

of technical analysis, so, too, is the identification of the reversal of a trend; a 30-day moving average crossing a 90-day moving average might be said to possibly confirm a trend reversal. This approach is said to help "time the market." Timing the market (i.e., identifying entry or exit points) is one area in which technicians attempt to add value for traders and portfolio managers.

Similarly, if prices are subject to a degree of randomness, then one might acknowledge that there is some range of uncertainty associated with the data at which one looks; the source of the variability arises from a variety of sources, including fickle investors, delayed data reporting, bad information, and so on. Some techniques seek to identify when prices break out of a range. One of the more popular approaches involves **Bollinger bands**, but there are also **cloud patterns** and other techniques that help define breakouts to the upside and downside.

One of the more popular schools of technical analysis is **Elliott Wave Theory**. This discipline, pioneered by Ralph Nelson Elliott in the 1930s, examines price data in an effort to discern a certain commonly recurring configuration; this pattern is generally thought to consist of five waves with the trend (e.g., in the case of a "bullish" market, up-down-up-down-up) known as a "motion wave" followed by three corrective waves (e.g., a "bearish" retracement, down-up-down). These waves are given identifying labels; the trend wave is generally designated 1-2-3-4-5 and the corrective wave, A-B-C or a-b-c. It is most easily described on a graph; see Figure 13.5.

It is said that financial data often exhibits this pattern in a "fractal" way in the sense that you can identify the five up waves followed by three down waves within each leg of a larger five-upward, three-downward pattern.

There are other methods of analysis for cyclical financial data such as **Dow Theory**. Another common technical analysis approach is **pattern recognition** that look at some commonly recurring shapes or tendencies in financial data, identified by such names as head-and-shoulders, pennants,

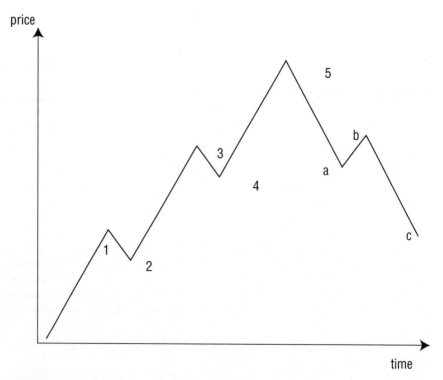

FIGURE 13.5   A Typical Elliott Wave

flags, double tops, triple bottoms, and so on. As an example, a formulating head-and-shoulders pattern may suggest, as in Figure 13.6a, that the price will continue rising until the "shoulder" or "neck line" and then "retrace" (as suggested by the dotted line). A "pennant" is a "consolidating" pattern that supposedly suggests that the price will run (one way or the other— again suggested by the dotted lines) once either the upper resistance line or lower support line is broken; see Figure 13.6b.

Patterns may be one way to understand qualitative price behavior, but having some quantitative sense of where those prices may go, or, having an understanding of what a specific percentage price move might mean for future directional price changes, one needs a numerical foundation. The most cited numbers in technical analysis are **Fibonacci numbers**. Attributed to Leonardo Fibonacci's work of the 1200s, a Fibonacci sequence is formed by adding the two previous numbers in a sequence. For example:

$$1, 2, 3, 5, 8, 13, 21, 34, 55, 89, 144, 233, 377, \ldots$$

In the limit, the ratio of one term to the following term is approximately .618. Followers of Fibonacci place great significance on relative price moves of .618, .382 (which happens to be $1 - .618$), and .50.

The analyses, techniques, or theories that we have mentioned so far

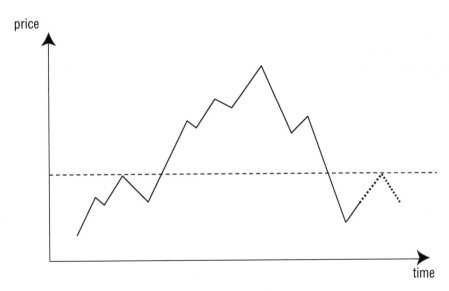

FIGURE 13.6a A Head-and-Shoulders Pattern

price

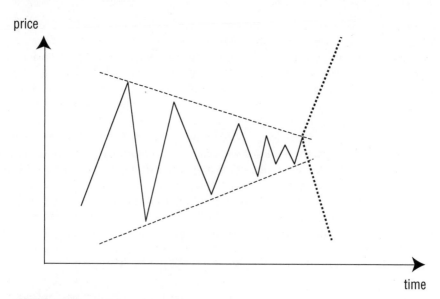

time

FIGURE 13.6b   A Pennant Pattern

are in no way exhaustive. There are also Gann Studies or Gann Angles, point and figure charts, stochastics, relative strength indices (RSI), and a number of other approaches.

TECHNICAL ANALYSIS IN FOREIGN EXCHANGE

It would be difficult to find many market professionals in foreign exchange who do not look at technicals in one way or another. Some of the more sophisticated may identify their approach as "statistical arbitrage" at the same time others (who are less convinced of the "free lunch") refer to "black-box trading." Is there more to technical analysis in foreign exchange than in other markets? Good question.

At the end of the day, I am an economist and I believe that if you see USD|JPY bouncing off 120.00 from below, there's a reason for that. If net buying drives prices up, then it must be selling that forces the exchange rate down. How do I know that somebody is selling Dollars at 120? As an institution that accepts limit orders for contingent execution, we may know there will be selling at 120 because we are going to sell (on behalf of one of our clients) if USD|JPY ever gets there. Furthermore, there is occasionally, though less frequently, central bank intervention (and this may transpire because the Bank of Japan has decided to sell U.S. Dollars at 120). Moreover, in order to hedge an exotic out-strike (that is, a large position from a barrier option with an out-strike, for example, at 120), market participants (like UBS) may have to sell a huge amount of Dollars as we approach that level in order to maintain a dynamically "delta neutral" position or "flat" book. If our counterparties were to randomly choose their barriers (at, for example, 119.73), perhaps we would not see the large trading activity at 120, but market participants often choose their barriers at nice round (or significant) numbers (e.g., 120, the figure). For all of these reasons, ultimately founded on and explainable by the actual underlying trading activity, there may well be a resistance level at 120.00. See Figure 13.7. Finally, over and above limit orders, central bank intervention, and barrier options, there may also be some psychology at work in the market; this is the notion of a "self-fulfilling prophecy" in which, because a sufficiently large number of foreign exchange participants think something will happen, then it actually will happen.[3]

Technical analysts sometimes suggest that if a significant resistance level (like 120) is breached, then there could be a sharp rise in the exchange rate. If the Bank of Japan were to stop defending that level (120) or if all the limit orders (to sell Dollars at 120) were filled, perhaps it would be no

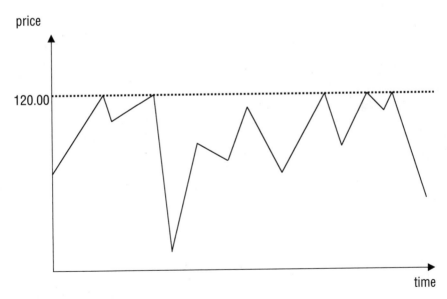

FIGURE 13.7 USD|JPY Resistance Level at 120.00

surprise that there would be an upward jump in the exchange rate (possibly to the next significant level).

Even some of those client-facing individuals at banks/broker dealers who are not believers in technical analysis still look at the charts—for two reasons. First, they know that some of their clients are watching these numbers and patterns; they want to be involved in that exchange and they also want to be informed when discussing market strategy. Just because a waiter can't stand Brussels sprouts, it should not preclude him from serving them to a customer who does want them. Second, some salespeople understand that technical analysis may provide them with something interesting to talk about (a "story") that may lead to a positive interaction with a client (e.g., "Did you see that the three-month moving average just crossed the one-month moving average?").

TECHNICAL ANALYSIS TODAY

The number of individuals who are actively involved in the FX markets has exploded [as a result of ubiquitous computing power, electronic communications networks (ECNs), direct market access tools and firms, the proliferation of information, and so on]. The market has responded by supplying trading tools to these day traders and smaller investors. There are more technical systems available than one can count. Each presumes to represent the holy grail for the individual investor/trader (up to the fiduciary responsibility disclaimer, that is). Nevertheless, technical analysis software seems to be proliferating at an incredible rate. Even the professional traders and marketmakers are engaging in "algorithmic trading," which, at its core, attempts to expedite market orders at a lower cost and in more efficient ways by taking into account patterns, such as trends, trading volumes, and other data.

Dave Toth, former U.S. head of technical analysis at UBS (who has gone on to manage money himself at CEC Capital, LLC in Chicago) stressed that the different approaches or theories on technical analysis do not compete with one another, but rather are simply different ways of saying the same thing. After all, Dave notes, "various technical theories like Elliott Wave, Dow, and candlesticks, for the most part, simply use different terminology to describe where any market may be within one of its three technical states—trending, consolidating, or reversing." "Elliott is to Dow is to candlesticks as English is to French is to Spanish."

SUMMARY

There is no doubt that one would be hard-pressed to find a trader, portfolio manager, hedge fund principal, or investment professional who would not want an edge or advantage over the market if such was legally available and cost effective. For that reason alone, many individuals in the financial markets look at some sort of technical analysis.

The representations, tools, techniques, systems, graphs, and screens may take on very different looks, but, in the end, they are all intended to summarize past price action with the goal of obtaining some insight into where the price will be in the future.

Whether one looks at charts, Japanese candlesticks, Elliott waves, Fibonacci numbers, moving averages, pattern recognition, Dow cycles, Gann Studies, relative strength indices (RSI), stochastics, cloud patterns, Bollinger bands, or some other more statistically-grounded approach, technical analysis is meant to discern market direction.

Ultimately, Jason Perl, global head of the technical strategy group at UBS has stated that although some may have the impression that technical analysis assumes some sort of market inefficiency, he starts from the presumption that the FX markets are extremely efficient, which is why he feels very comfortable focusing on past prices and does not feel the need to employ multifactor econometric models. I might add that, as an economist, I believe the foreign exchange markets are very efficient (by just about any criteria one might consider). Furthermore, as an economist, I am a believer in the theory of "revealed preference"; this means that you can infer an individual's or organization's preferences (what they value) by observing what they do, how they spend, and so on. Most of the major currency dealing banks employ a team of technical analysts who serve as a resource for their employees and their clients. Somebody believes in the value of technical analysis.[4]

For a discipline that purports to be quantitative in nature, though, one would think that technical analysis and its predictions could be utterly and directly evaluated by simple (or at least straightforward) statistical analyses, but these techniques, for years, avoided the scrutiny of careful and sophisticated statistical analyses driven, I believe, in large part by two factors: the disdain held for technical analysis on the part of the academic community, which is responsible for the majority of published research, and the fact that there are very few schools that seriously teach these approaches, techniques, and disciplines (and so the academic world has remained extremely ignorant of technical analysis).[5] Blake LeBaron and others in the academic community have only relatively recently (and increasingly) sought to either confirm or rule out the effectiveness (as gauged by overall net expected, and statistically significantly, positive returns) associated with a variety of classes of FX trading rules.[6] But things are changing; Felix Gasser writes:

> *Technical analysis (TA) is defined as the analysis of pure market price movement as time series called charts. Although this is a*

clear definition, anyone who has read a book on TA knows it's not necessarily straightforward. If we include all the tools and theories labeled technical—from the highly scientific to the rather eso-teric—the subject can become controversial and confusing. The flood of technical instruments has turned TA into an alchemist's melting pot, resulting in skepticism especially among the academic community. On the other hand, the influx from other disciplines, most of all statistics and the computer sciences, have added pow-erful analytical tools, strengthening the position of TA as a valid discipline in the investment community and increasingly in acade-mia as well.[7]

CHAPTER 14

Where Do We Go from Here?

In the last Triennial Survey of Foreign Exchange, the BIS noted that average daily turnover in FX between 2001 and 2004 rose by 57% at current exchange rates. Moreover, average daily turnover in the FX derivatives market and the OTC derivatives market generally were both up around 110% over the same time span. The factors contributing to that impressive surge in traded volume include "the growing importance of hedge funds," "investors' interest in foreign exchange as an asset class alternative to equity and fixed income," "the more active role of asset managers," "clear trends" leading to "momentum trading," "higher volatility," which "induced an increase in hedging activity," and "interest rate differentials," which drove "carry" trades. Other factors are also identified as significant; these involve a trend for global institutional (or "real") money (as opposed to hedge fund or leveraged capital) to seek offshore opportunities, the relaxation of restrictions on foreign exchange exposures for pension funds, and the increase in trading activities by commodity trading advisors (CTAs). Overall, this explosion in volume can be attributed to an expansion in FX transactions across the range of foreign exchange markets participants.

Although market conditions will continue to change, and international trade and capital flows will, as always, have direct and significant repercussions on the FX markets, there is no reason to believe that the realm of foreign exchange will not continue to expand in a way consistent with past developments.

Having said that, the *BIS Quarterly Review* is extremely circumspect. In their assessment, Galati and Melvin posit the lack of a clear future direction for the FX markets:

> So while the evidence supports the relative attractiveness of foreign exchange as an asset class, the level of investor interest in currencies is not certain to persist in the future.[1]

The FX markets will continue to be shaped by the factors that drive currency flows: international trade, global investing, capital market flows, multinational businesses, government policy (both trade policy and monetary policy), inflationary expectations, economic performance and productivity, technological advances, natural resources, comparative advantages, tariffs and trade barriers, transportation technology, consumer and corporate confidence, interest rates and interest rate differentials, accounting rules and reporting requirements, volatility, trading execution systems and communications technology, political considerations, rumors, and so on. In short, everything that moves markets.

What are the issues going forward? Will these markets continue to be essentially unregulated or will they (as we are seeing, for example, with the hedge fund industry) become the focus of increased scrutiny and regulatory supervision? Will the trend in the reduction of the number of world currencies continue? How will advances in information technology change the FX landscape—especially in terms of trading? What will the continuing consolidation in the banking and financial services industry mean for FX market spreads, profitability, and product innovation? How will the "currency area" of the Euro fare—both economically and politically?

What's next?

Good question.

One of the things that will be interesting to follow is whether the Euro challenges the position of the U.S. Dollar as the reserve currency of choice around the world. For some time, the Dollar has dominated financial markets (even in London, gold has been quoted in Dollars per ounce and, globally, crude oil has also typically been quoted in Dollars per barrel). We have seen a recent drift toward quoting these prices in Euro. No doubt the future likelihood of the Euro as a global reserve currency will depend critically on the ongoing behavior and credibility of the European Central Bank as well as the performance of the national economies in the Euro-Zone. Obviously, there are a great many countries that would benefit from insider status with respect to the Euro, but the critical issue on this topic centers on the acquiescence of the EuroZone members to adapt to and to embrace the common ECB monetary policy. Can the ECB satisfactorily convince Ireland, Germany, and Slovakia that their monetary policy is indeed "one size fits all"?

But why stop at Europe? As former Federal Reserve Governor Paul Volcker once noted, "A global economy needs a global currency."[2] Robert Mundell, a Nobel Prize-winning economist and Professor of Economics at

Columbia University, has admirably argued the case for a world currency. Mundell wrote:

> *My ideal and equilibrium solution would be a world currency (but not a single world currency) in which each country would produce its own unit that exchanges at par with the world unit. We could call it the international dollar or, to avoid the parochial national connotation, the intor, a contraction of 'international' and the French word for gold. . . . Everything would be priced in terms of intors . . .*[3]

Mundell believes that, "(t)he benefits from a world currency would be enormous."[4]

The downside of Mundell's proposed "intor"? Who would control the growth in the supply of intors? Back to the topic of monetary policy—and who's in charge. Mundell proposed that monetary policy could possibly be decided upon by a board of governors of the International Monetary Fund. But how many countries would like their monetary policy decided by a committee—on which they have but one vote (or a minority voice, at any rate)? Furthermore, in Mundell's recommendation, there would still be a need to identify who would be responsible for maintaining the par rate of exchange. As we saw in Chapter 12, it is often either the inability or the unwillingness of a country to maintain the value of their currency that leads to foreign exchange crises.

At some point, the economics ends and the egos and the politics begin. Mundell even admits:

> *I think that if we think in terms of a world currency, there is no need whatsoever to have a single currency. I think you could only do that with a complete rupture or change in political circumstances—maybe if we were invaded by Mars, they might impose on us a single currency, but each country would still want to keep its own currency.*[5]

In a bit more grounded proposal, Mundell has also suggested an alternative to the intor based on the three of the major currencies—Dollar, Euro, and Yen: the "**dey.**" Possibly a "currency basket" or "FX index."

There actually exists a group called the Single Global Currency

Association, which, as the name suggests, is intended to promote and implement a common worldwide monetary unit; some of the proposed names for the new currency: "global," "mundo," and "eartha." Whether we eventually end up with a single universal pazooza, who knows? But the trend toward currency consolidation is continuing. In 2005, a handful of West African nations (Gambia, Ghana, Guinea, Nigeria, and Sierra Leone) intend to adopt a new common currency called the "eco." There is also a planned launch of a common money for several Middle Eastern countries as well: Bahrain, Kuwait, Oman, Qatar, Saudi Arabia, and the United Arab Emirates.

Whether the world migrates to a single global currency or not, George Soros, a direct beneficiary (and an individual who has occasionally been identified as a cause) of past global currency crises, suggests that he perceives a need for "an international central bank"—or at least some overseeing regulatory institution. Soros wrote:

> *The inadequacies of the current architecture became glaringly obvious during the global financial crisis that was unleashed in Thailand. One deficiency was the lack of adequate international supervisory and regulatory authority.*[6]

He argues that it is not a new financial system that is needed (as ultimately, paraphrasing Winston Churchill, he believes that the market mechanism serves as the worst form of financial organization—except for all the others), nor periodic reforms or revisions of that system, but an active, ever-present monitor and guide that can assist in tempering the volatile events that arise in the natural course of global free market activity. And, if there were to be a single international money, Soros has proposed that the "unit of account would be based on oil."[7] Did Soros really think, when he made that suggestion in 1998, that this proposal would reduce market volatility?

Then again, Soros has clearly expressed his view "that financial markets are inherently unstable":[8]

> *Freely fluctuating currency rates are inherently unstable because of trend-following speculation; moreover, the instability is cumulative because trend-following speculation tends to grow in importance over time. On the other hand, fixed exchange rate regimes are dangerous because breakdowns can be catastrophic. The Asian*

crisis is a case in point. I often compare currency arrangements with matrimonial arrangements: Whatever regime prevails, its opposite looks more attractive.[9]

Where will the foreign exchange markets go from here? Most of us are uncertain, but, unless we move to a single worldwide money, it will likely involve a number of ups and downs—and some of the ups and downs may be large ones!

CHAPTER 15

Conclusion

Although foreign exchange may be confusing, in today's global marketplace, there is a critical need for almost everyone to understand foreign exchange like never before. As the world shrinks, there is an ever-increasing likelihood that we will be required to address the risks associated with the fact that there are different currencies used all around the world and that these currencies will have an immediate impact on *our* world. We must be able to evaluate the effects of, and actively respond to, changes in exchange rates with respect to our consumption decisions, investment portfolios, business plans, government policies, and other life choices (both financial and otherwise). Moreover, there is an ever-increasing probability that we will have to transact in these foreign exchange markets—in our personal or professional life. This book has been intended to assist with this potentially new and doubtlessly confusing milieu.

The words that were written by Claude Tygier some 20 years ago are as true today as they were then:

> To *most people, the arena where the world's major currencies fluctuate against each other remains very much of a mystery.*[1]

Perhaps that is why I enjoy teaching foreign exchange. It is gratifying to empower people with a new language and to assist them in entering and actively participating in a world that I believe is truly fascinating.

At this closing stage, let me summarize what we've attempted to accomplish in this book by stating why I think teaching (and learning about) foreign exchange is so tough.

First, the quoting conventions are convoluted at best. Even the meaning of the expressions "American quote" and "European quote" are generally misunderstood. And the distinctions between "direct" and "indirect," "base" and "counter," "foreign" and "domestic" do nothing to help. Moreover, the quoting conventions are neither consistent, uniform, nor rational. Sometimes it's Peso per Dollar. Sometimes it's Dollar per Euro. And "Dollar-Yen" means Yen per Dollar. That's always sounded backwards to me. (Again, don't blame any of this on me. I didn't make this up.) Further, the fact that the Interbank or OTC market uses one convention (Swiss Francs per Dollar) while the exchanges use the exact opposite (Dollars per Swiss Francs) only makes it worse. And, finally, the financial press doesn't seem to help with this confusion and often seems content to add to the obfuscation.

Second, we use money when we buy and sell things. Most of us are not used to buying and selling money. "After all, what's the price of a Dollar?" "A Dollar." Put another way, we are used to seeing prices quoted in terms of monetary units; money is usually not thought of as the traded asset or underlying.

Third, the language of the currency markets and the associated jargon used by the FX professionals are as foreign to most of us as anything else in foreign exchange. What is "Cable"? The obvious ambiguities and the use of different names for the same thing don't help. A "yard" of Japanese Yen? "He just said 'paid.' Did I buy or sell?" "Yes."

Fourth and finally, as by now I trust you have been made painfully aware, there is always an exception to "the rule" in FX. Forewarned is forearmed!

Hopefully, if you've gotten this far, you've gained a handle on FX conventions; you've been exposed to the jargon (though genuine familiarity and comfort only comes, as with swimming or riding a bicycle, with practice); you've gained an understanding of how this market and it's instruments work; you've acquired an ability to comprehend the reports, stories, and presentations in the popular and financial media; and you also now know some of the more common mistakes to be avoided.

The one thing that this book, unfortunately, cannot tell you is which way the Dollar (or Euro or Yen) is going to go in the future! And that's one of the reasons why I find following the foreign exchange markets to be so interesting, puzzling, and entertaining.

Just remember, the foreign exchange markets are all about buying and selling money, and, as Mignon McLaughlin tells us, "Money is much more exciting than anything it buys."[2] Ultimately, it is our hope that this book has been educational and that what we have conveyed is practical, memorable, and useful.

Precious Metals

The history of money and precious metals are inexorably linked.[1]
—Peter Bernstein

Even though gold and silver have served as money in the past, they are generally recognized today as commodities and are not categorized as money (unless "minted" as in the case of South African Krugerrands and Canadian Maple Leaf coins, and even then, the market values of such coins are based on their metal content and not contingent upon their struck denominations).[2] Having said that, gold is still sometimes employed in international trade settlements and often linked to the foreign exchange departments of banks and broker/dealers.

When the major currencies abandoned the gold standard (that is, when the paper currencies of these countries were no longer redeemable or convertible into gold), a disconnect occurred. To this day, some economists believe that severing the link between precious metals and fiat currency is regrettable, as it affords a far more capricious approach to monetary expansion (and therefore the possibility of inflation) than before. Increasing the money supply by 10% under a gold standard could only happen if the supply of precious metal was comparably increased. This requirement imposed a discipline on governments and politicians which, under most modern forms of monetary creation and expansion, is unthinkable (or at least unnecessary).

Some economists have even gone so far as to suggest that for every X units of currency printed and spent by the government, there should be placed on deposit Y bricks. This does not refer to a brick or ingot of gold or silver, but to an ordinary masonry brick. Even though it may sound like a rather odd idea, the presumption is that at least there would be some restraint imposed on the monetary authorities.

Gold continues to be a global investment vehicle—for both individuals and countries. Robert Mundell tells us that gold is second only to the U.S. Dollar as a reserve asset of the world's central banks and monetary authorities.

Why would an investor want to hold gold? Gold has been identified as playing the dual role as a harbinger of inflation and as a possible hedge against such a general rise in the price level. After all, when we see the price of gold rise from USD 400 to USD 450, our natural thought may be that the shiny yellow metal has gone up in price or strengthened, but it can alternatively be said that the U.S. Dollar has weakened or gone down. Anyone with assets fixed in U.S. Dollar terms will lose purchasing power as the aggregate level of prices rises, but people invested in gold (whose price would presumably move with that of all the other goods and services) could preserve the relative level of their wealth.

Also, since gold is not highly correlated with other asset classes, it has been identified as an attractive diversification component for one's portfolio.

Whether it is rational or not, gold continues to dazzle and draw investors.

In an earlier chapter, we documented some FX crises; there is no dearth of disasters in the world of metals. In a recent article by Rose-Smith and Barber,[3] two of the top five trading blowups of all time (out of an eclectically chosen 30) were metals-related (though one was copper-based, and therefore could be exempted as a commodity crisis).

The other involved the attempt (and in large part, success) by the Hunt brothers (Bunker and Herbert) to corner the silver market throughout the 1970s. At one point, the Hunts were said to own half of the world's deliverable supply. Changes in margin requirements by the Chicago Board of Trade (CBOT) and the Commodity Exchange (COMEX) in New York, reduced maximum contract position size on the exchanges, and the explicit support of regulators eventually helped "burst the bubble." Nevertheless, gold and silver continue to have a staunch following.

How important gold will be in the future, from an economic perspective, will depend on demand and supply. Gold maintains interest as an investment; gold apparently continues to matter to central banks; and gold has real uses in electronics products, jewelry, dental work, and so on. On the financial front, interest in gold and the other precious metals (silver, platinum, palladium) may depend on the expectation of inflation, the belief that gold and its cousins will protect one's wealth from those seemingly ever increasing prices (and even those fickle paper securities), the deterioration of the Dollar, and the degree of risk-aversion in the economy. Back to faith!

In order to understand the appeal for gold and other precious metals, we don't have to make reference to Fred C. Dobbs (Humphrey Bogart's character in the movie *The Treasure of the Sierra Madre*), gold fever, or alternative behavioral-finance explanations. One web site that currently advocates investing in hard gold states:[4]

- "The primary reason to own physical gold is to protect a core portion of your portfolio from all kinds of nonlinear contingencies."
- "Gold is the insurance part of a gold-related investment portfolio because gold itself will always maintain at least some value, no matter what 'disaster may happen on earth' as King Solomon warned."
- "The values of all other financial instruments change, but gold itself is immutable and unchanging and will always hold real value."

These marketing statements contain the most commonly articulated defense for gold as an investment: that, unlike traditional securities denominated in traditional currency units, gold will preserve your purchasing power and serve as a hedge against inflation.

Although many people have gotten used to continuously rising prices, we might ask the questions, "How bad is inflation, really?" and "Is inflation really that devastating?" Let me quote three authorities on inflation. Robert Mundell, one of the foremost authorities on the relationship between gold and the global monetary system, has written,

> *When the international monetary system was linked to gold, the latter managed the interdependence of the currency system, established an anchor for fixed exchange rates and stabilized inflation. When the gold standard broke down, these valuable functions were no longer performed and the world moved into a regime of permanent inflation.*[5]

Alan Greenspan has said,

> *In the absence of the gold standard, there is no way to protect savings from confiscation through inflation. There is no safe store of value.*[6]

Milton and Rose Friedman have a succinct answer to the two questions posed above:

> *Inflation is a disease, a dangerous and sometimes fatal disease, a disease that if not checked in time can destroy a society. Examples abound.*[7]

Will gold continue to matter as we move to a world of plastic and electronic money? It remains to be seen. To the extent that there is more gold in the basement of the New York Fed than anywhere else, to the extent that the ECB holds gold reserves against the Euro (even if those reserves are not actively managed), to the extent that the European Central Bank Gold Agreement was renewed in 2004 (for five more years), and to the extent that central banks still consider gold a "currency" of its own, the precious metals aren't going to go away overnight and will likely not lose their luster for some time to come, but the longer-term prospects are less clear. When was the last time you came across some wampum? While there is certainly no apparent or impending (financial, economic, or political) need for a return to a commodity money at this time, gold will, no doubt, continue to have its proponents:

> *If a free society is to be restored to America, then gold and silver must become the fulcrum of our monetary reform.*[8]

One way or the other, it will be fun to watch!

Answers to the Chapter Exercises

CHAPTER 2   Markets Exercises

1. If you need to purchase 2,000 ounces of platinum, you can buy it where the marketmaker is willing to sell it—at USD 976 per ounce.

   You would respond to the market quote with, "I would like to buy 2,000 ounces of platinum at a spot price of USD 976 please," or, more simply, "Mine, 2,000 (ounces) at 976."

   In two business days, you will wire USD 1,952,000 to the dealer and receive delivery (in whatever manner has been arranged for this) of 2,000 ounces of platinum.

2. A marketmaker in spot platinum would want to know (among other things): last trade price, market direction (based on fundamental analysis and/or technical analysis), their position, order flow, news coming out, and other relevant information that might move the spot price of platinum.

CHAPTER 3   Interest Rate Exercises

1. The interest on USD 10,000,000 for 3 months (90 days) at $r = 4.80\%$ (where this is a simple actual/360 rate):

   $$\text{USD } 10,000,000 \times (.0480) \times (90/360) = \text{USD } 120,000$$

2. The Euros you would receive if you deposited 40 million Euros for 12 years at a quarterly compounded rate of $r = 6.00\%$ (treating each quarter as exactly $\frac{1}{4}$ of a year):

   $$\text{EUR } 40,000,000 \times [1 + \{(.06)/4\}]^{12\times4}$$
   $$= \text{EUR } 40,000,000 \times [1.015]^{48}$$
   $$= \text{EUR } 81,739,131.56$$

which should make sense if you know the Rule of 72, which says your money should approximately double when the time frame, t (here, 12 years), and the interest rate, r (here, 6.00%), if multiplied together, gives a number around 72; more on this in the answer to Question 4 of this section.

3. The amount of Pounds Sterling today that are equal to 20,000,000 Pounds in 200 days if the relevant U.K. interest rate (quoted annually) is 8.20% depends on how you discount: Either

GBP 20,000,000/[1 + (.0820)(200/365)] = GBP 19,140,010.48

or

GBP 20,000,000 × [1 − (.0820)(200/365)] = GBP 19,101,369.86

The former would be the more likely calculation for market purposes (because that number of Pounds, deposited at r = 8.20% with simple interest would grow to GBP 20,000,000 in 200 days), although U.S. Treasury Bills and commercial paper typically use the latter convention. (Recall: GBP interest rate calculations typically assume that a year consists of 365 days.)

4. How long will it take for your money to double? More concretely, if you are quoted a rate of interest of 6.00% (compounded annually), how long will it take for your money today (PV) to double (i.e., so that $FV = 2 \times PV$)? This answer explains the Rule of 72, mentioned earlier. This is most easily shown using the continuous interest convention: $FV = PV\, e^{rt}$. In effect, it asks, "What is that time frame, t^*, over which your money (PV) will double (turn into $2 \times PV$) with a given interest rate?" Writing this out, $FV = 2\, PV = PV\, e^{rt^*}$. We can cancel the PVs (as the initial amount of money does not matter for solving this math problem), and we get $2 = e^{rt^*}$; we can then take the natural logarithm (ln) of both sides: $ln(2) = .69314718 = ln(e^{rt^*}) = rt^*$. Rounding off the left-hand side to .70, we get $.70 = rt^*$ . . . which says, for example, that, with continuous interest, if r = 5%, then it will take around t^* = 14 years for your money to double, whereas, if interest rates are 7%, it will only take around t^* = 10 years for your money to double. We said that not many financial institutions give continuous interest, so it may take a little longer; that fact, in conjunction with the observation that 72 seems nicely divisible by a larger number of integers, gives us the Rule of '72': One's money should approximately double depending on the rate of interest received according to the following general rule of thumb: $r \times t^* = .72$.

CHAPTER 5   Spot Exercise #1

1. The name of the exchange rate quoting convention between U.S. Dollars and Canadian Dollars if we quote USD|CAD: a European quote—

even though neither currency has anything to do with Europe. [If, on the other hand, someone wanted this currency pair quoted CAD|USD, it would be referred to as an American quote.]

2. If USD|CAD is quoted S = 1.2000, it means that USD 1 (1 U.S. Dollar) will trade for (e.g., can be bought or sold for) CAD 1.2000 (1.20 Canadian Dollars).

3. If USD|CAD S = 1.2000, then CAD|USD S = (1/1.2000) = .83333333 . . . (though we usually only quote spot prices out four decimal places, so, CAD|USD S = .8333).

4. The name of the foreign exchange rate quoting convention between Australian Dollars and U.S. Dollars ("Aussie") if we quote AUD|USD (as we do in the interbank market) is an American quote (because it reflects how many American (U.S.) Dollars per one Australian Dollar.

5. If AUD|USD S = .7500, then one Australian Dollar will trade for .75 U.S. Dollars.

Spot Exercise #2

One might guess that the exchange rate between Japanese Yen and Swiss Francs (knowing that Yen are small) would be quoted CHF|JPY or Swiss-Yen or Japanese Yen per one Swiss Franc (as, indeed, it typically is).

One might further guess that the exchange rate between Euros and Swiss Francs is quoted EUR|CHF or Euro-Swiss or Swiss Francs per one Euro.

Spot Exercise #3

1. The price of a Dollar could fall against the Swiss Franc and rise against the Japanese Yen; this would imply USD|CHF went down (the U.S. Dollar weakened against the Swiss Franc) and USD|JPY went up (the U.S. Dollar strengthened against the Japanese Yen). If this is the case, there is no doubt that the Swiss Franc just strengthened against the Japanese Yen (i.e., that CHF|JPY went up).

2. Can you buy U.S. Dollars with Pounds Sterling? Yes, and no, and yes! Of course you can buy Dollars with British Pounds, but, in the interbank market, a professional dealer would never say that; since the quoting convention between U.S. Dollars and Great Britain Pounds in the marketplace involves GBP|USD (i.e., Dollars per Pound), what you trade (that is, the underlying asset) is Pounds. If you want to buy Dol-

lars with Pounds, one would say, "I sell Sterling-Dollar," or "I sell Cable." Confusing, isn't it?

If you wanted to sell Japanese Yen in exchange for Dollars, what would you say?

Spot Exercise #4

Complete the following table of foreign exchange (cross) rates (**bold numbers given**):

	USD	EUR	JPY	GBP	CHF
USD	—	**1.2500**	.009091	2.0945	.8727
EUR	.8000	—	.007273	1.6756	.6982
JPY	110.00	137.50	—	230.40	**96.00**
GBP	.4774	.5968	.004340	—	.4167
CHF	1.1458	1.4323	.010417	**2.4000**	—

(*Hint:* Look back at Figure 1.9. To get oriented, start with USD and JPY.) Start by "inverting" all the quotes you are given (e.g., EUR|USD = 1.2500 so USD|EUR = (1/1.2500) = .8000). Then start looking for other pairs; knowing USD|EUR = .8000 and USD|JPY = 110.00, then EUR|JPY = 110.00/.8000 = 137.50. Similarly, knowing it takes 2.40 CHF per GBP 1 and 96 JPY per CHF 1, then it should take 230.40 JPY per GBP 1. (Answers are rounded to two, four, or six decimal places.)

Spot Triangular Arbitrage Exercises #5

1. Given the following spot prices:

> USD|JPY 110.00
> USD|CHF 1.2500
> CHF|JPY 85.00

triangular arbitrage starts by identifying where one currency pair is (i.e., too high or too low) in relation to the other two. Given the first quote USD 1 = JPY 110.00 and the second quote USD 1 = CHF 1.2500, then the exchange rate between CHF and JPY should follow from CHF 1.2500 = JPY 110.00 or, to put it in market terms, CHF|JPY should = 88.00. If CHF|JPY S = 85.00 in the market, it is too low (relative to where it should be trading). More precisely, the price of one Swiss Franc is lower (in terms of Japanese Yen) than it should be; one would want to BUY CHF and SELL JPY (as a single trade). If you start with CHF, you don't want to sell them for JPY, so sell them for USD, then sell the USD for JPY, and finally, sell the JPY for CHF. The cash flows would look like this:

Start: CHF 40,000,000 to USD 32,000,000 to JPY 3,520,000,000 back to CHF 41,411,764.71. Your profit in Swiss Francs is CHF 1,411,764.71 (or in percentage terms, you make 3.529412%, which, coincidentally, is exactly

$$[.8800/.8500 - 1].$$

See Figure A.1.

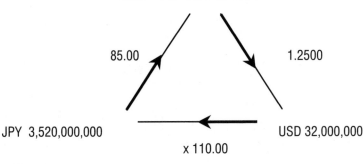

FIGURE A.1   Triangular Arbitrage

2. Given the following spot quotes:

   EUR|GBP .6850
   GBP|USD 1.8420
   EUR|USD 1.2500

   a triangular arbitrage starting with EUR 100,000,000 and realizing your profit in USD can be done two ways. One could simply do a regular triangular arbitrage starting with EUR and ending with EUR and then converting your EUR profit back into Dollars, or you can "take" your profit along the way.

   Let's try to consider the latter: First, looking at the first two quotes, EUR|USD should = 1.26177 (so the market price is too low; therefore, BUY EUR = SELL USD). Since we start with Euro, this would mean we go from EUR to GBP to USD to EUR. Starting with

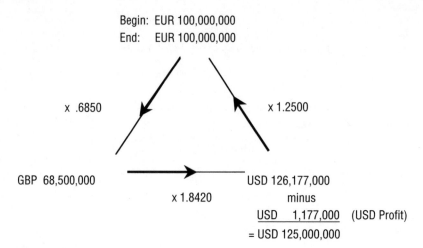

FIGURE A.2   Triangular Arbitrage

EUR 100,000,000 gives GBP 68,500,000, which subsequently gives USD 126,177,000.

At this stage, you might recognize that with EUR|USD S = 1.2500, all you should have to give up is USD 125,000,000 to get EUR 100,000,000. This would mean that you could take your profit in USD. That amount is USD 1,177,000.

If instead one had gone through the entire triangular arbitrage: EUR to GBP to USD to EUR, the resultant Euro position would have been EUR 100,941,600.00, which, net of the original EUR 100,000,000, gives a profit (in Euro) of EUR 941,600, which, translated at EUR|USD S = 1.2500 gives (as expected) USD 1,177,000. Reality check: 1.26177/1.2500 − 1 = .009416%, which is obvious enough in Euro—but that's also the ratio of the USD profit to the magnitude of the USD trade: USD 1,177,000/125,000,000. (See Figure A.2.)

CHAPTER 6   Forward Exercise #1

If a stock is trading at S = 100.00, interest rates are r = 4.00 percent, we are thinking about a one-year time frame (t = 1), and, over the course of the year, this stock will pay a quarterly dividend of Div = 0.25, where would the one-year forward price be quoted?

Using our forward relationship:

$$F = S + Srt - \text{Div}$$

we would have

$$F = 100 + 100(.04)(1) - (.25) \times 4 = 103$$

Forward Exercise #2

If USD|JPY is trading in the spot market at $S = 110.00$, Japanese interest rates are $r_J = 1.00\%$, U.S. rates are $r_{US} = 5\%$, then where would you expect to see the one-year USD|JPY forward price to be quoted?

$$F = \frac{S(1 + r_J t)}{(1 + r_{US} t)} = \frac{110.00(1.01)}{(1.05)} = 105.8095238 \quad \text{or} \quad 105.81$$

Forward Pricing/Forward Point Exercises #3

1. The one-year forward outright market in Cable (GBP|USD):

Spot Price	1.8021 – 1.8025	(4 pips wide)
Forward Points	118 – 115	(3 pips wide)
Forward Price	1.7903 – 1.7910	(7 pips wide)

2. The six-month forward market in USD|JPY:

Spot Price	112.49 – 112.57	(8 pips wide)
Forward Points	310 – 308	(2 pips wide)
Forward Price	109.39 – 109.49	(10 pips wide)

3. The one-month forward in USD|CHF:

Spot Price	1.2498 – 1.2504	(6 pips wide)
Forward Points	27.25 – 26.75	($1/2$ pip wide)
Forward Price	1.247075 – 1.247725	($6^{1}/_{2}$ pips wide)

4. If you wanted to sell USD 10,000,000 in one month, how many CHF you would get? Selling USD 10,000,000 with $F = 1.247075$ (*note:* You sell on the marketmaker's bid) means you will get CHF 12,470,750.

Foreign Exchange Forward Exercises #4

1. Undertake a spot-forward arbitrage in the following circumstances:

   $$EUR|USD \; S = 1.2940$$
   $$t = 1 \text{ year}$$
   $$r_{US} = 3.00\%$$
   $$r_{EU} = 4.00\%$$

   the one-year EUR|USD $F = 1.2750$

Do this on a spot notional of EUR 100,000,000 and check your answer.

The one-year forward *should* be $F = 1.2940 \ (1.03)/(1.04) = 1.28155769$

so, BUY EURO FORWARD.
   What this means:

   BUY EUR FORWARD = SELL USD FORWARD
   and SELL EUR SPOT = BUY USD SPOT.

Let's look at the cash flows.
   In the spot market

   Borrow and *sell* EURO *spot* = *buy* and deposit USD *spot*
   Sell EUR 100,000,000 and Buy USD 129,400,000

In one year, you'll *owe* EUR 104,000,000 and *own* USD 133,282,000.
   Now, if you sell all the USD you have at a forward price of $F = 1.2750$,

                BUY EURO FORWARD = SELL USD FORWARD

it will translate into EUR 104,534,902 or a Euro profit of EUR 534,902.
   If you had chosen to take your profit in Dollars, you'd get USD 682,000.
   (Reality check: You made a little more than .5%;
   $1.28156/1.2750 - 1 = .005+\%$.)

2. What could you say about Turkish interest rates versus U.S. interest rates if the forward points in USD|TRY are positive?
   If the USD|TRY forward points are positive, then $F > S$, which means (given the way this currency pair is quoted) that Turkish interest rates are higher than U.S. interest rates (for the time horizon under consideration).

3. What can you say about the forward points for USD|CHF if the respective (zero) interest rate curves in the respective countries currencies are as pictured in Figure 6.8 (reproduced here as Figure A.3)?
   At the short end of the curve, $r_{US} > r_{CH}$, so F will be $< S$ and forward points will be negative. Where the interest rate curves first cross, forward points will be zero. In that range in which $r_{CH} > r_{US}$, F will be $> S$ and forward points will be positive. They will go to zero once again where the interest rate curves cross a second time, and for longer-dated forwards, the forward points will again be negative (where $r_{US} > r_{CH}$).

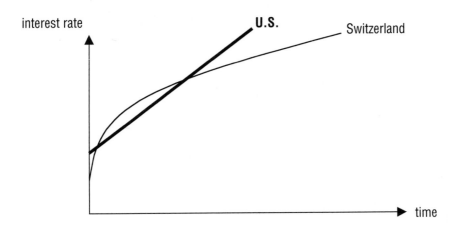

interest rate

U.S.

Switzerland

time

FIGURE A.3 Interest Rate Curves

4. If GBP|USD three-month forward is $F = 1.7568$, U.S. interest rates are 4.00%, U.K. interest rates 7.00%, and we assume three months involves 91 days, then

   ■ What is the GBP|USD spot price? Working our spot-forward relationship backward:

   $$F = 1.7568 = S(1 + (.04)(91/360))/(1 + (.07)(91/365))$$

   so

   GBP|USD $S = 1.76956748$ or probably $S = 1.7696$

   Note: For U.S. rates, we used an "actual/360" day count convention and for U.K. interest rates, we used an "actual/365" day count convention.

   ■ What do you think would happen to this forward price if the Bank of England raises interest rates? It depends on whether the rate hike was anticipated, and whether the magnitude of the rate hike was in line with expectations. If the rate hike was either unanticipated or greater than expected, S will likely go up; on the other hand, if the interest rate hike was anticipated, but the actual increase in U.K. rates was less than expected, S will likely fall. If the spot price is unchanged, though, then we can say that F will go down.

   ■ How much would you have to pay (today) for a three-month off-market forward of $F = 1.7200$ on a notional of GBP 10,000,000? If paying in USD, it will be the $PV(USD.0368$ per GBP 1$) \times$ GBP

10,000,000 (where this is discounted using r_{US}) = USD 364,316.36.

CHAPTER 7   Currency Futures Exercises

1. If a U.S. corporation had a firm commitment of two billion in Japanese Yen receivables arriving in December of that year

   What futures contracts could they use to "hedge"?
   Would they buy or sell them?
   How many would they want to trade?

   The corporation should SELL 160 (JPY 2,000,000,000/12,500,000) December Japanese Yen futures contracts.

2. In what ways do FX futures contracts differ from FX forward contracts? Exchange-traded versus OTC, standardized versus tailored (with respect to contract size, maturity, delivery dates, and processes, etc.), margined or marked-to-market daily versus (possibly) no cash flows, and the majority of futures contracts do not result in delivery, whereas many forwards do.

CHAPTER 8   Cross-Currency Swaps Exercise

Using the numbers in our earlier example: USD|CHF S = 1.2500, r_{US} = 5.00% and r_{CH} = 3.00% (for all maturities):

1. Show, in two different ways, that if the U.S. corporation issues a 3.00% annual coupon bond in CHF in Switzerland and does a cross-currency swap, then, effectively, it will be borrowing at 5.00% in USD.

   PVing the CHF cash flows (scaling for a notional of CHF 100):

   $$(.9709)(3) + (.9426)(3) + (.9151)(3) + (.8885)(3)$$
   $$+ (.8626)(103) = 100 \text{ (CHF)}$$

   PVing the USD cash flows on an equivalent amount of Dollars = USD 80:

   $$(.9524)(4) + (.9070)(4) + (.8638)(4) + (.8227)(4)$$
   $$+ (.7835)(84) = \text{USD } 80$$

   (*Note:* The USD coupon of "4" is 5% of the notional of USD 80.)

   We can alternatively use the FX forward rates (calculated earlier in Chapter 8), turn all the cash flows into one currency (say, CHF here),

PV (using Swiss interest rates), and sum. If the result = 0, then there is no "savings" from issuing abroad.

In Year 1 – CHF 3 + USD 4 × F_1 (1.2262) = + CHF 1.9048
In Year 2 – CHF 3 + USD 4 × F_2 (1.2028) = + CHF 1.8112
In Year 3 – CHF 3 + USD 4 × F_3 (1.1799) = + CHF 1.7196
In Year 4 – CHF 3 + USD 4 × F_4 (1.1574) = + CHF 1.6296
In Year 5 – CHF 103 + USD 84 × F_5 (1.1354) = – CHF 7.6264

PVing and summing

$$(.9709)(1.9048) + (.9426)(1.8112) + (.9151)(1.7196)$$
$$+ (.8885)(1.6296) - (.8626)(7.6264) = 0$$

2. Determine the fair USD coupon for a five-year coupon-only FX swap where one counterparty receives the 3.00% CHF on a notional of CHF 125,000,000.

$$[(.9709) + (.9426) + (.9151) + (.8885) + (.8626)](3)/(1.2500)$$
$$= USD\ 10.9913$$
$$= [(.9524) + (.9070) + (.8638) + (.8227) + (.7835)]c$$

Here, USD c = 2.53875%

CHAPTER 9   Put-Call Parity Exercise #1

If a nondividend-paying stock is trading S = 78.50, the time frame is one year; interest rates are 4.00%, and the one-year 80 strike European call is trading at 80C = 3.75, where should the one-year 80 strike European put be trading?

$$C - P - S + X/(1 + rt) = 0$$
$$3.75 - P - 78.50 + 80/(1.04) = 0$$
$$80P = 2.17$$

Alternatively, If S = 78.50, the one-year F = 81.64 (F = $S(1 + rt)$ = 78.50(1.04)), so the 80 call has value or is in-the-money with respect to the forward and has an intrinsic value of 1.64. If you present value the 1.64 (= 1.58) (recalling equation [9.8]) and take that away from the 80 call, you get 2.17.

If it's trading for .50 more than you think that it should, what trades would you do?

Sell high. Sell the 80 put (+2.67), buy the 80 call (–3.75), and sell the spot (+78.50). This results in a net cash inflow today of 77.42. Deposited in the bank (at 4.00%), it will grow into 80.52. At expiration, you would have to buy back the underlying at the strike price of $X = 80.00$, so your profit is .52. Why did you make more than .50 (your original "edge")? Because you waited to "capture your profits," you would realize an amount equal to the future value of your original "edge": $.50 \times (1.04) = .52$.

FX Put-Call Parity Exercise #2

USD|JPY $S = 110.00$, $r_J = 1.00$ percent, $r_{US} = 3.00$ percent, $t = 3$ months $(t = \frac{1}{4} = .25)$

1. For the 107.50 strike $(X = 107.50)$ three-month European options, by how much will the call and put differ and which will be more valuable?

     Using equation [9.11]:

$$C - P = S/(1 + r_2 t) - X/(1 + r_1 t)$$
$$C - P = 110/(1 + (.03)(.25)) + 107.50/(1 + (.01)(.25))$$
$$C - P = 109.18 - 107.23 = 1.95$$

Since the call is in-the-money (forward), the 107.50 C is more valuable than the 107.50 put.

     Alternatively, using equation [9.12]:

$$C - P = (F - X)/(1 + r_1 t)$$
$$F = 110.00(1 + (.01)(.25))/(1 + (.03)(.25)) = 109.454$$
$$(F - X) = (109.454 - 107.50) = 1.954$$

and

$$(F - X)/(1 + r_1 t) = 1.954/1.0025 = 1.95$$

2. If the 107.50 call is trading at JPY 2.62 per USD 1, where should the put be trading? The 107.50 call is in-the-money forward, so it should be trading over the put by 1.95, or the 107.50 put should be trading for JPY .67.

FX Option Premium Exercise #3

You telephone an FX option dealer/bank and ask for a three-month $(t = \frac{3}{12} = .25)$ at-the-money European option on EUR|JPY on a notional of EUR 40,000,000. Spot is currently trading at $S = 140.00$, Japanese interest rates are 1.00%, and Euro rates are 5.00%.

The dealer/bank quotes the premium in Yen pips: 263.

1. What is the strike price, X?

> Using simple interest: $X = F = 138.62$ (rounded)
> (more precisely 138.617284)

2. What is this option (i.e., call or put, on what currency)?

> This is either a Euro call or a Euro put;
> > for valuation, it doesn't matter; at-the-money (forward) European calls and puts have the same value.
>
> This is an option to exchange EUR 40,000,000 for JPY 5,544,800,000.

3. Calculate the option premium in terms of

> Total EUR: EUR 751,428.57; total JPY: JPY 105,200,000.
> Percent of Euro face: 1.88% (really 1.87857%);
> > percent of Yen face: 1.90% (really 1.89727%).
>
> Euro pips per Yen: (remember, Euro-Yen pips go out 6 decimal places): 135.52.

FX Option Breakeven Graph Exercise #4

1. Sketch the P/L (profit/loss) or breakeven graph of a long three-month 125.00 put with a premium of 6.58. Identify the breakeven spot price, S^*. Does it matter whether this is a three-month option or a one-year option? Briefly explain. See Figure A.4.

Breakeven graphs are typically drawn independent of the expiration date (so it doesn't matter, for our graph, whether expiration is in three months or one year), but it will impact the cash flows and, therefore, our actual profit/loss.

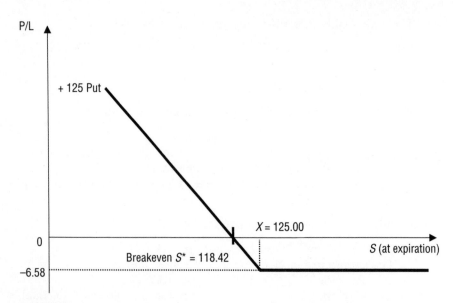

FIGURE A.4   Solution to FX Option Breakeven Graph Exercise #4
Profit/Loss Graph for the 125 Put.

CHAPTER 10   Exotic Option Exercise

What would you label a put option with spot at $S = 22.50$, strike price
at $X = 20.00$, and an out barrier at 21.00? What if, instead, it was
a call?

I would label this option "Stupid." Think about it. If spot trades down
to or past 21.00, the option disappears, and this put would only have value
if the spot price ends up below the strike price of $X = 20.00$. Nevertheless,
we would label such an option, which goes out as the spot price moves in
the in-the-money direction a "kick out" put. With these same parameters
$(S = 22.50, X = 20.00, B = 21.00)$, a call option would be referred to,
among other things, as a "knock out call."

Notes

CHAPTER 1   Trading Money

1. R. A. Radford, "The Economic Organization of a P.O.W. Camp," *Economica* 12 (1945): 189–201.
2. Adam Smith based his title on the following passage found in the Bible:

   > *Lift up your eyes, look around and see; they all gather together, they come to you; your sons shall come from afar, and your daughters shall be carried in their nurses' arms. Then you shall see and be radiant; your heart shall thrill and rejoice, because the abundance of the sea shall be poured out to you, the* **wealth of nations** *shall come to you. A multitude of camels shall cover you, the young camels of Midian and Ephah; all those from Sheba shall come. They shall bring gold and frankincense, and shall proclaim the praise of the Lord.*
   > —Isaiah 60: 4–6

3. There may be other limitations on the requirement of acceptance of money as a vehicle of payment. In the United States, an automobile dealer may refuse payment of 2,000,000 pennies for a $20,000 automobile. And a fast-food restaurant or convenience store may, if a notice is posted, refuse to accept any currency larger than, say, a $20 bill.
4. This example may seem rather exaggerated, but moves of this magnitude have actually occurred.

   > *On 12 January 1994, for example, the 14 countries of the African Financial Community (whose currencies were tied to the French franc) devalued their currencies by 50%. This move, of course, did not cut the real output of these countries by half.*

   (See: http://www.cia.gov/cia/publications/factbook/docs/notesanddefs .html#2001)

   Similarly, the Turkish Lira lost over 40% of its value in one day in 2001 and 50% of its value within three months when forced to float against the U.S. Dollar. This was solely because of currency revaluation; the Turkish economy had not collapsed.

5. Paul Samuelson suggests that people would save even if the rate of interest were negative! See Paul A. Samuelson, "An Exact Consumption-Loan Model of Interest with or without the Social Contrivance of Money," *Journal of Political Economy* 66, no. 6 (1958): 467–482.

6. Working at UBS, which is headquartered in Switzerland, many of my colleagues speak several languages. There is a running joke: "What do you call someone who speaks three languages? Trilingual. What do you call someone who speaks two languages? Bilingual. What do you call someone who speaks one language? American."

7. The countries of the former Soviet Union (or U.S.S.R.): Armenia, Azerbaijan, Belarus, Estonia, Georgia, Kazakhstan, Kyrgyzstan, Latvia, Lithuania, Moldova, Russia, Tajikistan, Turkmenistan, Ukraine, and Uzbekistan; Germany (formerly West Germany and East Germany); the successors of Yugoslavia: Bosnia and Herzegovina (one country), Croatia, Macedonia, Serbia and Montenegro (again, one country), and Slovenia; the Czech Republic and Slovakia (formerly Czechoslovakia); Eritrea; Namibia; Yemen; Palau; Marshall Islands; Micronesia; and East Timor.

8. See www.geography.about.com/cs/countries and www.cia.gov/cia/publications/factbook.

9. There have been some interesting studies of different facets of money throughout history. One of the more interesting is *The Big Problem of Small Change* by Thomas J. Sargent and Francois R. Velde (Princeton University Press, 2002).

10. Needless to say, a cursory inspection of money from around the world provides a microcosm of significant people and events from a country's past, a panoply of art, and a showcase for nationalistic chauvinism. Although contemporary political leaders, monarchs, government officials, and the occasional dictator appear on money around the world, a law has been passed in the United States that forbids the likeness of a living person to appear on U.S. currency.

   Because of the artistic, historical, and patriotic aspects of currency, individuals around the world collect money, and there has been a recent upsurge in interest in (and therefore prices of) paper currency. Not surprisingly, there are books detailing the engravers' art that has gone into the design of many of the major and minor currencies around the world, such as *The Art of Money* by David Standish (Chronicle Books, 2000).

11. "Why Didn't I Think of That?" *The Economist* (December 18, 2004).
12. For example, I have never heard of the U.S. government actively buying or selling IBM stock, though a friend of mine, who happens to be an economist, was quick to point out that every time the government sponsors a corporate bailout, it is doing just that.

CHAPTER 2   Markets, Prices, and Marketmaking

1. For others in equities, OTC might be interpreted as referring to the "pink sheets"—a listing of stocks that trade very infrequently, illiquidly, or, as one of my colleagues likes to put it, "by appointment." Just another financial expression with multiple meanings.
2. One of the primary reasons that UBS has been ranked #1 in foreign exchange in 2003 and 2004 is because of the electronic trading tools that have been put into the hands (really, onto the computers) of UBS clients, who can trade relatively large quantities of foreign exchange directly—without requiring a telephone call to a salesperson or any other form of execution intermediation.
3. The U.S. securities markets are recognized as one of the most highly regulated in the world.
4. Numerically, this simply involves using the "1/x" button on your calculator, but being able to go back and forth in foreign exchange (even though it is not mathematically complicated or sophisticated) is essential because sometimes in FX we quote Dollar per Euro, though sometimes we might like to figure out Euro per Dollar. Confusing isn't it?
5. We will tend to use S to refer to the spot price; we will see later that there are other types of prices. Also, just for the record, around the world (even in London), the price of gold is typically quoted in USD per ounce.
6. If I were to say, "My wife is long on patience," it would mean that she has a great deal of that virtue. "Long" means to have, to possess, to own, or to have bought something. "Short" is the opposite of long; if something is in short supply, there isn't much around. In the financial markets, "short," more precisely, means that you have sold something that you did not have or do not own (and, therefore, will have to borrow in order to make delivery).
7. U.S. Secretary of Defense Donald H. Rumsfeld is known for the following statement: "Reports that say that something hasn't happened are always interesting to me, because, as we know, there are known knowns; there are things we know we know. We also know there are known unknowns; that is to say, we know there are some things we do

not know. But there are also unknown unknowns—the ones we don't know we don't know." (Quoted from a Department of Defense news briefing, February 12, 2002.)

8. In Sonny Kleinfield, *The Traders* (New York: Holt, Rinehart and Winston, 1983), 138.

CHAPTER 3   Interest Rates

1. Deflation refers to a general decline in the average level of prices over time.
2. One of my colleagues in Education once asked a class of relative newcomers to the financial markets why they thought U.S. interest rates were quoted out of London. One individual conjectured, "Because they wake up before we do?"

CHAPTER 4   Brief History of Foreign Exchange

1. Example: Country ABC's coin is worth 10 Thalers and is 1/8 of an ounce of gold. Country XYZ's coin is worth 8,000 Lira and is 1/2 of an ounce of gold. Then the exchange rate ought to be 200 Lira per 1 Thaler (otherwise an arbitrage would exist); we will look at several examples of arbitrage throughout this book.
2. Glyn Davies, *A History of Money: From Ancient Times to Present Day* (University of Wales Press, 2003); Jack Weatherford, *The History of Money* (Three Rivers Press, 1997/1978); Jonathan Williams, ed. *Money: A History* (New York: St. Martin's Press, 1997).
3. John Kenneth Galbraith, *Money: Whence It Came, Where It Went* (Boston: Houghton Mifflin, 1975). Then again, Robert Mundell, a Nobel Prize winning economist, might challenge Galbraith's assertion; see his "Uses and Abuses of Gresham's Law in the History of Money," Zagreb, *Journal of Economics* 2 (1998).
4. The Bank for International Settlements (BIS) was established for the proximate goal of coordinating the reparation payments by the German government to the Allies following World War I and the more lasting objective of promoting cooperation among the central banks in various counties. Founded in 1930, the BIS claims to be the oldest international financial institution in the world. Its headquarters are located in Basel, Switzerland. Most recently, working with the national central banks and regulatory agencies, the BIS has endeavored to help establish global banking guidelines addressing such topics as capital

reserves and risk management on the part of international banks in a continually consolidating financial world.

5. Kenneth A. Froot and Richard H. Thaler, "Foreign Exchange," *Journal of Economic Perspectives* 4, no. 3 (1990): 179–192, reproduced in Richard H. Thaler, *The Winner's Curse* (Russell Sage Foundation, 1992).

6. There is more than one OCC. This could indicate the Office of the Comptroller of the Currency or it could refer to the Options Clearing Corporation (the issuer, guarantor, and registered clearing facility for all U.S. exchange-listed securities options).

7. From Chapter 4, "The Federal Reserve in the International Sphere," in *The Federal Reserve System: Purposes and Functions*, 9th ed., Board of Governors of the Federal Reserve System (2005), 51.

8. Lucio Sarno and Mark P. Taylor, "Official Intervention in the Foreign Exchange Market: Is It Effective and, If So, How Does It Work?" *Journal of Economic Literature* 39, no. 3 (September 2001): 839–868.

CHAPTER 5   The Foreign Exchange Spot Market

1. Li Lian Ong, *The Big Mac Index: Applications of Purchasing Power Parity*, Chapter 3, "The Economics of the Big Mac Standard" (Palgrave Macmillan, 2003), 77.

2. As is usually the case in FX, there are exceptions to the rule. In North America, a U.S. Dollar versus Mexican Peso or U.S. Dollar versus Canadian Dollar spot trade can be arranged to settle "T + 1" (note the different ISO codes for such transactions in the Appendix to Chapter 1) or even "T + 0" (if done early enough in the day)!

3. Ron Marr, from Copp Clark, publisher of the Euromarket Day Finder, has indicated the continued popularity of these calendars even though electronic versions are available.

CHAPTER 6   Foreign Exchange Forwards

1. As mentioned earlier, if the two interest rates are the same, then spot = forward.

2. In short, whether the U.S. interest rate goes on the top or the bottom (or more generally, which interest rate is on top and which interest rate is on the bottom) in our relationship depends on how the currency pair is quoted.

3. When we consider longer dated trades that span several years, then we must take compounding of interest into account. We will see examples of this in Chapter 8.

4. See "Wonton Fireworks in CNY NDFs Should Dim Sum" by Thomas Birkhold and Thomas Kane (October 8, 2005), UBS Foreign Exchange web site and "An Overview of Non-Deliverable Foreign Exchange Forward Markets" by Laura Lipscomb, Federal Reserve Bank of New York (May 2005).

CHAPTER 7 Foreign Exchange Futures

1. See Leo Melamed, "Evolution of the International Monetary Market," *Cato Journal* 8, no. 2 (1988): 393–404, and Leo Melamed, "The Birth and Development of Financial Futures," presented at the China Futures Seminar (1996) and accessible on his web site: www.leomelamed.com/Speeches/96-china.htm.
2. These quotes come from Leo Melamed, "Evolution of the International Monetary Market," *Cato Journal* 8 (1988): 393. Friedman was surely a driving force behind the promotion and early success of FX futures contracts. Melamed wrote, "In those days, Professor Milton Friedman was singular in his loud and unabashed prediction about the demise of the Bretton Woods system. Moreover, to the consternation of the world's central bankers, Dr. Friedman proclaimed this eventuality a good thing. . . . As I often stated, 'Professor Friedman gave my idea the credibility without which the concept might never have become a reality.' " [From Leo Melamed, "The Birth and Development of Financial Futures" (1996).]
3. From the "Clearing Membership" section of "Trade CME Products" on the Chicago Mercantile Exchange web site: www.cme.com. (author's emphasis added).
4. The CME proudly notes the following: "Throughout its history, the CME Clearing House has never experienced a default, a claim that not all commodity clearing houses can make." From the "What Is a Futures Clearing House?" section of "Education" on the Chicago Mercantile Exchange web site: www.cme.com.
5. In almost every textbook I have seen (e.g., John Hull's popular *Options, Futures, and Other Derivatives*, p. 110), forwards are identified as having "counterparty risk," while futures contracts—because they are backed or "guaranteed" by the exchange and the clearing houses— are said to have less or no counterparty risk. While bankruptcy remote, exchanges themselves are not riskless entities, and whether the credit risk of a large global bank is necessarily worse than that of an exchange is, at best, a point for discussion. Banks will sometimes incorporate "credit mitigation vehicles" (similar to marking-to-market,

though possibly without daily adjustments) with some of their counterparties in the context of forward contracts as well.

6. For the general case, see John C. Cox, Jonathan E. Ingersoll Jr., and
Stephen A. Ross, "The Relationship between Forward and Futures
Prices," *Journal of Financial Economics* 9 (1981): 321–346, and for
the classic reference on foreign exchange, see Bradford Cornell and
Marc R. Reinganum, "Forward and Futures Prices: Evidence from
the Foreign Exchange Markets," *Journal of Finance* 36 (1981):
1035–1045.

7. Although we understand EuroDollar to be an FX exchange rate, here
EuroDollar refers to three-month USD interest rate futures contracts
(also traded at the CME in the United States); the name derives from
the fact that this rate is obtained by a polling carried out by the British
Bankers Association (BBA) in London among a group of large global
banks, and, as such, could be characterized as identifying where European banks will lend their U.S. Dollars (to other strong credit—
"AA"—quality banks). Hence the name LIBOR (often used
synonymously with EuroDollar): the London InterBank Offer Rate.

CHAPTER 8 Foreign Exchange Swaps or Cross-Currency Swaps or Cross-Currency Interest Rate Swap or . . .

1. The (.9151) for example in the third term of this expression is the
three-year discount factor for Swiss Francs (CHF) at 3.00% per year
(i.e., $(1/(1.03))^3$ = (.9151)]. In other words, it converts CHF in three
years' time into the equivalent number of Swiss Francs today.

2. Here, the (.8638) for example in the third term of this expression is the
three-year discount factor for U.S. Dollars (USD) at 5.00% per year
[i.e., $(1/(1.05))^3$ = (.8638)].

3. While it is beyond the scope of this book to go into more detail here
on the relationship between zero rates and swap rates, the interested
reader can follow up on interest rate relationships in any good interest
rate primer such as Joe Troccolo's *Just Enough Interest Rates and Foreign Exchange*.

CHAPTER 9 Foreign Exchange Options

1. For a very brief introduction to options (though admittedly with an equity slant), see Tim Weithers, "Options Fundamentals," Chapter 1 of
The Handbook of Equity Derivatives, rev. ed., ed. Jack Clark Francis,

William W. Toy, and J. Gregg Whittaker (New York: John Wiley & Sons, 2000).

2. In UBS's *Options: The Fundamentals*, Gary Gastineau contributes an interesting explanation for the original choice of the terms American and European, p. 28.

3. See the Philadelphia Stock Exchange (PHLX) web site: www.phlx.com and more specifically, the contract "specs" and terms for their currency options: www.phlx.com/products/currency/currency.html.

4. If the stock price moves enough (up or down), the exchange will "open" or start listing new strike prices. Also, for stocks trading at lower prices, for example $S = 20$, the difference between the standardized strike prices also shrinks (e.g., $X = 15$, $X = 17.50$, $X = 20$, $X = 22.50$, $X = 25$).

5. See Hans R. Stoll, "The Relationship between Put and Call Option Prices," *Journal of Finance* 23: 801–824 (1969).

6. The Shad-Johnson Accord (1982) banned single stock futures (and other narrowly defined equity futures contracts). This law was superseded as part of the Commodity Futures Modernization Act (2000), and single stock futures now trade in the United States and elsewhere around the world.

7. Traders also use the notion of delta colloquially. "Are you coming golfing this weekend?" "It's my spouse's birthday; I'm a 10 delta (e.g., I have only a 10% chance of coming)."

8. In the United Kingdom, it is typical for exchange-traded options to be written on 1,000 shares. In Switzerland (as well as other parts of the world), the notional may be different still.

9. Because of the way in which we define volatility for use in the Black–Scholes and Garman–Kohlhagen models (as the annualized standard deviation of returns where returns are defined as the logarithm of consecutive price ratios or relatives), the math of it is such that if USD|CHF volatility is 10.00%, then CHF|USD volatility is also exactly 10.00%.

10. I write this out as a formula, but this conversion exhibiting equivalence between a call on one currency and the corresponding put on another currency obviously depends on how the currency pairs are quoted.

11. At first, this might look like a rather large spread, but, as a percentage of the notional, it is less than eight basis points (on a one-year option).

12. See Ian Giddy, "Six Common Myths about FX Options," *Derivatives Strategies* 1 (February 1996) and the response that his article generated from Christopher S. Bourdain, "FX Option Myths That Aren't," *Derivatives Strategies* 1 (April 1996).

APPENDIX TO CHAPTER 9   Option Valuation Models

1. See p. 8 of Fischer Black's "How We Came Up with the Option Formula," *Journal of Portfolio Management* 15, no. 2 (1989): 4–8.
2. John Cox, Stephen Ross, and Mark Rubinstein, "Option Pricing: A Simplified Approach," *Journal of Financial Economics* 7 (1979): 229–263, compared to Fischer Black and Myron Scholes, "The Pricing of Options and Corporate Liabilities," *Journal of Political Economy* 81 (1973): 637–654. It's interesting that exchange-traded options first began trading in the United States in 1973 on the Chicago Board Options Exchange (CBOE), the same year that the Black–Scholes paper was published, even if that was purely coincidental.

CHAPTER 10   Exotic Options and Structured Products

1. Gary L. Gastineau and Mark P. Kritzman, *The Dictionary of Financial Risk Management*, rev. ed. (Frank J. Fabozzi Associates, 1996), 92.
2. The best explanation I have heard for the use of the expression "Asian" involves the process used for the cash settlement of the Hang Seng stock index in Hong Kong. Because some of the stocks in this index traded thinly, there was the belief that some unscrupulous index traders would occasionally attempt to manipulate the index by trading the underlying stocks in large size on the close. The market response was to cash settle the index, not to its constituents' closing stock prices, but to the hourly averages on the last day of trading (providing some buffer from alleged tampering). Therefore, Asian came to refer "averaging."
3. This summary from "Greenspan Sick?" http://www.slobokan.com/archives/2004/03/.

CHAPTER 11   The Economics of Exchange Rates and International Trade

1. See Bill Gross, *Everything You've Heard About Investing Is Wrong!* (New York: Times Books/Random House, 1997), 43.
2. At this point, we should understand the factors driving foreign exchange forward quotes (i.e., recalling interest rate parity from Chapter 6).
3. From McDonald's Corporation Form 10-K for the fiscal year ending December 31, 2004 (also in McDonald's Corporation 2004 Financial Report, pp. 7, 15).

4. John Train, *The New Money Masters* (New York: Harper & Row, 1989), 68.

5. Alexander M. Ineichen, *Absolute Returns: The Risk and Opportunities of Hedge Fund Investing* (New York: John Wiley & Sons, 2002).

6. From the Introduction, *Exchange Rate Regimes: Choices and Consequences* by Atish R. Ghosh, Anne-Marie Gulde, and Holger C. Wolf (Cambridge, MA: MIT Press, 2002), 1.

7. Milton Friedman, "The Case for Flexible Exchange Rates," in *Essays in Positive Economics* (Chicago: University of Chicago Press, 1953).

8. "The Tyranny of Controls," in *Free to Choose: A Personal Statement* by Milton and Rose Friedman (1980), 47.

9. "Exchange Rates" by Paul Krugman, from *The Concise Encyclopedia of Economics*, Liberty Fund (2005).

10. H. Robert Heller, *International Trade: Theory and Empirical Evidence*, 2nd ed., Chapter 11, "Welfare Aspects of International Trade" (Englewood Cliffs, NJ: Prentice-Hall, 1973), 197.

11. Milton and Rose Friedman, *Free to Choose: A Personal Statement*, 47.

12. Ibid., p. 90.

CHAPTER 12   Currency Crises

1. Charles P. Kindleberger, *Manias, Panics, and Crashes: A History of Financial Crises*, 3rd ed. (New York: John Wiley & Sons, 1996), 97.

2. Abbigail J. Chiodo and Michael T. Owyang, "A Case Study of a Currency Crisis: The Russian Default of 1998," *Federal Reserve Bank of St. Louis Review* (2002): 7–17.

3. See *The Practice of Risk Management*, Exhibit 3.6, "Case Note: The Collapse of Bankhaus Herstatt, 1974," 35.

4. See "Settlement Risk," at riskglossary.com: www.riskglossary.com.

5. For CLS, see www.cls-group.com/about_cls/.

6. For a very detailed and well-documented account of the events leading up to Black Wednesday, see Robert Slater's *Soros: The Unauthorized Biography*, McGraw-Hill (1996), especially Chapters 18–20.

7. See Robert Slater's *Soros: The Unauthorized Biography*, 183.

8. George Soros, *The Alchemy of Finance: Reading the Mind of the Market* (New York: John Wiley & Sons, 1994), 324–325.

9. Stanley Fischer, "The Asian Crisis: A View from the IMF," Washington, D.C., January 22, 1998.

10. For those who would like to obtain further details on LTCM and the Russian Crisis, there are two very readable, but very different, publications. The first, Roger Lowenstein's *When Genius Failed*, gives some

fascinating insights into the personalities and an anecdotal account of the events surrounding the collapse and bailout of LTCM. The second, written by a derivatives expert and technical editor of *Risk* magazine—Nicholas Dunbar—gives more of a market insider's view into the specific trades and actual financial circumstances relevant to Long Term Capital Management; it is entitled *Inventing Money*. Both were published in 2000 and are in the References.

11. For those who would like to learn more about credit default swaps and other credit derivatives, see Antulio N. Bomfim's *Understanding Credit Derivatives and Related Instruments* (Academic Press, 2004).

12. See Abigail J. Chiodo and Michael T. Owyang's "A Case Study of a Currency Crisis: The Russian Default of 1998" (2002) for their taxonomy of classes of academic/theoretical models purporting to "explain" currency crises. Another excellent reference is Andre Fourcans and Raphael Franck's *Currency Crises—A Theoretical and Empirical Perspective* (2003). Both identify first-generation, second-generation, and third-generation models of currency crises.

13. See Bill Gross, *Everything You've Heard About Investing Is Wrong!*, 20.

14. See Bill Gross, *Everything You've Heard About Investing Is Wrong!*, 42–43.

15. Dick K. Nanto, "The 1997–1998 Asian Financial Crisis," www.fas .org/man/crs/crs-asia2.htm (February 6, 1998).

16. Milton Friedman and Anna Jacobson Schwartz, *A Monetary History of the United States, 1867–1960* (Princeton, NJ: Princeton University Press, 1971).

CHAPTER 13   Technical Analysis

1. In Bill Gross's *Everything You've Heard About Investing Is Wrong!*, 53–54.

2. Robert Amzallag in the Foreward to *Advanced Trading Rules*, 2nd ed., edited by E. Acar and S. Satchell (Butterworth–Heinemann, 2002).

3. There has been relatively recent interest in and attempts to model "self-fulfilling prophecies." See Roger E. A. Farmer's *Macroeconomics of Self-Fulfilling Prophecies*, 2nd ed. (Cambridge, MA: MIT Press, 1999). Paul Krugman has also written on this topic: "Are Currency Crises Self-Fulfilling?" (1996).

4. As another example, there are a number of trade publications, web sites, and newsletters (such as "Technical Analysis of Stocks and Commodities," www.cqg.com) dedicated to this area.

5. One of the shining exceptions to this statement is the research of Carol Osler. Carol worked for 10 years in Capital Markets at the New York Fed and has a distinguished academic career (currently an Associate Professor of Finance at Brandeis University). Some of her relevant publications include "Identifying Noise Traders: The Head-and-Shoulders Pattern in U.S. Equities," Federal Reserve Bank of New York Staff Report (1998); "Support for Resistance: Technical Analysis and Intraday Exchange Rates," *Economic Policy Review* 6 (2000); and "Currency Orders and Exchange Rate Dynamics: Explaining the Success of Technical Analysis," *Journal of Finance* 58 (2003). Any academic who can garner both the attention and admiration of Victor Niederhoffer is noteworthy in itself: "Don't bet the rent on technical analysis":http://moneycentral.msn.com/content/Investing/Powertools/P79688.asp.

6. See Blake LeBaron, "Technical Trading Rule Profitability and Foreign Exchange Intervention," *Journal of International Economics* 49 (1999): 125–143; John Okunev and Derek White, "Do Momentum-Based Strategies Still Work in Foreign Currency Markets," *Journal of Financial and Quantitative Analysis* (2002); John Okunev and Derek White, "The Profits to Technical Analysis in Foreign Exchange Markets Have Not Disappeared."

7. "The Need for Performance Evaluation in Technical Analysis," Chapter 15 in *Advanced Trading Rules*, 2nd ed., ed. Emmanuel Arca and Stephen Satchell (Butterworth–Heinemann, 2002): 419.

CHAPTER 14   Where Do We Go From Here?

1. From "Why has FX trading surged? Explaining the 2004 triennial survey," by Gabriele Galati and Michael Melvin, *BIS Quarterly Review* (December 2004): 73.

2. Paul Volcker quoted by Robert Mundell in "Currency Areas and International Monetary Reform at the Dawn of a New Century," *Review of International Economics* 9 (2001): 595–607.

3. Robert Mundell.

4. Robert Mundell.

5. Robert Mundell.

6. George Soros, *The Crisis of Global Capitalism* (New York: Public Affairs: 1998), 179.

7. George Soros, *The Alchemy of Finance* (1994).

8. Ibid., 318, 329, 338.

9. Soros, *Crisis of Global Capitalism*, 176, 184.

CHAPTER 15 Conclusion

1. Claude Tygier, "The Foreign Exchange Market: A Descriptive Study," Program on Information Resources Policy (1986).
2. From Mignon McLaughlin, "The Second Neurotic's Notebook" (Bobbs-Merrill, 1966).

APPENDIX Precious Metals

1. Readers interested in the historical connection between gold and money are referred to Peter Bernstein's, *The Power of Gold: The History of an Obsession* (John Wiley & Sons, 2001) and "The Anatomy of Crisis," Chapter 3 of Milton and Rose Friedman's *Free to Choose: A Personal Statement* (Harcourt, 1980).
2. There is a Canadian Maple Leaf gold bullion coin that is stamped "50 Dollars" (meaning 50 Canadian Dollars) and similarly stamped "1 OZ OR PUR," which has a current market value of well over 460 Dollars (and that is U.S. Dollars).
3. See Imogen Rose-Smith and Andrew Barber's "The 30 Biggest Trading Blowups of All Time (And What You Can Learn From Them)," *Trader Monthly* (October/November 2005): 78–85.
4. See www.zealllc.com/2002/gold101.htm.
5. Robert A. Mundell, "The International Monetary System in the 21st Century: Could Gold Make a Comeback?" Lecture delivered at St. Vincent College (March 12, 1997).
6. Alan Greenspan, "Gold and Economic Freedom," *The Objectivist* (1966).
7. Milton and Rose Friedman, *Free To Choose: A Personal Statement* (1980), 253.
8. Nelson Hultberg, "The Future of Gold as Money," Financial Sense OnLine, www.financialsense.com/editorials/hultberg/2005/0203.html (2005).

References

CHAPTER 1   Trading Money

Written References

Bishop, Paul, and Don Dixon. 1994. *Foreign exchange handbook*. New York: McGraw-Hill.

Goodwin, Jason. 2003. *Greenback*. New York: Henry Holt.

Reinfeld, Fred. 1957. *The story of paper money*. New York: Sterling Publishing Company.

Web Sites

Geography   www.geography.about.com/cs/countries/

International Organization for Standardization (ISO)   www.iso.org/iso/en/prods-services/popstds/currencycodes.html

The CIA Factbook   www.cia.gov/cia/publications/factbook

The United Nations   www.un.org

CHAPTER 2   Markets, Prices, and Marketmaking

Written References

Fenton-O'Creevy, Mark, Nigel Nicholson, Emma Soane, and Paul Willman. 2005. *Traders: Risks, decisions, and management in financial markets*. Oxford University Press.

Francis, Jack C. and Roger Ibbotson. 2002. *Investments: A global perspective*. Upper Saddle River, NJ: Prentice-Hall.

Gastineau, Gary L., and Mark P. Kritzman. 1996. *The dictionary of financial risk management*. rev. ed. Frank J. Fabozzi Associates.

Harris, Larry. 2003. *Trading and exchanges: Market microstructure for practitioners*. New York: Oxford University Press.

Harris, Sunny J. 1996. *Trading 101*. New York: John Wiley & Sons.

Kleinfield, Sonny. 1983. *The traders*. New York: Holt, Rinehart and Winston.

CHAPTER 3   Interest Rates

Written References

Gordon, John Steele. 1997. *Hamilton's blessing: The extraordinary life and times of our national debt.* New York: Walker.

Stigum, Marcia. 1990. *The money market.* 3rd ed. New York: McGraw-Hill.

Troccolo, Joe. 2004. *Just enough interest rates and foreign exchange.* UBS.

CHAPTER 4   Brief History of Foreign Exchange

Written References

Baker, James. 2002. The Bank for International Settlements—Evolution and Evaluation. Quorum Books.

DeRosa, David F. 1996. *Managing foreign exchange risk: Advanced strategies for global investors, corporations and financial institutions.* rev. ed. Irwin.

DeRosa, David F. 2001. *In defense of free capital markets—The case against a new international financial architecture.* Princeton, NJ: Bloomberg Press.

FX Week (business periodical/magazine). Market professionals trade publication (where tomorrow's FX history is being recorded today).

Levi, Maurice D. 2004. *International finance.* 4th ed. Routledge.

Tygier, Claude. 1988. *Basic handbook of foreign exchange.* Euromoney.

Web Sites

Bank for International Settlements (BIS)   www.bis.org
The European Central Bank   www.ecb.int
Federal Reserve Bank of New York   www.newyorkfed.org/markets/foreignex.html
Federal Reserve System   www.federalreserve.gov
International Monetary Fund (IMF)   www.imf.org

CHAPTER 5   The Foreign Exchange Spot Market

Written References

Mavrides, Marios. *Triangular arbitrage in the foreign exchange market: Inefficiencies, technology, and investment opportunities.*

Ong, Li Lian. 2003. *The Big Mac Index: Applications of purchasing power parity.* Palgrave Macmillan.

Reuters. 1999. *An introduction to foreign exchange and money markets.* New York: John Wiley & Sons.

Von Ronik, Wolf. 1995. Currency squares, *Futures Magazine* (September): 38.
Weisweiller, Rudi. 1986. *Arbitrage: Opportunities and techniques in the financial and commodity markets*. New York: John Wiley & Sons.
Weisweiller, Rudi. 1990. *How the foreign exchange market works*. New York: New York Institute of Finance.

Web Sites
Bank for International Settlements (BIS)   www.bis.org
Federal Reserve Bank of New York   www.newyorkfed.org/fxc/
Foreign Exchange Committee

CHAPTER 6   Foreign Exchange Forwards

Written References
DeRosa, David F. 1992. *Managing foreign exchange risk*. Probus.
DeRosa, David F., ed. 1998. *Currency derivatives*. New York: John Wiley & Sons.
Froot, Kenneth A., and Jeffrey A. Frankel. 1989. Forward discount bias: Is it an exchange risk premium? *Quarterly Journal of Economics* (February): 139–161; reproduced as Chapter 13 in Richard H. Thaler's *Advances in Behavioral Finance* (Russell Sage, 1993).
Kritzman, Mark P. 2000. *Puzzles in finance: Six practical problems and their remarkable solutions*. Chapter 1, "Siegel's Paradox," 1–21. New York: John Wiley & Sons.
Shamah, Shani. 2003. *A foreign exchange primer*. New York: John Wiley & Sons.
Siegel, Jeremy. 1972. Risk, interest rates, and the forward exchange. *Quarterly Journal of Economics* 86: 303–309.
Thaler, Richard H. 1992. *The winner's curse: Paradoxes and anomalies of economic life*, Chapter 14 (with Ken Froot) "Foreign Exchange," 182–196 (New York: Free Press). Originally published as "Foreign Exchange," *Journal of Economic Perspectives* 4 (3): 179–192.

Web Sites
UBS, Reuters, Telerate, . . .

CHAPTER 7   Foreign Exchange Futures

Written References
Chicago Board of Trade. 1998. *Commodity trading manual*, Fitzroy Dearborn.

Cornell, Bradford, and Marc R. Reinganum. 1981. Forward and futures prices: Evidence from the foreign exchange markets. *Journal of Finance* 36: 1035–1045.

Cox, John C., Jonathan E. Ingersol Jr., and Stephen A. Ross. 1981. The relationship between forward and futures prices. *Journal of Financial Economics* 9: 321–346.

Friedman, Milton. 1971. The need for futures markets in currencies. In *The futures market in foreign currencies*, 6–12. Chicago: Chicago Mercantile Exchange.

Melamed, Leo. 1988. Evolution of the international monetary market. *Cato Journal* 8 (2): 393–404.

Melamed, Leo. 1996. The birth and development of financial futures, China Futures Seminar.

Telser, Lester G. 2000. Classic futures: Lessons from the past for the electronic age. London: Risk Books.

Whaley, Robert E., ed. 1992. *Selected writings on futures markets: Book VI*. Chicago: CBOT.

Web Sites

The Chicago Mercantile Exchange (the CME or the "Merc"), which houses the International Monetary Market (IMM)   www.cme.com

The Commodity Futures Trading Commission (the CFTC), which regulates the futures markets in the United States   www.cftc.gov

CHAPTER 8   Foreign Exchange Swaps or Cross-Currency Swaps or Cross-Currency Interest Rate Swaps or . . .

Written References

Beidleman, Carl R., ed. 1992. *Cross currency swaps*. Irwin.

Coyle, Brian. 2001. *Currency swaps*. Fitzroy Dearborn Publishers.

Dattatreya, Ravi E., Raj E.S.Venkatesh, and Vijaya E. Venkatesh. 1993. *Interest rates and currency swaps: The markets, products and applications*. Probus.

CHAPTER 9   Foreign Exchange Options

Written References on Options

Cox, John, and Mark Rubinstein. 1985. *Options markets*. Prentice-Hall.

Hull, John C. 2006. *Options, futures, and other derivatives*. 6th ed. Upper Saddle River, NJ: Prentice-Hall.

Jarrow, Robert, and Andrew Rudd. 1983. *Option pricing*. Irwin.

Natenberg, Sheldon. 1994. *Option volatility & pricing: Advanced trading strategies and techniques*. rev. ed. New York: Irwin/McGraw-Hill.

Stoll, Hans R., and Robert E. Whaley. 1992. *Futures and options: Theory and applications*. Southwestern Educational Publishing.

Troccolo, Joe. 1999. *Options: The fundamentals*. UBS.

Weithers, Tim. 2000. Options fundamentals. In *The handbook of equity derivatives*, rev. ed., ed. Jack Clark Francis, William Toy, and J. Gregg Whittaker, chap. 1. New York: John Wiley & Sons.

Classic Options References

Black, Fischer. 1988. The holes in Black–Scholes. *Risk* 1.

Black, Fischer, and Myron Scholes. 1973. The pricing of options and corporate liabilities. *Journal of Political Economy* 81: 637–654.

Merton, Robert C. 1973. Theory of rational option pricing. *Bell Journal of Economics and Management Science* 4: 141–183.

Stoll, Hans. 1969. The relationship between put and call option prices. *Journal of Finance* 23: 801–824.

Classic FX Option References

Biger, Nahum, and John C. Hull. 1983. The valuation of currency options. *Financial Management* 12: 24–28.

Garman, Mark B., and Steven W. Kohlhagen. 1983. Foreign currency option values. *Journal of International Money and Finance* 2: 231–237.

Giddy, Ian. 1983. Foreign exchange options. *The Journal of Futures Markets* 3: 143–166.

Grabbe, J. Orlin. 1983. The pricing of call and put options on foreign exchange. *Journal of International Money and Finance* 2: 239–253.

FX Option Books

Bourdain, Christopher S. 1996. FX option myths that aren't. *Derivatives Strategies* 1 (April).

DeRosa, David F., ed. 1998. *Currency derivatives: Pricing theory, exotic options, and hedging applications*. New York: John Wiley & Sons.

DeRosa, David F. 2000. *Options on foreign exchange*. New York: John Wiley & Sons.

Giddy, Ian. 1996. Six common myths about FX options. *Derivatives Strategies* 1 (February).

Hakala, Jurgen, and Uwe Wystup. 2002. *Foreign exchange risk: Models, instruments and strategies*. Risk Books.

Web Site

"The Derivatives 'Zine" of William Margrabe Group   www.margrabe.com

APPENDIX TO CHAPTER 9   Option Valuation Models

Written References

Boyle, Phelim P. 1977. Options: A Monte Carlo approach. *Journal of Financial Economics* 4: 323–338.

Cox, John C., Stephen Ross, and Mark Rubinstein. 1979. Option pricing: A simplified approach. *Journal of Financial Economics* 7: 229–263.

Kholodnyi, Valery, and John F. Price. 1998. *Foreign exchange option symmetry*. World Scientific Publishing Company.

Lipton, Alexander. 2001. *Mathematical methods for foreign exchange: A financial engineer's approach*. World Scientific Publishers.

Neftci, Saleh. 2000. *An introduction to the mathematics of financial derivatives*. 2nd ed. Academic Press.

Smith, Clifford W. 1976. Option pricing: A review. *Journal of Financial Economics* 3: 3–54.

CHAPTER 10   Exotic Options and Structured Products

Written References

Briys, Eric, Huu Minh Mai, Mondher Bellalah, and Francois de Varenne. 1998. *Options, futures, and exotic options: Theory, application and practice*. New York: John Wiley & Sons.

Jarrow, Robert. 1996. *Over the rainbow: Developments in exotic options and complex swaps*. Risk Books.

Lipton, Alexander, ed. 2003. *Exotic options: The cutting edge collection technical papers published in risk 1999–2003*. Risk Books.

Reiner, Eric. 1992. Quanto Mechanics. *Risk* 5: 59–63.

Rubinstein, Mark, and Eric Reiner. 1992. Exotic options [Many of the sections of this manuscript, one of the most highly referenced, unpublished works on derivatives, appeared as short articles in *Risk* magazine.]

Zhang, Peter G. 1998. *Exotic options: A guide to second generation options*. 2nd ed. World Scientific Publishing Company.

Web Sites

The William Margrabe Group   www.margrabe.com

Mark Rubinstein's web site   www.in-the-money.com/pages/author.htm

CHAPTER 11   The Economics of Exchange Rates and International Trade

Written References

Caves, Richard E., and Ronald W. Jones. 1984. *World trade and payments: An introduction*. Little, Brown.

Frenkel, Jacob A., and Harry G. Johnson, eds. 1976. *The monetary approach to the balance of payments*. Allen and Unwin.

Friedman, Milton. 1953. The case for flexible exchange rates. In his *Essays in positive economics*, 157–203. Chicago: University of Chicago Press.

Ghosh, Atish R., Anne-Marie Gulde, and Holger C. Wolf. 2002. *Exchange rate regimes: Choices and consequences*. Cambridge, MA: MIT Press.

Grabbe, J. Orlin. 1996. *International financial markets*. 3rd ed. Upper Saddle River, NJ: Prentice-Hall.

Johnson, Harry G. 1977. The monetary approach to the balance of payments: A nontechnical guide. *Journal of International Economics*: 251–268.

Kenen, Peter B. 1994. *The international economy* 3rd ed. Cambridge University Press.

Krugman, Paul R., and Maurice Obstfeld. 1991 *International economics: Theory and policy*. 2nd ed. New York: HarperCollins.

Xin, Hai. 2003. *Currency overlay: A practical guide*. Risk Books.

CHAPTER 12   Currency Crises

Written References

Desai, Padma. 2003. *Financial crisis, contagion, and containment: From Asia to Argentina*. Princeton, NJ: Princeton University Press.

Dunbar, Nicholas. 2000. *Inventing money: The story of long-term capital management and the legends behind it*. New York: John Wiley & Sons.

Fourcans, Andre, and Raphael Franck. 2003. *Currency crises—A theoretical and empirical perspective*. Edward Elgar.

Galbraith, John Kenneth. 1993. *A short history of financial euphoria*. Whittle.

Goldman, Sachs & Company and SBC Warburg Dillon Read. 1998. *The practice of risk management*. Euromoney Books.

Kindleberger, Charles P. 1996. *Manias, panics, and crashes: A history of financial crises*. 3rd ed. New York: John Wiley & Sons.

Krugman, Paul R. 1998. *Currencies and crises*. Cambridge, MA: MIT Press.

Lowenstein, Roger. 2000. *When genius failed: The rise and fall of long-term capital management*. New York: Random House.

Mackay, Charles. 1841. *Extraordinary popular delusions and the madness of crowds*. London.

Slater, Robert. 1996. *Soros: The unauthorized biography*. New York: McGraw-Hill.

Soros, George, with Byron Wein and Krisztina Koenen. 1995. *Soros on Soros: Staying ahead of the curve*. New York: John Wiley & Sons.

Soros, George. 2003. *The alchemy of finance*. New York: John Wiley & Sons.

CHAPTER 13   Technical Analysis

Written References

Frankel, Jeffrey A., and Kenneth A. Froot. 1990. Chartists, fundamentalists, and trading in the foreign exchange market. *American Economic Review* 80(2): 181–185.

Murphy, John J. 1999. *Technical analysis of the financial markets*. New York: New York Institute of Finance.

Okunev, John, and Derek White. 2002. The profits to technical analysis in foreign exchange markets have not disappeared. In *Advanced trading rules*, 2nd ed., ed. E. Acar and S. Satchell, Chapter 7.

Pring, Martin J. 1985. *Technical analysis explained: The successful investor's guide to spotting investment trends and turning points*. 3rd ed. New York: McGraw-Hill.

Pring, Martin J. 2002. *Candlesticks explained*. New York: McGraw-Hill.

Reuters. 1999. *Introduction to technical analysis*. New York: John Wiley & Sons.

Schlossberg, Boris. 2006. *Technical analysis of the currency market*. New York: John Wiley & Sons.

Schwager, Jack D. 1999. *Getting started in technical analysis*. New York: John Wiley & Sons.

CHAPTER 14   Where Do We Go From Here?

Written References

Mundell, Robert

Soros, George. 1998. *The crisis of global capitalism*. New York: PublicAffairs.

Web Site

The Works of Robert Mundell   www.robertmundell.net

CHAPTER 15   Conclusion

Written References

Gross, William H. 1997. *Everything You've heard about investing is wrong!* New York: Times Books/Random House.

Xin, Hai. 2003. *Currency overlay: A practical guide.* Risk Books.

APPENDIX   Precious Metals

Written References

Bernstein, Peter L. 2001. *The power of gold: The history of an obsession.* New York: John Wiley & Sons.

Risk Books/UBS. 2004. *Managing metals price risk.* Risk Books in association with UBS.

Web Site

U.S. Geological Survey   http://minerals.usgs.gov/minerals/pubs/commodity/gold/

About the Author

Tim Weithers is a Managing Director at UBS and runs a team of professional educators based out of UBS's primary U.S. office in Stamford, Connecticut, which houses the largest trading floor in the world. Prior to working at UBS, he worked at O'Connor and Associates, Swiss Bank Corporation, as well as NationsBanc-CRT. Before joining the world of the practitioner, Tim was a part of the academic community; he taught at the University of Chicago and at Fordham University in New York for several years. He continues to teach (Foreign Exchange among other things) in the University of Chicago's Graduate Program on Financial Mathematics. Tim received his Ph.D. in Economics from the University of Chicago a long time ago.

Index